Successful Professional Women of the Americas

Successful Professional Women of the Americas

From Polar Winds to Tropical Breezes

Betty Jane Punnett

Professor of International Business and Management, University of the West Indies, Barbados

Jo Ann Duffy

Professor of Management, Sam Houston State University, Texas, USA

Suzy Fox

Associate Professor, Institute of Human Resources and Industrial Relations, Loyola University Chicago, USA

Ann Gregory

Honorary Research Professor, Memorial University of Newfoundland, St John's, Canada

Terri R. Lituchy

Associate Professor of Management, John Molson School of Business, Concordia University, Montreal, Canada

Silvia Inés Monserrat

Professor of Business and Private Law, Universidad Nacional del Centro de la Provincia de Buenos Aires, Argentina

Miguel R. Olivas-Luján

Professor of Management, Clarion University of Pennsylvania, USA and Member of the Business Faculty, Tecnológico de Monterrey, Mexico

Neusa Maria Bastos F. Santos

Professor of Management and Accounting and Director of the Graduate Programme in Accounting and Finance, Pontifícia Universidade Católica de São Paulo, Brazil

Edward Elgar

Cheltenham, UK • Northampton, MA, USA

Published by
Edward Elgar Publishing Limited
Glensanda House
Montpellier Parade
Cheltenham
Glos GL50 1UA
UK

Edward Elgar Publishing, Inc.
136 West Street
Suite 202
Northampton
Massachusetts 01060
USA

A catalogue record for this book
is available from the British Library

Library of Congress Cataloguing in Publication Data

Successful professional women of the Americas: from polar winds to tropical
   breezes/Betty Jane Punnett . . . [et al.].
      p. cm.
   Includes bibliographical references and index.
   1. Women in the professions—America. 2. Women—America—History.
I. Punnett, Betty Jane.
   HD6054.2.A45S83   2006
   650.1082'097–dc22   2005031734

ISBN-13: 978 1 84542 437 4
ISBN-10: 1 84542 437 9

Printed and bound in Great Britain by MPG Books Ltd, Bodmin, Cornwall

Contents

List of figures   vii
List of tables   viii
List of contributors   ix

1   From polar winds to tropical breezes: the evolution
of the Successful Women project   1
Suzy Fox

2   Successful women professionals in the Americas:
theoretical perspectives and empirical findings   28
*Ann Gregory, Catherine Mossop and
Neusa Maria Bastos F. Santos*

3   Culture and personal characteristics for professional
success   60
Miguel R. Olivas-Luján and Betty Jane Punnett

4   Beginning the research in a tropical breeze   76
Betty Jane Punnett and Lawrence Nurse

5   Personality, management/leadership styles and
views on great leadership   97
Suzy Fox and Ann Gregory

6   What the successful women said about professional and
life experiences: barriers, social support and mentors   114
Terri R. Lituchy and Jo Ann Duffy

7   Successful women in the polar winds of Canada   131
*Terri R. Lituchy, Ann Gregory, Joan Dewling and
Robert Oppenheimer*

8   Successful women of the United States of America   149
Jo Ann Duffy, Suzy Fox and John Miller

9   Successful professional women in Mexico   161
Miguel R. Olivas-Luján and Leticia Ramos Garza

10   Successful women: a vision of Brazil   183
     Neusa Maria Bastos F. Santos

11   Argentina: returning to its glorious past   195
     Silvia Inés Monserrat, Griselda Lassaga and
     Claudia D'Annunzio

12   The successful women of Chile   210
     Mahia S. Saracostti, Silvia Inés Monserrat and
     ComunidadMujer

13   The big picture from polar winds to tropical breezes   220
     Betty Jane Punnett, John Miller and Donald Wood

Appendix A   Successful Women Worldwide e-mail survey for
             the USA   228

Appendix B   Form A: interview questions – Successful
             Women Project   242

Appendix C   Milestones of the project: presentation of the
             SWW Core Team   244

Appendix D   Statistical results: successful women and
             comparison groups   246

Appendix E   Women in the workforce worldwide: trends   248
             Ann Gregory

References   251
Index   277

Figures

1.1	Concentric influences model	6
1.2	Empirical model	8
1.3	Map highlighting the Americas	16
3.1	Comparison of scores on Hofstede variables	72
4.1	Map of the West Indies	79
4.2	Comparison of successful women and students	93
7.1	Map: location of Canada	132
8.1	Map: location of the USA	150
9.1	Map: location of Mexico	162
9.2	*Maquiladora* line workers by sex	166
10.1	Map: location of Brazil	184
11.1	Map: location of Argentina	196
12.1	Map: location of Chile	211
E.1	Labour force participation rates, by sex and region, 1993 and 2003	249

Tables

2.1 Economic activity and women's share of the labour force
in the Americas   29
2.2 Changes in labour force participation rates of women in
eight Latin American countries   31
2.3 Women's share as administrative and managerial workers
and high officials in the Americas   32
2.4 Index of women holding executive, technical and academic
positions for Latin American countries included in the study   33
3.1 Cultural dimensions/personal characteristics   71
3.2 Scores on Hofstede values for countries in the Americas   73
3.3 Scores on Successful Women survey for countries in the
Americas   74
4.1 Comparison of scores in the Caribbean countries   90
5.1 Personality and other internal factors   99
5.2 Management and leadership styles   105
5.3 Great leaders   110
6.1 Demographic factors   115
6.2 External factors   116
9.1 Some famous women in Mexican history   163
9.2 Cities and states of origin of participants   171

Contributors

Jo Ann Duffy (MA, PhD, University of Texas at Austin) is Professor of Management at Sam Houston State University, Texas and Director of the Gibson D. Lewis Center of Business and Economic Development. She is the Editor in Chief of the *Journal of Business Strategies* and past President of the Southwest Academy of Management. She has published in numerous journals including *Benchmarking: An International Journal, Journal of Service Marketing, Journal of Managerial Issues, Journal of Educational Administration* and *Journal of Management*. Jo Ann is partner in Sower, Duffy and Associates, a management consultancy firm specializing in healthcare quality improvement.

Suzy Fox, Associate Professor in the Institute of Human Resources and Industrial Relations, Graduate School of Business, Loyola University Chicago, teaches Global Human Research Management, Ethics of Employment and Diversity and Organizational Behaviour. She received her PhD in Industrial/Organizational Psychology from the University of South Florida in 1998 and an MBA in 1993. Her primary research areas are counterproductive work behaviour (with her colleague and mentor, Paul Spector, she has just published *Counterproductive Work Behaviour: Investigations of Actors and Targets*, APA Press), racial/ethnic workplace bullying (with Lamont Stallworth), and the Successful Women Worldwide research group. She has presented research at many international conferences, taught executive programmes internationally and has published widely in academic journals. She has acted as Associate Editor of *Human Relations* for the past three years.

Ann Gregory, Honorary Research Professor and supposedly retired, teaches at the Faculty of Business Administration, Memorial University of Newfoundland, St John's and coaches in the online executive MBA programme at Athabasca University in Alberta. She has also taught in Barbados, China, Indonesia and Israel. Her PhD is from Columbia University in political science, and she subsequently received her MBA from New York University. In management, her second field, her initial publications were on political risk management and, later, in gender and diversity studies.

Terri R. Lituchy has a PhD from the University of Arizona. She is Associate Professor of Management at John Molson School of Business, Concordia University in Montreal, Canada. She has taught in the USA, Mexico, Trinidad, the Czech Republic, France, Malaysia, Thailand, China and Japan. Terri's research interests are cross-cultural and comparative issues in organizational settings. Recent articles appear in the *International Journal of Cross Cultural Management*, the *International Journal of Entrepreneurship and Small Business*, *Leadership Quarterly*, *Canadian Journal of Administrative Sciences*, *International Journal of Organizational Behaviour*, *International Business Review* and the *Journal of Organizational Behaviour*.

Miguel R. Olivas-Luján, Professor of Management, Clarion University of Pennsylvania, USA and Member of the Business Faculty, Tecnológico de Monterrey, Mexico, earned his PhD in Human Resources and Organizational Behaviour from the Katz School of Business (University of Pittsburgh, 2003), an MBA (1992), and a Computer Engineering bachelor's degree (1989) from Tecnológico de Monterrey. His research focuses on women in management, on the diffusion of information technology for human resource purposes around the world, and on the ways culture affects business. He has published several refereed articles in scientific journals, and has refereed for a variety of top academic associations since 1989. He was admitted to Mexico's selective National Researchers' System in 2004. He has offered a variety of university courses, seminars, conferences and talks in three continents. Before entering the academic world, Dr Olivas worked as a manager in the field of International Education, co-ordinating student exchanges between higher education institutions from around the world.

Silvia Inés Monserrat, Professor of Business and Private Law, Universidad Nacional del Centro de la Provincia de Buenos Aires, Tandil, Argentina. Silvia holds an MBA from Universidad Nacional del Centro, with a California State University LA Bachelor in Law. She is a Full Professor and teaches undergraduate and graduate courses and is a Visiting Professor at California State, San Bernardino University. Monserrat's research interests are in women, entrepreneurs and cross-cultural organizational behaviour.

Betty Jane Punnett, Professor of International Business and Management and Head, Department of Management Studies, University of the West Indies, Cave Hill Campus, Barbados. Betty Jane has a PhD in International Business from New York University and her major research interest is cross-cultural issues in management. Betty Jane is a native of St Vincent and the Grenadines and she does research and consulting in the English-speaking Caribbean. She recently published *International Perspectives on*

Organizational Behaviour and Human Resource Management, Experiencing International Business and Management and *The Handbook for International Management Research.*

Neusa Maria Bastos F. Santos, Professor of Management and Accounting and Director of the Graduate Programme in Accounting and Finance, Pontifícia Universidade Católica, de São Paulo, Brazil.

This book was the work of many people, in addition to the core research team. Successful Women Worldwide Partners and others who have contributed to the book are briefly described next.

Claudia D'Annunzio, MBA Universidad Nacional del Centro with California State University LA. She is associate professor on undergraduate and graduate courses. Her research interests are entrepreneurship and small business development.

Joan Dewling received her MBA from Memorial University of Newfoundland and Labrador. Her experience includes 14 years of management in the retail sector. She has helped develop and teach a variety of accounting and budgeting seminars through the Centre for Management Development of the Faculty of Business, Memorial University. She consults with various companies in the film industry, small business and organizations in the not-for-profit sector.

Griselda Lassaga is a PhD candidate in Sociology Studies, Master in Business Administration, Universidad de Belgrano and since 1994 works with women in corporations, and professional women development. She has given seminars to women in Colombia, Peru and Argentina.

John Miller holds a PhD from Rice University and a JD from the University of Houston. He is Assistant Professor of Economics, Sam Houston State University, and founder of Benchmark Research Consultancy. His research interest is applied statistical analysis.

Catherine Mossop, President, Sage Mentors Inc., Toronto, Ontario, Canada. She designs large-scale mentorship programmes to accelerate leadership talent development. Catherine is co-author of *Mentoring and the World of Work in Canada*, 2003, Sage Mentors Inc., Toronto, Ontario, Canada.

Lawrence Nurse, University of the West Indies, Cave Hill Campus, Barbados. Lawrence is a native of Barbados who teaches Industrial Relations and Organizational Development. He does research on organizational justice and effectiveness in the Caribbean public and private sectors.

Robert Oppenheimer, Professor of Management in the John Molson School of Business, Concordia University, Montreal, Quebec, Canada. Robert has been teaching for 32 years, and he is Director of the Centre for Mature Students. He has developed courses in Managerial Skills, Organizational Behaviour and Human Resource Management, and provides consulting services in issues relating to individual, team and organizational effectiveness.

Margarita María Errázuriz Ossa, ComunidadMujer President, Santiago, Chile. She is a sociologist and for the past 20 years she has worked as a consultant. Her expertise is in gender and poverty. She has also worked with UNICEF, FAO and CEPAL.

Leticia Ramos Garza has an MA and PhD from Tulane University and is Associate Professor of Management and Director of Research at ITESM. She has received the Premio a la Labor Docente, for outstanding professor of the year, and the Best Article award at the II International Conference of the Iberoamerican Academy of Management. As well as being an educator and researcher, she is an active adviser to management in the human resource area.

Mahia S. Saracostti is a social worker with a Master's in Business Administration from Pontificia Universidad Católica de Chile, and she is a PhD candidate in Social Welfare, City University of New York. She is Project and Studies Director of ComunidadMujer. She is a Professor at Hunter College, New York, and different Chilean universities – Pontificia Universidad Católica de Chile, Universidad Alberto Hurtado and Universidad del Desarrollo. She has participated in several studies, and published in newspapers and specialized journals.

Donald Wood is a management consultant with Eureka Management Consultants of Barbados and St Vincent and the Grenadines. He holds a Master's degree from Massachusetts Institute of Technology and studied in the DBA programme at Harvard.

1. From polar winds to tropical breezes: the evolution of the Successful Women project[1]

Suzy Fox

If you were to ask a successful businesswoman, 'Just what made you so successful?' what do you think she would say? Do you think a successful professional woman in Chicago would tell you the same thing as one in Buenos Aires, Monterrey or Montreal? Listen to the voices of successful women in South America, North America and the Caribbean. Can you guess what countries they come from?[2]

> As a person I'm very much a fighter. I always wanted to have my financial independence, because for me, it is the most important thing – not to depend on other people.
>
> I pursued success – asked for promotions, aggressive career planning, worked very, very, very hard.
>
> I always knew I could do anything I wanted.
>
> I'm a hard worker, I'm a perfectionist. It has to be done right . . . If something has to be done it will get done. I'm driven.
>
> I don't believe in chance. I believe in hard work, opportunity, the ability to take risks and timing. People often confuse those factors with luck.
>
> I worked hard. I have a strong personality but also a positive view of life.
>
> I have a very, very strong work ethic, very strong conviction of who I am – very confident and secure in my management style and my abilities to do my job and do it well.
>
> Family education gave me the ability and desire to struggle to achieve my objectives . . . and the support and co-operation I've received from my husband has always been a motivation in my career.

What do these women scattered across the western hemisphere have in common? How do they differ from one another? How do they differ from their compatriots in their respective countries? To what can we attribute the miracle of success, in the face of personal, social, organizational, cultural and economic barriers facing women everywhere?

This book is the story of successful women, women who are managers, business owners, tenured professors, university administrators, doctors, lawyers and government ministers. They come from the mountains of Mexico, the fishing towns of Newfoundland; rural Texas, downtown Toronto and the suburbs of Chicago; the mountains of Jamaica and the financial centres of Barbados; the centre of São Paulo and the outskirts of Buenos Aires. What each has in common is a certain spirit and the knack for grabbing opportunity where it arises. Each has become a rising star in the face of statistics that predict a more mediocre career for most women. The women in our study come from tropical paradises, with warm tropical breezes, from cold northern climes, with polar winds, and from places in between.

The women and men researchers of the Successful Women of the Americas (SWA) project began our acquaintance at a professional development workshop of the Academy of Management. We began by asking the simplest of questions – how do those women do it? What are the characteristics of individuals and their environments that enable some women, and not others, to reach the heights of their business and professional fields? And in light of the urgent need for talent and leadership in the changing societies of the Americas, what can be done to draw more women into positions of power and influence?

WHY STUDY WOMEN IN THE AMERICAS?

We find very little published research about efforts to explore characteristics of women at the top of their fields in different national contexts. We have searched in vain to find information about successful women in Latin America and the Caribbean. We have plenty of stereotypes – but very few facts! A failure to understand how women succeed in widely differing cultures puts corporations and educators at a disadvantage in this time of globalization. Trade agreements such as the North American Free Trade Agreement (NAFTA) are pushing countries together in business and making it important to understand what characteristics are associated with leadership and professional success. The increasing push towards business partnerships among companies in Canada, the USA, Mexico, the Caribbean, Central and South America suggests that firms that understand the characteristics and experiences of successful women in these countries could turn the development of leadership talent into a major competitive advantage.

Positioning Women in a Period of Economic Change

Social, political, and economic relationships among Mexico, the USA and Canada have changed dramatically since the signing of the North American Free Trade Agreement in 1992. In the current period, there is much activity and debate around the expansion of the concept to encompass the entire western hemisphere. Mexico, for example, has already signed bilateral and multilateral Free Trade Agreements (FTAs) with 32 countries, modelled on NAFTA in form and substance (Diaz, 2001). There is concrete activity under way to develop a Dominican Republic–Central American Free Trade Area or DR-CAFTA (USTR, 2004). For many, the ultimate goal is a Free Trade Area of the Americas (FTAA), including 34 national economies (WOLA, 2005).

It has been noted that the current debate about FTAs does not sufficiently include potential effects on women in the Americas. Critics predict differential effects of the ensuing economic changes on women and men. Specific issues include the violence and working conditions experienced by women in the *maquiladora* districts since NAFTA; the migration of the female labour force in Latin America to the service sector, and effects of the expanded trade agreements on health, education and social services (US Gender and Trade Network, 2005). Clearly these changes will affect women at every layer of the economies of all countries affected. One of the driving motivations in the initial stage of the Successful Women of the Americas project was to understand how the social and economic changes projected for the coming period of Free Trade Agreements would affect the endeavours of women to reach the top echelons of business and the professions. This initial question morphed into a proactive desire to understand the factors underlying women's success, in order to help women position themselves advantageously to respond to the opportunities presented in the coming period of change.

The economies and societies of the nations of the Americas will become increasingly interdependent. There will be a dramatically increased need for strong business and professional leadership, capable of leading economic changes within each country, and, more particularly, capable of working across borders. The ability of women to participate in this leadership role is crucial.

Where Do We Stand Today?

In every country of the Americas, to a greater or lesser degree, women have trailed behind men in access to power and resources. In this book we look at some of the similarities and differences in the successes and failures of women in nine countries, in their efforts to achieve success in business and the professions. Barriers exist in every society we have looked at; every cultural heritage contains seeds of frustration for women who aspire to leadership roles in their careers. These barriers may differ over time and across borders but, without exception, women in each country must overcome hurdles that their male counterparts do not encounter. Few women have advanced to senior levels of their organizations. The wage gap has actually widened over the past ten years. Globally, the promotion of women is not even seen as beneficial by the leaders of many organizations, as reported in a study by the International Labor Organization. Yet many organizations have found, as recent research suggests (for example, Stroh et al., 2000; Tyler, 2001), that women may be uniquely advantaged over their male counterparts in bridging cultural distances in their business relationships. Understanding the unique strengths of successful women may prove to be a priceless competitive advantage for companies involved in joint ventures, trade negotiations, international mergers and expatriate assignments.

The anthropologist Desmond Morris says in his introduction to *The Naked Woman* (2004) that he was disturbed and angry with the way women were treated in many countries around the world – 'considered the "property" of males and as inferior members of society' (p. x). He goes on to say that as a zoologist who has studied the evolution of humans 'this trend to male domination is simply not in keeping with the way in which *Homo sapiens* has developed'. It may not fit with evolutionary development, but it is the reality of the world that today women face many barriers in society generally, and in the business world particularly.

Finally, the commonalities we find across geo-cultural boundaries may offer insights into the kinds of experiences, perceptions, beliefs, and assumptions we may wish to encourage in young girls, in order to enhance their prospects of achieving professional success. Managerial skills in which women appear to excel can be promoted; skills in which women tend to lag behind can be developed.

This book is the story of an ongoing research project about women in the Americas. A cross-cultural, interdisciplinary team of scholars from Canada, the USA, Mexico, the West Indies, Brazil and Argentina have formed a core research team, devoted to exploring successful women in each of our countries and across countries. The intent of this project is to gain an understanding of the similarities and dissimilarities of successful women living in different parts of the Americas, in order to foster the development of business, professional, and global leadership among the next generations of young girls throughout the region.

What Determines Women's Success? A Theoretical Approach

The foundation of any project that hopes to gain insight into the experiences of successful women must be a notion of the myriad of factors that contribute to success. As organizational and social scientists, we do not believe these factors are random or accidental. We like to be guided by a sense of things being systemically related, and we ask questions to help us understand these relationships.

- How do the national cultures we grow up in help us or hurt us in our professional lives?
- Why do some organizations seem to nurture us and others seem so forbidding? Is there something about the cultures in organizations that helps or hinders us from achieving our professional goals?
- What kinds of life experiences help or hurt us?
- How do our personalities help or hurt us?
- Which of these factors are the same for men and women? Which national, organizational and personal factors help or hurt women in particular?
- What sets successful women apart and enables them to overcome the obstacles to success?
- Are personal characteristics and experiences that enable women to succeed in one national culture the same as those that enable women to succeed in other countries?
- In which respects will successful women in one country more closely resemble successful women in a different country than they resemble their own compatriots?

These are the kinds of questions we attempted to answer systematically when we developed a theoretical model. The purpose of our empirical study was to test the relationships in the model, and from these results to come to understand what kinds of factors really play a role in professional success in general, and successful women in particular. We sought to understand why a small minority of women manage to overcome barriers to the top levels of their professions. Once we understand that, we can begin to find ways to help more women enjoy the fruits of success.

Different kinds of models provide different ways of looking at the same sets of relationships. We found two models most useful as we developed our survey and interview materials. The first is more general, and helped us prioritize the myriad of influences on people's work lives. From this model, we were able to derive a more specific model that incorporates gender, nationality, national culture, organizational structure and culture, and personal characteristics into our study.

CONCENTRIC INFLUENCES MODEL

The first way to see the theory driving this research is shown in Figure 1.1. This concentric influences model looks at different kinds of influences on women's careers, and organizes them in concentric circles, according to the proximity of the factor and the extent of its influence on women's success. Thus the model begins with the individual at the centre and works outward towards the environment. Each successive circle is somewhat less proximate, less intense in its effect on the individual women we are studying, but nevertheless provides the context and socialization for each previous circle. 'Individual factors' – at the core of the model – are those characteristics that are most immediate in determining success; examples of these are personality, inner drive, abilities and education. Even within a unified, cohesive workgroup, within a strong organizational culture, located in a relatively homogenous national environment, individuals differ from one another. These differences are the individual factors that make one person a leader, another a follower; one person will stop at a roadblock, another will go around it; one person will achieve his or her goals, another will not. These are the differences we see at the core of success.

Individual factors are nested within the 'Departmental/workgroup' factors. Features at this level might include a collegial group environment, a supportive and empowering boss and co-operative subordinates. The

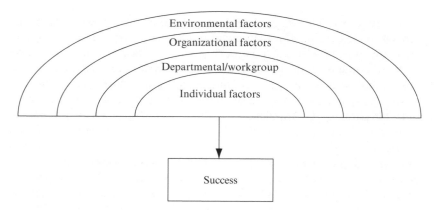

Figure 1.1   Concentric influences model

workgroup factors are followed in proximity and intensity by 'Organizational factors', which might include equalitarian company policies and the presence of female managers in the executive suite. Finally, shown in the outmost circle as the most distant influences, are the 'Environmental factors' that might include effective Equal Employment Opportunity legislation, a non-discriminatory national culture and room for economic mobility. These environmental factors would still have a significant impact, yet not as strong as the types of factors that are closer to the centre.

Clearly, there are dozens of characteristics that one could include within each of the circles in the model. We have mentioned only a few in the paragraph above. Additionally, we expect that some of the characteristics *interact* (in other words, the combination of two characteristics might be more powerful than the sum of isolated effects of each one). For example, having an internal locus of control (an individual factor) *and* working for a participative boss (a workgroup-level factor) together, might contribute to success in a stronger fashion than an internal locus of control or a participative boss contribute by themselves. Also, some interactions may be *negative*: for example, a woman with strong self-efficacy (an individual factor) might plausibly feel her confidence undermined by being perceived as taking advantage of Equal Opportunity quotas or policies (an environmental factor), and that might negatively impact her chances to succeed. These kinds of interactions should become clearer as we move to the next model.

EMPIRICAL MODEL

While the concentric circles model emphasizes the relative strength of different kinds of influences, we recognized the need for a more complex model that emphasizes the interconnectedness of the different factors (see Figure 1.2). We would draw upon this model to develop the hypotheses and choose the study variables for our empirical research. The centrality of personal factors from the concentric influences model is seen here in the initial, direct link from personality to success – we propose that this is the first, most immediate difference between successful and unsuccessful individuals. We focus on three of many possible personality and personal belief variables: locus of control, self-efficacy and need for achievement.

In addition to personal factors, there is a direct link between success and the kinds of support individuals receive from their organizations and external environments. A person who feels supported by the workgroup, organization or society is more likely to experience satisfaction and success. But what constitutes support? What factors affect the kinds of support or lack

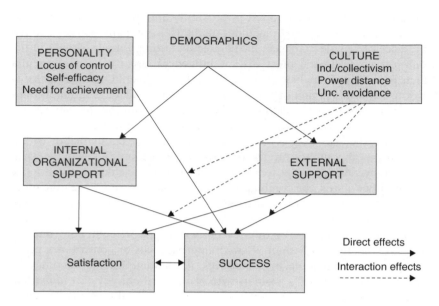

Figure 1.2   Empirical model

of support available to people in their careers? We focus on two of many possible demographic factors (gender and national origin) and on three of many possible national/cultural dimensions (individualism/collectivism, power distance and uncertainty avoidance) as we examine their impact on internal organizational and external environmental support and, in turn, on satisfaction and success.

As in the concentric influences model, often the factors do not work in isolation, but rather in complex interaction with other factors. For example, culture and personality may interact in their effect upon success. Imagine a scenario in which a person who is high in self-efficacy may be quite successful in an individual-oriented job within an individualistic national culture. That same person may clash and flounder in a team-based work environment within a collectivist national culture. In Figure 1.2, dotted lines suggest these kinds of interactions.

STUDY VARIABLES DERIVED FROM THE MODELS

From a review of the literature we identified a set of individual, cultural and experiential characteristics likely to influence success. We were particularly interested in variables that were likely to vary from country to country.

We made the strategic decision to include in our survey only measures that had been developed and validated by previous researchers. As we developed the theoretical basis of our project, we were able to choose the specific measures for our written survey that we felt would best help us test our model of successful women. We would love to have included many additional measures, but were realistic about how much time our very busy successful women would be willing to spend filling out a questionnaire. We came up with the best compromise we could between covering the most essential characteristics within a reasonably short, interesting survey. At the same time, we were well aware that such a questionnaire would only give us part of the picture. The rigour of an empirical study based on a handful of pre-chosen, narrowly constricted measures needed to be supplemented with the voices of the women themselves. We developed a semi-structured interview protocol, in order to tap characteristics not covered in the written survey, and to allow new insights and experiences to emerge from the words of the successful women themselves.

In the next section, we identify the study variables we chose to represent the empirical theoretical model. The specific variables we used in the written survey are described, followed by some broader concepts we incorporated into the personal interviews.

The English form of the written survey is presented in Appendix A. The semi-structured interview protocol is presented in Appendix B.

Demographics

Our review of research literature on careers, leadership, entrepreneurship, gender roles, women, international management and organizational behaviour helped us to identify several demographic variables we expected to influence professional success. Included in the survey were gender, year of birth, place of birth, nationality, ethnicity, birth order, gender of siblings, educational level attained, parents' education and profession, marital status, and number and age of children. Additional information was collected on current professional status, including profession, title, business ownership, number of employees, salary, level of managerial responsibility and occupational sector.

Personality

The personal characteristics we measure in our studies of organizational behaviour typically include personality and other kinds of individual differences, such as abilities, belief systems, personal values and need structures. For our survey, we chose three measures that the research literature has identified as among the most likely to influence success: self-efficacy, locus of control and need for achievement.

Self-efficacy

Self-efficacy is the belief in one's capability to perform successfully in a specific task domain (Bandura, 1986). Research suggests that motivation and achievement of goals are determined in part by how effective people believe they can be. Individuals with higher self-efficacy tend to try harder to master the challenge of difficult situations, show more persistence in the face of obstacles, respond to negative feedback with increased effort, set more challenging goals, and work harder and longer to achieve them. Perceived self-efficacy has been shown to predict effective use of analytic strategies in managerial decision-making (Wood et al., 1990). Bandura (1986) also suggests that individuals with high self-efficacy may be more resilient in potentially stressful or threatening environments. This factor may also influence the kinds of careers people choose. Jex and Bliese (1999) suggest that individuals with high self-efficacy often self-select into high-scope jobs and work environments that offer a greater degree of autonomy.

There is some research on gender and self-efficacy, suggesting that self-efficacy predicts women's ability to handle effectively work–family role conflict (Erdwins et al., 2001) and, conversely, that gender role socialization can effect a woman's level of self-efficacy (Hackett and Betz, 1981). The measure used in the current study (Sherer et al., 1982) consists of 17 items. An example of these items is 'If I can't do a job the first time, I keep trying until I can'.

Locus of control

This is a personal belief system about the extent to which success and failure, rewards and punishments are contingent upon one's own actions or external factors. An individual with an internal locus of control believes his or her actions are key, while an individual with an external locus of control believes that success and failure are products of outside forces (fate, luck, deity, other people). Internals are more likely to engage in actions to improve or control their environment, place greater emphasis on striving for achievement, have more position mobility, are more active in managing their own careers and engage in more entrepreneurial activity. Internals report greater job satisfaction (Spector, 1988), are less alienated from the work environment and less likely to commit counterproductive behaviours in response to work frustration (Fox and Spector, 1999). A body of research has demonstrated that individuals with internal locus of control perceive less work stress and are better able to cope with the stress they experience (Anderson, 1977; Judge et al., 1999; Kobasa, 1979; Spector, 1988).

Gender differences have been demonstrated as well: external locus of control has been demonstrated to be positively related to stressors and symptoms of ill-health, and negatively related to job satisfaction for women, and moderates the relation between job stress and ill health for women but not for men (Muhonen and Torkelson, 2004). Locus of control has also been studied cross-culturally (Spector et al., 2002) and has shown wide variability between national samples. Our survey used Spector's (1988) work locus of control, a 16-item scale which measures locus of control specifically in the work domain. An example is 'People who perform their jobs well generally get rewarded for it'.

Need for achievement

This personality characteristic is a preference for challenging but achievable tasks and a willingness to work harder than required. Individuals with a high need for achievement are motivated to overcome barriers to success; they want specific feedback on how they are performing (McClelland et al., 1976). Recent organizational research has linked need for achievement with job performance, prosocial organizational behaviour (Baruch et al., 2004) and career commitment (Goulet and Singh, 2002). This personal characteristic has been studied cross-culturally as well (Punnett, 1998). The 16-item measure used in the current study (Jackson, 1989) includes items such as 'I will not be satisfied until I am the best in my field of work'.

Additional personal variables

To capture key characteristics our survey missed, each woman we interviewed was asked, in an open-ended question, to discuss anything about herself as a person that had contributed to her success. We will see in later chapters that the women were certainly not shy in pinpointing the locus of their success on what they believed were defining personal characteristics. They emphasized self-confidence, a positive attitude, high energy, persistence and, above all, 'hard, hard, hard work'. These characteristics should be incorporated into future models and surveys.

Culture

Three variables were chosen to represent national cultural dimensions. Based on the work of Hofstede (1980a), we chose the three most widely researched cross-cultural variables: individualism/collectivism, power distance and uncertainty avoidance. These dimensions, which will be discussed at length in Chapter 3, were measured with the scale developed by Dorfman and Howell (1988). Here we present a brief overview of the three variables.

Individualism/collectivism
This most widely studied cultural dimension is the tendency for a person to be motivated by his/her own preferences and goals, while collectivism is the tendency for a person to view him/herself as part of a network of social groups. A scale item representing collectivism is 'Employees should only pursue their goals after considering the welfare of the group'.

Power distance
Cultures with high power distance exhibit a greater acceptance of inequality, special privileges for those of higher status and an organizational hierarchy. An item representing high power distance is 'It is frequently necessary for a manager to use authority and power when dealing with subordinates'.

Uncertainty avoidance
This dimension is an aversion to risk. This comprises beliefs that dissidence is dangerous, written rules and regulations are needed, and experts are to be followed. An item representing uncertainty avoidance is 'Managers expect employees to closely follow instructions and procedures'.

Support

Figure 1.2 illustrates the theoretical premise that demographics (in our study, gender and nationality) affect success primarily through their influence on the types and levels of support people receive in life and in their professional endeavours. Support might come from within the work organization, or from external sources such as family, educational and religious institutions, professional associations, government programmes, and so on. Support might be formal (such as formal mentoring programmes) or informal (such as social networks), current or past. In Chapter 6, we hear from women about the kinds of support or lack of support they received in their early family and educational experiences, in the early stages of their careers and currently. We also look in greater depth at research on mentoring of women in organizations, and what our women said about their mentoring experiences.

In the written survey, a 16-item scale (Tepper et al., 1996) measured two types of mentoring: psychosocial and career oriented. Psychosocial mentoring includes emotional and social support, role models and access to social networks. A sample item is 'encouraged you to talk openly about anxieties and fears that detract from your work'. In contrast, career-oriented mentoring includes sharing of information and know-how, sponsorship and visibility, and political power and resources. A sample item is 'assigned responsibilities to you that have increased your contact with people who will judge your potential for future advancement'. Additional survey questions asked how many mentors the women had had, the gender and age of the mentors, and whether the mentors had been internal or external to the organization.

The personal interviews tapped several aspects of support. Work–life balance is generally considered to be one of the most overwhelming stressors for working women, and one manifestation of the difficulties women have in managing this conflict is the amount of assistance they have in managing their homes. One interview question asks about the level and kinds of current housekeeping help available to the woman (for example, contributions by the spouse, children, household help, mother/father or extended family).

At a more general level, open-ended questions asked what factors external to themselves had contributed to their success, what other people, if any, had contributed to their success and, in particular, in what ways gender and nationality/ethnicity had helped or hindered their professional careers.

Outcomes: Satisfaction and Success

The ongoing debates in organizational studies and industrial/organizational psychology concerning the complex relationships among job satisfaction, performance, success and life satisfaction are beyond the scope of this endeavour. We believe that both satisfaction and success are important, and decided to consider them as separate but related outcomes of the model.

Job satisfaction
This is arguably the most studied variable in organizational behaviour research. We measured job satisfaction with a three-item scale derived from the Michigan organizational assessment scale (Cammann et al., 1979). A straightforward example is 'All in all, I am satisfied with my job'. To this we added a parallel item measuring general life satisfaction.

Success
Rather than directly measuring success in the written survey, we defined success as a criterion of inclusion in the study. We operationalizd success as having reached a certain level in one's professional career (see description of participants, below). In the interview, we asked our respondents whether they felt they had succeeded in achieving their goals and ambitions, and whether they considered themselves to be successful people.

PARTICIPANTS IN THE STUDY

Participants were 'successful women' in Argentina, Brazil and Chile in South America, St Vincent and the Grenadines (SVG), Jamaica and Barbados in the West Indies, and Mexico, the USA and Canada in North America. Because we needed a relatively objective and roughly comparable indicator of success, we defined successful women as women who have reached a relatively high level in their professions or occupations. Our goal was to sample women who were representative of professional success in contrasting occupational sectors and countries. More specifically, we set the following criteria for participation in the study:

- *Private sector*: managers of managers
- *Academic sector*: tenured, full professors or senior university administrators
- *Entrepreneurial sector*: women who have owned a business for at least two years
- *Additional optional groups*: government ministers/officials, legal, engineering and medical professionals.

More details about the methods of selecting participants in each country and descriptions of the women who responded follow in Chapters 7–12, each of which focuses on a single country.

We recognized that in order to draw conclusions about the characteristics of successful women, we needed to survey a comparison group. We chose to survey a group in each country consisting of both male and female undergraduate students. The students completed the same instrument as the women, except that the mentoring scale was not included (because we assumed some students would have little work experience). Students were selected as a comparison group because it seemed that this was a likely base from which successful women would emerge. Since students are likely to be high on the personal characteristics identified, relative to the general population, and since future successful women would presumably be included in this group, differences in obtained scores would represent an underestimate of true differences, and would thus provide powerful evidence of the importance of these characteristics to the success of women. We intentionally chose personality variables (self-efficacy, need for achievement and locus of control) that tend to be relatively stable over a person's lifetime, so that differences between students and successful professionals could not be attributed primarily to age. The students and the successful women came from the same cultural backgrounds, and thus scores on these measures were not expected to be significantly different for the women and the students.

The Countries Studied

The countries involved in the Successful Women of the Americas project are Argentina, Brazil, Chile, St Vincent and the Grenadines, Jamaica, Barbados, Mexico, the USA and Canada (see Figure 1.3). Each of these countries is considered in its own chapter, as we look to unique historical, political, economic and cultural factors that intertwine with the story of women in that society. What follows here is a brief sketch of each country, just to give a flavour of the excitement we have experienced working with people from all these great places – and the tremendous challenges women face in each of them.

South America and the Caribbean

We begin with a brief discussion of the South American and Caribbean countries included in the study.

Argentina

To the rest of the world, Argentina probably means 'tango' 'pampas', 'meat' and 'soccer'. In the past few years Argentina has also meant 'crisis and default'. In fact Argentina is all of the above – but much, much more.

Argentina is a land of tremendous geographic and climatic contrasts, from the immense eastern plains to the impressive Andes mountain range. Culturally, Argentineans feel European. It is said that Argentineans grow up looking beyond the Atlantic Ocean. When asked about their ethnicity, Argentina's women feel proud to answer 'European' because, in almost every family, Spain or Italy are somehow part of their inheritance. From Spain, Argentineans received not only their language and religion (89.87 per cent are Catholics, but also the third largest Jewish community in the world lives there), but also their architecture, music, literature and lifestyle. Argentineans inherited their love of gastronomy from their European background as well. No matter how many hours a woman works, and how successful she is, her family will expect a 'hand-crafted' meal on the table. Argentineans are friendly, and love to invite friends to their homes. Lunch and dinner are good opportunities to gather families and friends around the table.

Politically and economically, the turbulence of Argentina's past continues to this day. Despite legal prohibitions, Argentina's patriarchal society still encourages discrimination against women, from unequal pay to gender-specific recruitment advertising. Even the language itself may play a role, as the words denoting each profession have masculine and feminine forms, and may carry gendered connotations. But there has been some

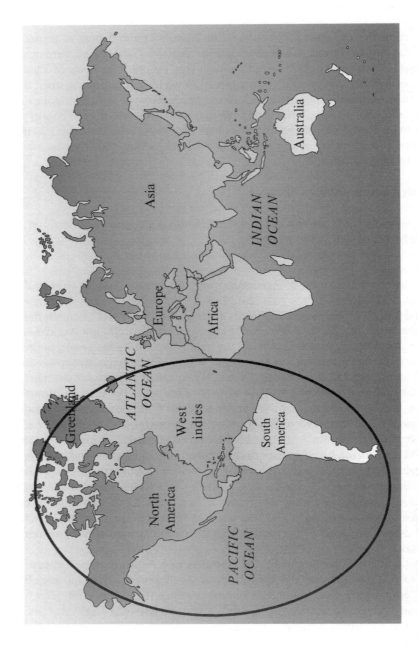

Figure 1.3   Map highlighting the Americas

16

improvement over the past few years. Today women hold the same number of higher academic degrees as men, and women are attending universities at a higher rate than men. However, on academic faculties, women are concentrated in lower and mid-level positions. Women's political representation is among the highest in Latin America, centred in mid-level ministerial positions and the judiciary. Women hold close to 30 per cent of managerial positions, but represent a very small proportion of board directors, presidents, vice-presidents or general directors.

As with women in much of Latin America, Argentinean women often employ outside services for domestic help and childcare. Nevertheless, the responsibility for the household is not shared with men in this culture, and Argentinean women continue to struggle between their need to be professionally successful and their household obligations. Perhaps their biggest task is not feeling guilty because of their professional success.

Brazil
Brazil is the largest country in South America and the fifth largest country in the world. It possesses the fourth largest population on the planet with a total of 169 799 170 inhabitants (Brazilian Institute of Geography and Statistics, 2005).

The coast of Brazil extends 7408 km along the Atlantic Ocean. Brazil borders all of the nations of South America, except for Ecuador and Chile. The Brazilian population comprises several races: in the south and southeast areas the population is predominantly German, Italian and Japanese, while in the north it is predominantly African and Dutch. In spite of this great heterogeneity, Brazil does not possess any dominant racial group. Portuguese is the official language of the country, and English is the second language, the latter more commonly spoken in areas in which the tourist industry is concentrated. The main religion of the country is Catholicism, but Protestantism, Candomblé, Macumba and Umbada are also practised. The climate is tropical, varying from 18 to 30 °C, allowing the use of light and airy clothes. The largest Brazilian city is São Paulo with about 18 million inhabitants, and is considered the centre of the manufacturing industry.

Between 1985 and 2002, the participation of Brazilian women in the labour market grew from 32 per cent to 40 per cent (Bruschini and Lombardi, 2004). Women's jobs are concentrated in public service, education and health. The general level of education has continued to increase over the past few years, more so for women than for men. In 1999, 54.2 per cent of Brazilian women had completed 12 years of study, compared with 45.8 per cent of men. By 2002, that had risen to 55.4 per cent for women, but declined to 44.6 per cent for men. In higher education and professional education, women's participation is concentrated in a few specific areas, forming feminine 'niches' or occupational 'ghettos' (Ministério Da Educação E Cultura, 2005). Their strongest concentration is in the areas of education, services, health and social well-being, humanities and arts, social sciences, business and law, and weakest in precisely those disciplines leading to the higher-paid careers: science, mathematics, computing, agriculture, veterinary, engineering, production and construction. Although women continue to obtain increasingly higher levels of education than men, their salary levels continue to lag behind those of men.

Chile

We proceed to south-west South America, stretching far south to Antarctica, with its true polar winds. Chile is a country of startling contrasts and extreme beauty, with attractions ranging from the towering volcanic peaks of the Andes to the ancient forests of the Lake District. Chile has become known as the Land of Poets because of Pablo Neruda and Gabriela Mistral. Gabriela Mistral was the first Latin American woman to win the Nobel Prize for Literature, in 1945, and in her acceptance speech said: 'At this moment, by an undeserved stroke of fortune, I am the direct voice of the poets of my race and the indirect voice for the noble Spanish and Portuguese tongues.' With a mixed European and native American heritage, she represents the Chilean culture: a heterogeneous combination of Hispanic and European elements brought by soldiers and missionaries who colonized the Chilean territory from 1535, intermarried with the indigenous people from the civilizations that were already established in that territory: Aymaras, Diaguitas, Changes, Quechuas, Mapuches, Picunches, Pehuenches, Onas and Yamana, among others.

A majority of the original indigenous peoples no longer exist, except for the Aymara (close to 90 000) and Atacameños (around 10 000) in the north; Mapuche, or people of the earth (around a million) in the south-central zone; Rapanui (3500); and some Kawaskhar and Yagans on the islands of the extreme south. Their customs and cultural heritage are protected by the Indigenous Law, which recognizes the unique character of these people and their right to live according to their own customs and cultural patterns.

The overwhelming majority of the Chilean people live in the middle of Chile. Roman Catholicism is the dominant religion, and continues to exert a strong influence over the lives of Chilean women. For example, owing to strong opposition from the Catholic Church, Chile had remained, until recently, one of only three countries in the world where divorce was banned.

Chile is one of the leading industrialized nations of Latin America. It has a strong economy based on mining, especially copper mining, and agricultural goods, largely for export. Chile is the world's largest producer and exporter of copper. It also exports fruits and vegetables, and its wines have become popular in many countries.

Over 81 per cent of women's employment is concentrated in the tertiary sector – including social, personal and community services, financial services, transportation, retailing and communication (Selamé, 2004). Total average income of women is about 65 per cent that of men's, but the gap declines for lower educational levels. Women with low education receive 83 per cent of corresponding men's income, but educated women (who have studied at university) receive only 43.8 per cent. Over the past decade and a half, women's participation in the job market has been slowly growing from 31.3 per cent to 35.6 per cent, according to the 2002 national census.

The English-speaking Caribbean
The West Indies are a string of small islands in the Caribbean sea, usually associated with sea, sun and sand. These island countries are rightfully known for their tropical lushness, wonderful weather, and some of the best sailing and diving in the world. Less often do we think of these countries from the world of work point of view but, of course, people in the Caribbean work, just as people do around the world. And women in the Caribbean face many of the same issues as do women around the world.

The map of the island countries of the Caribbean (see Chapter 3) shows the range of islands from the Bahamas in the north, off the coast of south Florida, to Trinidad and Tobago in the south, off the coast of Venezuela. This region is fascinating because of the diversity that exists in a relatively small geographic area. The Caribbean region was very important to the European economies, following Columbus's discovery of the 'New World', and the colonial powers fought over the countries of the region. The result is that there are several different languages spoken – Dutch, English, French and Spanish. There is also a local creole language in all of the islands, which reflects a mix of African and European speech. In most islands, descendants of African slaves make up the majority of the population, but there are European descendants, as well as a substantial number of Indian and Chinese residents. The original inhabitants found by the Europeans were called the Caribs but, unfortunately, only a few survive today.

The economies in the countries vary quite dramatically, from centrally planned in Cuba to essentially a free market in Trinidad and Tobago; others, such as St Vincent and the Grenadines have leaders who lean towards socialism. Some are rich (the Bahamas), some close to the first world (Barbados) and others are very poor (Haiti). Some islands remain colonies, others are closely allied with Europe (the French islands are Departments of France), but most are independent, democratic countries. The three countries included in our study were Barbados, Jamaica and

St Vincent and the Grenadines. Jamaica is the largest of these countries, with a population of approximately 2.5 million; Barbados has a population of about 300 000 and St Vincent and the Grenadines is the smallest, with a population of only 100 000. Economically, Barbados is better off than either Jamaica or SVG; both Barbados and Jamaica depend substantially on tourism for foreign earnings, while SVG is more dependent on agriculture and offshore financial services.

In many of the Caribbean countries, women are the main breadwinners, and approximately 80 per cent of the graduates of the University of the West Indies are women; thus one might expect the role of women to be better in the Caribbean than elsewhere. It is certainly true that in the English-speaking countries there are substantial numbers of women at middle levels, as well as substantial numbers of women professionals. Women do face similar challenges, however, here as elsewhere, and it is still unusual to find women at top levels, and there are relatively few women in fields such as engineering. While women still face some barriers in the world of work in the Caribbean, there has been more concern recently about the apparent marginalization of young men in the region. The current situation, where a large number of young men opt out of school, university and the legal workforce, preferring not to work or to become involved in the underground or illegal economy, means that companies are increasingly turning to young women. Many younger women work at jobs traditionally thought of as 'male', such as pumping gas.

North America

The following is a brief description of the North American countries in the study.

Canada

This second largest country in the world spans the northern portion of North America from ocean to ocean to ocean (the Atlantic, Arctic and Pacific). With polar winds in the far north, 90 per cent of its 32.5 million people live as far south as possible, within 100 miles of the US border. Canada has two official languages, English, which is the first language of 59.3 per cent and French, which is the first language of 23.2 per cent of the population. The balance, 17.5 per cent is indicative of the varied nature of Canada often termed the 'Canadian mosaic' (www.cia.gov/cia/publications/factbook/geos/ca.html).

Canada is a nation of distinct cultural regions. Newfoundland, the eastern-most province and an independent country for many years, only joined Canada in 1949 after two referenda, the results of which are still being questioned today. Although there is no sizeable separatist movement as in Quebec, there are separatist sentiments and the Newfoundlanders do have a common culture and strong ethnic identity. This has been facilitated by the homogeneous population base, originating in England and Ireland. Few women have reached upper management positions owing to vertical and institutional segregation prominent in the culture.

Quebec accounts for 25 per cent of Canada's population. French is the mother tongue of more than 80 per cent of Quebecois. A provincial law requires all external signs to be only in French. French Quebecois generally insist they are culturally different from the rest of Canada. Threats of secession from the rest of Canada, which have decreased since an unsuccessful referendum in 1995, have caused tension in Quebec and the rest of Canada.

On the whole, Canadians strongly value equality and this is reflected in its laws and programmes offering access to national health care and education. Canadians favour pragmatic over ideological thinking, which leads to a weaker sense of nationalism than is found in the USA. Women in Canada make up 46.2 per cent of the labour force (Little, 2002) and just under 50 per cent of the 15 to 64 sector of the population. However, women comprise only 32 per cent of the managerial roles, 12 per cent of senior management and 7.5 per cent of directorships. In fact, the situation is getting worse rather than better! The proportion of women legislators, senior officials and managers decreased from 37 per cent in 1996–99 to 34 per cent in 2000–02, and women's share of senior management positions has dropped by 23 per cent since 2001 (Statistics Canada, 2005). Fifty-seven per cent of Canadians holding graduate degrees are women, but half of Canada's companies do not have any women in their senior ranks (McQueen, 2001). In academic institutions, women comprise less than 30 per cent of full-time faculty members, and their wages are only 90 per cent of their male counterparts' (CFHSS-FCSH, 2002). On a more positive note for women, they are starting businesses at a rate of three to four times more than that of men (Chatelaine, 1999).

Mexico
Malinche, Sor Juana Inés de la Cruz, Josefa Ortiz de Domínguez, Margarita Maza de Juárez, Frida Kahlo, Martha Sahagún de Fox: these are the names of a few of the most revered, and at the same time criticized, Mexican women. From pre-colonial times to the twenty-first century, women in Mexico have played central, if mostly veiled and sometimes rejected, roles in all facets of society. Within this machista society (borrowing a characterization from Nobel Prize winner Octavio Paz) Mexican women have increased their labour force participation rate rapidly in the past few years. Modernity, feminism, international attention and local

support are some of the forces that might be increasing interest both within and outside the country in the development of professional and business success among Mexican women.

The land of machismo, as many call this large, diverse country, has traditionally done a poor job of offering equal opportunity to more than half of its citizens – according to the 2000 national population census, the country comprised 49.89 million women and 47.59 million men. Paradoxically, Mexico's legislation was one of the first in the Americas to outlaw gender discrimination in labour markets: as far back as 1917, the Mexican constitution stated that 'to like work must correspond like salary, regardless of sex or nationality' (Article 123, Section A, Paragraph VII).

The country's traditional culture has favoured the conventional view that women are the nurturers that have to stay and work at home, while men are the 'breadwinners' that have to work outside and enjoy the housekeeping done by the females in the family. Labour force participation rates have thus been quite different for males and females: 93.6 per cent of Mexican women aged 20 or older work at home, but only 38.7 per cent work in conventional labour markets; on the other hand, 90.4 per cent of comparable men work (or, one could say, 'help out') at home, while 41.9 per cent participate in workforce activities (INEGI, 2004a). Additionally, migratory flows statistics suggest that domestic migration within Mexico (typically from smaller population areas into the larger cities) is almost equally divided among the sexes: 52 per cent of 2.3 million migrants between 1995 and 2000 were female (INEGI, 2004a), but international emigration is dominated by male migrants: 75.3 per cent of almost 1.57 million people who left Mexico to live in the USA in the same period were males (INEGI, 2004a). These statistics paint a picture showing that Mexican women tend to participate in labour markets less than males, and that they also tend to travel shorter distances and in lesser numbers.

Some improvement can be seen over the past 35 years. In 1970, only 17 per cent of women aged 12 and older worked outside their home; between 1991 and 1997, female participation in the workforce increased from almost 35 per cent to close to 40 per cent (NAALC, 2003). Nevertheless, related figures, such as women's schooling between the ages of 15 and 29 show a perturbing disparity: 23.5 per cent attend school, compared with 26.1 per cent of men. Fortunately, the gap between the sexes in terms of higher education attendance has been narrowing in the past years, in addition to showing strong gains for both sexes: in 1990, of 1.1 million students at the undergraduate level, 41 per cent were women, while in 2002 of the 1.9 million undergraduate students, 48.5 per cent were women. At the graduate level, there were almost 46 000 students in 1990, 34 per cent of them female; in 2002, the number had increased to over 138 000, 44.5 per cent of them being women.

Thus, while some improvements have been made in the past decades, it is easy to see that women in Mexico's labour markets have yet to see the level playing field that the country's latest revolution intended to create. It is in this context that studying the characteristics of successful women in this country takes on a special importance: what does it take to succeed in an environment that has so systematically made it difficult for women to advance in the workplace?

The USA

As the third largest country in the world in population, and fourth in area, the USA is a country of diversity in terms of geography, cultures, economy, natural resources, religious beliefs and political philosophies. Commonalities are limited to respect for the democratic government system and free enterprise system, and identification as an American citizen. Besides the Native American culture, European, African, Asian and other Spanish American cultures blend and coexist to varying degrees owing to the influx of peoples from throughout the world. Politically the country encompasses views from conservatism to liberalism. Religious affiliation tends to be either Protestant or Roman Catholic with smaller representation in the Jewish, Mormon, Muslim and Eastern Orthodox faiths. There are also small groups of Buddhists and Hindus. Economically, the USA enjoys a high standard of living because it is one of the most highly developed and productive counties in the world. There appears to be a continuing shift from the manufacturing industries to the service and information sectors.

Growing numbers of US women are entering the workforce. They represent 43 per cent of the total workforce in the USA. Women are starting their own businesses at a faster rate than men. They own over 10 million companies accounting for over 45 per cent of all US firms. However, they are not well represented in either the boardroom or in top management. In a study comparing men and women executives in the USA, Catalyst (2005b), a research, consulting and advocacy organization promoting women in business, found that men and women shared many of the same career obstacles and the same strategies to overcome them. However, women faced a layer of additional challenges that few men had to deal with, such as lack of general management or line experience, systematic exclusion from informal networks, gender-based stereotypes and preconceptions of women's roles and abilities (Catalyst, 2003a). At the highest level of corporate America, women hold 13.6 per cent of board seats in Fortune 500 companies (Catalyst, 2003a), and more than 54 Fortune 500 companies have no women on their boards of directors.

While women's earnings have been increasing over the past decade, estimates of women's salaries range from 76 per cent to 80 per cent of those
of their male counterparts. This pay inequity is even more pronounced for
college-educated women who work full time. A typical college-educated
woman working full time earns $44 200 a year compared with $61 800 for
college-educated male workers, averaging 71.5 cents to the men's dollar
(American Association of University Women, 2005). Although women are
now at parity with men in terms of the number of doctorates awarded,
they hold about one-third of tenure or tenure-track positions in US
colleges and an even lower percentage of full-tenured or administrative
positions.

Clearly, differences in institutional and cultural environments emerge
among the countries of the Americas. Each country offers unique opportunities and unique challenges to women in business and the professions.
Yet in each country, there are some women who have succeeded in their
chosen fields. Becoming successful in the face of substantial barriers to
success implies that these women have personal characteristics, belief
systems and backgrounds that set them apart within their own environments. Just what is it that enables some women, and not others, to succeed
in spite of all roadblocks? Is there some magical ingredient that helps
women regardless of the cultures and institutions in which they work, or
does it vary from country to country? Do successful women in a given
country more closely resemble successful women in other countries than
they resemble their own national compatriots?

These are the questions that intrigued a group of university professors
from around the Americas, who met serendipitously at a professional
development workshop in Chicago in 1999.

THE SUCCESSFUL WOMEN OF THE AMERICAS PROJECT

In 1998, Betty Jane Punnett, a professor of management at the University
of the West Indies came up with an idea for a professional development
workshop (PDW) for the annual meeting of the Academy of Management.
The workshop, with the gorgeous name 'From polar winds to tropical
breezes' was a hands-on experience in developing research questions
and strategies for doing management research in the Americas. Attendees
were professors and advanced doctoral students with an interest in international management issues of particular concern in light of NAFTA
and prospective additional Free Trade Agreements among the countries
of the Caribbean, North, Central and South Americas. The workshop

participants were divided into three or four groups by academic interest area, such as strategic management and organizational behaviour. Each group held a breakout session, in which they were to come up with an interesting research question and research plan related to international or cross-cultural management issues in the Americas.

No matter how internally driven professors may think we are, sometimes you have to chalk things up to pure, dumb luck. At the organizational behaviour discussion table, the problematic of barriers to the professional success of women in the various American countries was raised. The idea caught on fire, and when the group was reluctantly dragged back to the workshop debriefing, it had the seeds of an exciting international research project to report. Several members of different breakout groups, upon hearing our report, asked to join the group. By the end of the workshop, an amazing thing happened. A handful of academics from university campuses in lands of polar winds and tropical breezes, who had never met before nor come to the workshop with any expectations beyond a good learning experience, agreed to form the core of a serious research endeavour. Betty Jane Punnett tells the story of the early years of this project in Chapter 4, from our first meeting in Chicago to the pilot of our research project in the tropical breezes of the Caribbean.

Members of the Successful Women Worldwide (SWW) Core Team and Partners have talked about this project in workshops, symposia and presentations at academic and professional meetings throughout the Americas and in Europe. We have published papers in a number of conference proceedings, and have three papers under peer review by major academic journals. Appendix C has more information about our academic milestones to date. The Core Research Team consisted of those listed in the 'Contributors' section of this book.

In addition we would like to thank Martha Reavley, University of Windsor, Pamela Lirio, PhD student, McGill University, Monica Mancini, Pontifícia Universidade Católica de São Paulo and Mitchell Cohen, MSc student, Concordia University, for help with completing the book. We would like to note that Gina Arismendi, MBA Sam Houston State University, wrote the first qualitative paper. The College of Business Administration, Sam Houston State University supported the US data collection and collation and the SWW conference held at Sam Houston. The Faculty of Business Administration, Memorial University of Newfoundland, supported the Newfoundland data collection, and the University of the West Indies, Cave Hill Campus, funded the research in the Caribbean. The Canadian Social Sciences and Humanities Research Council and Concordia University supported the conference held at Concordia.

OVERVIEW OF BOOK

With this chapter, we hope we have piqued your curiosity about those all too few but extraordinary women across the Americas, who have managed to beat the odds and become role models of professional success. We have taken you through the process with which we theorized just exactly what we mean by success, and the kinds of factors that help or hurt women in their efforts to achieve it. We have noted the long road we have taken, from our initial curiosity, through the development of our core research questions, informal and formal establishment of an international research team, and development of a survey and interview project. In the chapters to come, we take you on a guided tour of the results and conclusions of this exciting project.

In Chapter 2, Ann Gregory, Catherine Mossop and Neusa Maria Bastos F. Santos look more closely at the current status of women in the Americas. What has their role been in their respective countries, and where do they stand today? More importantly, what roles can women expect to play in the free trade regions and turbulently changing national and global economies of the future? This chapter then summarizes what the research literature has to say about the questions we have asked in this project.

Chapter 3 elaborates one of the basic underlying themes of this book: culture matters! Miguel R. Olivas-Luján and Betty Jane Punnett take us through the theory and research literature of the role of culture in professional experience in general, and women's experience in particular. The cultural and personal factors we chose to investigate in the study will also be introduced.

Every story has a beginning. In Chapter 4, 'Beginning the research in a tropical breeze', Betty Jane Punnett and Lawrence Nurse describe the first stages of this project, from our chance meeting at a professional development workshop, the formation of the Successful Women Worldwide Core Team, up through the pilot study in the West Indies.

Chapters 5 and 6 allow the successful women of our study to speak to you in their own voices. These chapters summarize the findings of interviews with women from nine countries. In Chapter 5, Suzy Fox and Ann Gregory highlight what the women have to say about their own personalities, management styles and leadership. Terri R. Lituchy and Jo Ann Duffy present what the successful women had to say about their professional and life experiences, mentoring and social support in Chapter 6. Here the focus is on barriers they encountered along the way, and sources of social support that helped them to overcome these barriers to success.

Chapters 7 to 12 discuss the individual countries in our project. Each chapter includes background information about the country, and about the status of women in general and in business and professional leadership in particular. Each chapter describes the sample of women who participated in our study as well as any particular features of the procedures (for example, translation issues). Finally, the results for each country are presented and discussed. The country chapters are organized, from north to south as follows:

Chapter 7, Canada by Terri R. Lituchy, Ann Gregory, Joan Dewling and Robert Oppenheimer

Chapter 8, USA by Jo Ann Duffy, Suzy Fox and John Miller

Chapter 9, Mexico by Miguel R. Olivas-Luján and Leticia Ramos Garza

Chapter 10, Brazil by Neusa Maria Bastos F. Santos

Chapter 11, Argentina by Silvia Inés Monserrat, Griselda Lassaga and Claudia D'Annunzio

Chapter 12, Chile by Mahia S. Saracostti, Silvia Inés Monserrat and Margarita María Errázuriz Ossa, President, ComunidadMujer, Santiago, Chile

Finally, Betty Jane Punnett, John Miller and Donald Wood draw it all together in Chapter 13, giving us 'The big picture from polar winds to tropical breezes.'

NOTES

1. Shortly before this book went to press in early 2006, women were elected to the highest offices in Chile, Jamaica, Liberia, Germany and South Korea. The success of these women in achieving these positions underscores the success that women can achieve, as illustrated throughout this book.
2. The women quoted here, respectively, come from Brazil, the USA, the West Indies, Canada (Newfoundland), Canada, Argentina, the USA and Brazil.

2. Successful women professionals in the Americas: theoretical perspectives and empirical findings

Ann Gregory, Catherine Mossop and Neusa Maria Bastos F. Santos

Chapter 1 discussed the increase in women in the Americas entering non-traditional professions, and pointed out that only a small minority of these reach the top of their professions. In our study we include women entrepreneurs, women managers (including government, not for profit and for profit) and professional women (in medicine, academia, law and engineering). We ask:

- What are the characteristics of those who managed to reach the upper levels?
- What were the barriers they faced in attaining the top ranks?
- What support did they receive?

The focus of the chapter is on the existing literature, and the results of previous research, which points the way to answering these questions. Throughout the book we draw on aspects of the literature review presented here. In this chapter, the literature review can be related to many aspects of the theoretical model, introduced in Chapter 1.

We begin with a brief look at women in the workforce in the Americas. Appendix E presents some statistics and discussion on women in the workforce worldwide, for readers who want to compare the situation in the Americas with the rest of the world.

WOMEN IN THE WORKFORCE, MANAGEMENT AND PROFESSIONS IN THE AMERICAS

In this following section, we discuss overall workforce trends in the Americas, as well as workforce trends in Canada and the USA and in Latin America; then we look at trends in terms of management.

There have been changes in labour participation rates over the years; however, gender segregation and differential wages still remain. This is shown in Table 2.1 (for countries for which information was available).

The two developed countries of the Americas, the USA and Canada,

Table 2.1   Economic activity and women's share of the labour force in the Americas

Country	Year	Female adult (15+) economic activity rate (%)	Male adult (15+) economic activity (%)	Women's share of the labour force (%)
Argentina	2003	46	72	43
Bahamas	2002	62	76	48
Barbados	2002	62	76	48
Bolivia	2000	60	82	45
Brazil	2001	54	81	42
Canada	2002	61	73	46
Chile	2003	36	71	34
Colombia	2003	51	76	43
Costa Rica	2003	42	80	36
Dominica	1997	60	75	–
Ecuador	2003	54	81	41
El Salvador	2003	46	79	41
French Guiana	1999	53	68	44
Grenada	1997	62	75	–
Honduras	2001	43	85	36
Jamaica	2003	53	71	44
Mexico	2003	38	81	34
Netherlands Antilles	2000	53	67	49
Nicaragua	2000	36	91	30
Panama	2003	46	79	37
Peru	2003	56	75	44
Puerto Rico	2002	36	58	43
Saint Lucia	2001	54	76	43
Suriname	1999	33	61	37
Trinidad and Tobago	2002	48	75	39
USA	2003	60	74	47
Uruguay	2003	49	69	45
Venezuela	2002	55	84	40

Source: ILO (2003); LABORSTA database accessed in 2004; ILO Caribbean Office, Digest of Caribbean Labour Statistics 1998 (Port of Spain, Labour Office, 1999); and national statistics reports, United Nations Statistics Division, Demographic and Social Statistics, http://unstats.un.org/unsd/demographic/products/indwm/ww2005/tab5d.htm.

together, have the highest participation rate of women in the work-force (60.5 per cent); the Caribbean area, including French Guiana and Suriname, has the second highest (54 per cent), and the Latin American region the lowest (averages 50 per cent).

Workforce Trends in Canada and the USA

Over the last several decades, increasing proportions of women have been labour participants in those two countries. In 1970, only about 43 per cent of women participated in the labour force (US Department of Labor, 2004), whereas in 2004 women overall had a labour force partici-pation rate of 59.2 per cent, representing 46 per cent of the total US labour force (US Department of Labor, Women's Bureau, 2005), with black women having the highest participation rate (61.5 per cent) and Hispanic the lowest (56.1 per cent). They were employed in management, professional and related occupations (38 per cent), in sales and office occupations (35 per cent), in service occupations (20 per cent), and other occupations (7 per cent) (US Department of Labor, Women's Bureau, 2005). Women's real wages advanced from 1979 to 2002, increasing by 27 per cent, and they moved during that time period into higher-paying job categories (US Department of Labor, Women's Bureau, 2005, p. 1). Their unemployment rates are roughly similar to those of men. While women especially were more likely to work in a managerial or professional spe-cialty occupation by 2002, women 'still accounted for the lion's share of employment in some of the relatively lower-paying occupations within this broad category'. (ibid., p. 1) For example, only 11 per cent of engi-neers were women, but 98 per cent of preschool and kindergarten teach-ers were women (ibid., p. 1 and table 10). Black and Hispanic women had greater earnings parity with black and Hispanic men, 91 per cent and 88 per cent, versus 78 per cent for white women (ibid., p. 2 and table 13). In Canada, average income for women, in comparison with men's income, is relatively stable, with little narrowing of the wage gap. There has been little change from 1994 to 2002; in 1994 the differential for women was 62.0 per cent and in 2002 it only went up to 65.2 per cent. As in other countries, women in Canada continue to earn less than their male coun-terparts, regardless of age, education, experience, labour market attach-ment or occupation. At all educational levels, the income of working women, as compared with that of men, does not reach above 71 per cent. Part of the reason for the differential in wages is occupational segrega-tion, women are overrepresented in the lowest paid occupations and underrepresented in the highest paying occupations (in the latter, women comprise around 25 per cent of the total share of full-time full-year work). Owing to global structural changes, there is a secondary labour market in the growing service sector of low-paid contingent workers. Women remain overrepresented in this secondary market, and it is expected that this will remain the case. A secondary result of global restructuring affecting Canada is the decline of the public sector, which, in the past decades has been an important factor in women's integration into the labour market. A third area of growth has been in self-employment, but in Canada women are concentrated in a few service industries, such as childcare, sales and hairdressing, again located at the lower end (see www40.statcan.ca/101/cst01/labour01a.htm).

Workforce Trends in Latin America

Latin American women have similar educational backgrounds to men, but women participate less in the labour market, and many of those who do participate tend to be the least well paid and have bad working conditions. In the early 1980s, women's labour participation rate in Latin America was only 24.7 per cent, a rise from 1970, when it was only 19.9 per cent (Wirth, 2001). Table 2.2 compares the labour rate participation in the early 1990s and the late 1990s in eight Latin American countries, which have higher labour participation rates than the average.

For those women who are working in 18 Latin American countries, according to research reported in 2001, there has been substantial progress made, including the steady closing of the gender wage gap in Venezuela,

Table 2.2   Changes in labour force participation rates of women in eight Latin American countries

Country	Participation in early 1990s (%)	Participation in late 1990s (%)
Brazil	44	50
Chile	35	41
Colombia	36	45
Costa Rica	24	35
Honduras	37	51
Panama	30	41
Uruguay	52	58
Venezuela	35	48
Average	37	46

Source: Adapted from Duryea et al. (2001).

Costa Rica, Brazil and Uruguay (Duryea et al., 2001). Nevertheless, as in other parts of the world, most women are concentrated in a few occupations, while men are in a wider range of occupations (Oliveira, 2001). The level of women's education has increased in Latin America, but this has not resulted in proportionate wage increases. On average women earn 75 per cent of men's earnings in Argentina, Chile and Uruguay; the largest gender difference is among qualified professionals where women earn 65 per cent of what men earn, even when their educational attainments are higher than those of their male co-workers (Correla, 1998).

WOMEN MANAGERS IN THE AMERICAS

Table 2.3 shows women's share as a percentage of administrative and managerial workers in the Americas (in those countries for which there is information).

Table 2.3   Women's share as administrative and managerial workers and high officials in the Americas

Country	% of total employment	% of administrative and managerial workers	% of legislators, senior officials and managers
Argentina	48	–	27
Bermuda	58	43	–
Bolivia	48	–	37
Brazil	62	44	–
Canada	62	33	34
Chile	52	21	–
Colombia	50	38	–
Costa Rica	26	–	54
El Salvador	47	–	27
Mexico	35	–	26
Netherlands Antilles	52	–	30
Peru	53	–	28
Trinidad and Tobago	42	–	40
Venezuela	61	28	–
United States	55	48	–

Source: ILO (2004b).

The latest findings of Catalyst (2004) for the USA indicate that, although men and women equally aspire to be the CEO of an organization and they use the same strategies, women still face a host of stereotypes and environmental challenges. Some of the barriers are exclusion from informal networks, lack of role models, an inhospitable corporate culture and difficulty in achieving line experience. Women of colour were more concerned than were white women about the lack of mentors/sponsors and access to informal networks. According to Catalyst, among the Fortune 500 companies, there are eight women CEOs, 5.2 per cent of the top earners are women, and women comprise 7.9 per cent of those with the highest titles, 13.6 per cent of the boards of directors and 15.7 per cent of the corporate officers. Women's advancement into corporate upper levels in Canada is even slower, with 7.1 per cent in 2004 holding upper-level executive positions (Catalyst, 2005a).

Table 2.4 shows the proportion of women in executive, technical and academic positions for the Latin American countries that are included in the sample. However, it is not clear at which level they operate and what the definition of 'executive position' is.

According to an ILO study, in 1991 women in Latin America comprised only around 3 per cent of the top executives (Wirth, 2001). A recent study of seven countries in Latin America (Argentina, Brazil, Chile, Colombia, El Salvador, Mexico and Venezuela) noted that women have been successful in terms of achieving management positions in the private sector; however, they are not well represented among the highest levels of the corporate hierarchy (Maxfield, 2005). On average in the above countries, women make up almost 35 per cent of all corporate employees, but roughly 10 per cent of corporate presidents or vice-presidents. The report found

Table 2.4   *Index of women holding executive, technical and academic*
positions for Latin American countries included in the study

Country	Executive positions	Technical and academic positions
Argentina	–	–
Brazil	–	62
Chile	22	51
Mexico	21	40

Source: World Development Indicator 2000; World Bank, 2000; Report on Human Development, 1998, 2000; PNDU, 1998, 2000 (Publifolha, 2002, p. 36). The data is for 1998 of the last available year. Adapted by Neusa Santos.

that women were still a rarity in the boardroom, going from a low of 3 per cent in Mexico to a high of 7 per cent in Argentina (Maxfield, 2005). In Mexico there has also been growth of women in professional and managerial positions (20 per cent in 1993; see Muller and Rowell, 1997); however, the proportion of top-level positions was 7 per cent, around the same as Canada's; this was an increase of 2 per cent from 1993 to 2001 (Zabludovsky, 2001).

In Brazilian companies women who were directors, managers and department heads in the highest salary brackets comprised about 3 per cent of the total (Wirth, 2001). In Brazil there are salary differences between men and women with the same education, a phenomenon which is an extension of the concept of 'glass walls,' that is, the tendency towards gender segregation in certain corporate functions or occupations. Women are concentrated in professions characterized as 'feminine,' such as nursing and teaching and these occupations have a lower remuneration than do the 'masculine professions,' such as engineering, medicine, and law. The trend, though, is for more women to go into these masculine professions (Bruschini and Puppin, 2005). Even in the more masculine occupations, salary differentials increase as careers develop (Bruschini and Puppin, 2005). The fact that women have made inroads in Brazil is demonstrated by the fact that Brazilian women occupied 24 per cent of the directorial positions in 2000, but the majority of them worked in the area of community and social services (Bruschini and Puppin, 2005).

This relatively brief overview of women in the workforce and women in management provides a basis for understanding why we chose to examine successful women in the Americas. We were struck by the challenges that women face in the world of work, but also struck by the number that succeed professionally in spite of these challenges. The rest of the chapter examines theoretical perspectives and research findings concerning professional women.

REVIEW OF THE LITERATURE

Our samples are drawn from women defined as professionally successful. We begin, therefore, by defining success and discussing differing perceptions of success. Both the scholarly and popular literatures are filled with accounts of barriers women face in various professions and the slow pace of movement to the upper levels, and we examine the different types of barriers faced by women in reaching higher management levels. We conclude with a discussion of leadership styles.

The Meaning of Success

Success can be defined in a variety of ways. Our interest in this study was primarily professional success. Below we examine the success concept.

Gender variations

The traditional objective measures that have been used to define success are income and organizational level (O'Neil et al., 2003). Gender studies have urged that success should be more broadly defined, and some recent studies have included both objective and subjective measures, such as Kirchmeyer's (2002) study in which she included a subjective indicator, called 'perceived success'. She found that even though women had not achieved as much in terms of objective career success in comparison with men (measured by income over time), women managers perceived that their careers were even more successful than the comparison men.

The extent to which women themselves define success using more objective or subjective criteria may vary depending upon whether the women have ordered or emergent career patterns (O'Neil et al., 2003). Ordered career patterns can be defined as traditional career ladders where a career follows a linear, sequential or ladder-like advancement. In contrast, emergent careers are those which do not follow any clearly logical pattern; there may be interruptions, and unpredictable 'twists and turns, serendipitous events', designed to accommodate other aspects of life than traditional work (O'Neil et al., 2003, p. 2). Women with emergent career patterns were more likely to use subjective measures, such as 'personal growth, professional development, and meaningful work', to define success (O'Neil et al., 2003, p. 2). The researchers also suggested that women with external career loci may be more likely to define success using objective measures, whereas those with internal career loci may define their career success in terms of psychological success and self-realization (O'Neil et al., 2003). The authors also found that women who had ordered careers were more satisfied than those who had emergent careers, similar to White's finding (1995, p. 13) that, for women, 'continuous full-time employment appears to be a prerequisite for career success'.

Women's attributions for success and perceptions of others

To what do women attribute their success? The attributional theory of achievement motivation (see Weiner, 1992; Weiner et al. 1972), which differentiated between internal and external attributions of success, sparked a host of studies examining differences in individual attribution for success, explained by differences in women's and men's socialization (Deaux and Emswiller, 1974; Deaux and Farris, 1977). Many of these early studies reported that women usually attributed their performance successes to external factors, such as hard work, luck and the contribution of others, but they attributed their performance failures to internal factors, such as the lack of ability (Deaux and Emswiller, 1974; Deaux and Farris, 1977). In contrast, Florentine (1988) found no significant differences between women and men in terms of internal and external attributes; however, female pre-med students had less confidence in their ability to perform the role of physician than their male counterparts. Some other studies of managers did find significant differences between women and men, with women managers attributing their achievement to hard work and their subordinates' performance, rather than to their own ability, while men attributed their success to their own ability (Rosenthal, 1995).

Perceptions of women managers are also an important consideration. Early studies (Schein, 1973; 1975) noted that both men and women believed that successful managers possessed 'characteristics, attitudes, and temperaments more commonly ascribed to men in general than to women in general' (Brenner et al., 1989). The authors found that even though women had entered middle management positions, male middle managers still adhered to a male managerial stereotype (Brenner et al., 1989). This perception that the 'good manager' is masculine has been noted in other studies (Lueger et al., 1984; Rosen and Jerdee, 1974; White et al., 1981). The following section outlines the three major theoretical perspectives for understanding why women face difficulty in advancement.

Theoretical Perspectives

Three theoretical perspectives are used to explain the position of women in management and masculine-typed professions and why it is difficult for women to advance in management or their profession (for a discussion of these perspectives see Fagenson and Horowitz, 1985; Gregory, 1990; Riger and Galligan, 1980). These perspectives are presented in chronological order, indicating the evolution of thinking in the field.

The person-centred view
This perspective holds that internal characteristics of women (either due to socialization or biology) are responsible for women exhibiting traits and behaviours that are not conducive to holding management positions (see Hennig and Jardim, 1976; Horner, 1968). This view has given rise to many studies on the extent to which gender differences exist between men and women managers, especially studies on personality, motivation to manage and leadership. In general, there were no gender differences except in leadership studies. These differences arose from perception, not actual per-

formance; nevertheless, 'the perception still exists that women do not possess the personality attributes, motivation to manage, and leadership skills to manage' (Gregory, 1990, p. 259).

The organization-centred perspective
In contrast, according to Kanter (1977), it is not an individual's gender, but the position in organizational power hierarchies which influences their traits and behaviours. The women studied by Kanter rose to management positions from the secretarial level and they remained in low-level positions, and their femininity and exhibition of feminine traits were developed in response to these positions. According to Kanter, if these women had been in high-level positions, they would have exhibited behaviours and traits appropriate to those holding higher positions. Kanter stressed that the token representation of women in managerial roles had contributed to gender stereotyping, and believed this stereotyping would decrease if the proportion of women in managerial positions rose (see Heilman, 1980, as the first example of a study substantiating Kanter's thesis).

The gender context perspective
The third perspective is influenced by three streams of research: gender stereotyping, gender numerical proportions and gender-ascribed social status (Falkenberg and Rychel, 1985; Marshall, 1984; Schneer, 1985); conceptually these streams can be combined into one perspective. The gender context (see Schneer, 1985) is built on the earlier perspectives, especially Kanter, but is based on the idea that the ascribed social status of the group to which the individual belongs is important in determining the perception of others towards these individuals. Falkenberg and Rychel (1985) argued that women are stereotyped as having traits associated with being a homemaker, which has created the stereotype that women do not have the necessary traits to enter perceived masculine and/or higher status occupations. Compounding this is the perceived higher value ascribed to men and masculine traits than to women and feminine traits (Powell and Butterfield, 1979, cited in Falkenberg and Rychel, 1985). This perception prevents women from entering occupational groups on an equal footing with men (Falkenberg and Rychel, 1985; Schneer, 1985). People who are high in the power hierarchy are highly valued and are evaluated positively, and because men are dominant in the power hierarchy, they are more highly valued than females.

Marshall (1984) expanded the gender context theory by hypothesizing that any dominant majority (in terms of power) wants to maintain their positions of power and uses the psychological technique of labelling the sub-dominant group as sub-standard and restricting them to appropriate social roles. The sub-dominant group's response is to accommodate and adjust to its status. In addition, because the cultural, social and political systems are controlled by the dominant group, the members of the sub-dominant group define their own aspirations in terms of dominant group goals. In management, women, being lower-status members, are expected to provide encouragement and support for higher-status men (Falkenberg and Rychel, 1985).

RESEARCH ON PROFESSIONAL WOMEN

There is a substantial body of literature on professional women. In the following discussion we consider literature relating to managers, entrepreneurs, academics, lawyers, physicians and engineers.

Managers

The major theme at the onset of studies of women in management was the very limited number of women who held managerial ranks. This was so dramatic that a planned study in the USA in the 1960s had to be abandoned because there were so few women in managerial positions (Epstein, 1975, cited in Powell, 1999). The concept of the 'glass ceiling', to explain the few women in upper levels of management, facing women was introduced by Morrison (1992) and this concept became common in the 1980s and 1990s (see Dominguez, 1992; Hamlin, 1994; Wernick, 1994; Woody and Weiss, 1994). This term was amended to 'concrete ceiling' for African-American managers and the 'bamboo curtain' for Asian minorities in North America (see Ray, 1988; Shaw et al., 1994; Thomas and Gabarro, 1999; Woo, 1994). The growth of the women's movement in North America fuelled hopes that the situation for women would change. Progress, though, has been slow, from 3.2 per cent of corporate officers in 1995 to only 12.3 per cent in 2000 (Catalyst, 2000). For example:

> a breakthrough into the centers of organizational power seems even less likely today than it did twenty years ago. Women's increased investment in higher education and greater commitment to management as a career, as well as new equity opportunity legislation . . . did not result in a significant breakthrough into the executive ranks. Regardless of the proportion of women managers at lower levels, women in every country remain only a tiny fraction of those in senior positions. (Segal and Zellner, 1992, cited in Izraeli and Adler, 1994, p. 7).

Attention has focused in both the scholarly and the popular literatures on the reasons for the difficulties women had in reaching executive ranks.

One focus of attention has been the cultural and social system of business. Business has been characterized as inherently patriarchal, a system and culture which entails values and norms devaluing women, even when they adopt those masculine norms and values (see Marshall, 1984; Powell, 1993, Vilkinas, 2000); Powell (1999) says 'women's presence in top management positions violates the societal norm of men's higher status and superiority to a greater extent than women's presence in lower-level management positions' (p. 334).

Manifestations of this cultural system are seen in the criteria for promotion to top positions. Decision-makers, for example, are influenced by their conceptualization of those who comprise the executive suite, and this influences their choices for these positions. This is referred to as the homophily bias (Kanter, 1977; Lazarsfeld and Merton, 1954), and is based on the principle that people prefer contact with similar people and they make the most positive evaluations of people they see as similar to themselves (Ibarra, 1992). In upper-level management, this results in homosocial reproduction (Kanter, 1977) – that is, if an executive believes that men and women exhibit different behaviours in management positions, their actual behaviour and performance may have little impact upon the executive's evaluation of them. Another area where perception is key is the selection bias against women who want to be posted to expatriate assignments (Harris, 1995; Paik and Vance, 2002). Even though evidence shows that women have a high success rate, headquarters' management continue to be concerned about the likelihood of a woman's success.

Lower- and middle-level management positions have been freer from bias against women because the criteria for selection and promotion were more objective. Upper-level positions used criteria which were more subjective, and recent research has shown that women considered gender discrimination, stereotyping, and formal and informal organizational policies as contributing to women's inability to rise to upper-level positions (Liff and Ward, 2001; Wood and Lindorff, 2001). In the following discussion of women in other professions, we see that some of the themes mentioned above are echoed in the literature about women in those particular professions.

Entrepreneurs

There has been tremendous growth in women-owned firms in the Americas; for example, in the USA, between 1997 and 2002, the growth of these firms was twice as high as the overall growth of businesses and their revenues grew by 40 per cent (Winn, 2004). This is a dramatic contrast to the relatively stagnant, low percentage of women who are corporate CEOs (Catalyst, 2002). In Canada, women entrepreneurs form a major segment of Canada's small business sector, and represent the fastest growing segment (8 per cent growth in the number of women-led firms from 1996 to 2001), and nearly half of Canadian small businesses are wholly or partially owned by women (15 per cent are wholly owned by women). In contrast, the average income of women entrepreneurs is only about half of that of men – $18 400 per year compared with $33 400 for self-employed men (Church, 1998, cited in Foundation of Canadian Entrepreneurs, 2000, p. 3; see also www.edc.ca/docs/news/2004/2004_news_e_1904htm).

Many researchers have examined the differences between male and female entrepreneurs in the USA and Canada. Early studies found differences in demographics, personality characteristics and traits (Belcourt, 1987; Hisrich and Brush, 1983; Schwartz, 1979), education and experience (Birley et al., 1987; Hisrich and Brush, 1983), and in obtaining finances (Brush, 1992). The assumption in the research usually is that women's goals are similar to those of men's, that is, growth and expansion of their enterprises (see Campbell, 1992), although that is not necessarily the case (Lee-Gosselin and Grisè, 1990; Luthans et al., 1995). One study that looked at women in Quebec found that these women favoured small and stable firms, which would allow them to perform both entrepreneurial and family roles (Lee-Gosselin and Grisè, 1990).

Various approaches have been developed in the study of entrepreneurs. One approach (Goffee and Scase, 1985) classified female entrepreneurs into four groups, depending on acceptance of conventional gender roles and adherence to entrepreneurial ideals. The socialization approach has stressed the adoption of the masculine work ethic, including the sacrificing of family relationships for success (Goffee and Scase, 1989) and the prediction that 'innovators', women adhering to traditionally masculine entrepreneurial ideals, would become the most successful entrepreneurs.

Another research approach has focused on the structural barriers facing women entrepreneurs. Women's businesses prior to the 1980s were typically small and located mainly in unprofitable, labour-intensive service subsectors (Bowen and Hisrich, 1986). It was difficult for these women to obtain start-up capital owing to discrimination in terms of credit access and loans (Moore et al., 1992). In addition, the women were usually not educated in modern management methods and had not had prior business experience. In Canada, at that time, a high proportion of female-owned small businesses were run from home; these businesses were very small and in poorly paid sectors (Wehrell, 1996, cited in Marchandani, 1999, p. 231).

An alternative approach (Moore, 1999) classified entrepreneurs into two groups, 'traditionals' and the 'moderns or second generation'. Traditionals were those whose psychological and work profiles reflected traditional values associated with the roles of women. The types of businesses they were involved in were usually low income, low equity, small and slow growing (Vesper, 1983, cited in Moore, 1999). In contrast, the moderns, made up of women who left corporations in the 1980s with experience in finance, insurance, manufacturing and construction (sectors that had traditionally been dominated by men – Hisrich and O'Brien, 1981), tended to go into sectors related to their prior work experience and they were sophisticated in terms of management and strategic planning and analysis (Moore, 1999).

Mattis's (2004) study of women entrepreneurs, in which the 'moderns' predominated showed that the majority of the 650 women entrepreneurs sampled had been employed in corporations as upper-level managers. When asked why they left their former corporation, flexibility was mentioned, but the more important reasons were aspects of the glass ceiling and glass walls (for example, contributions not recognized or valued; isolation; lack of promotion; exclusion from informal networks, communications, and training opportunities). Family history was also important with 55 per cent having had at least one immediate family member who was an entrepreneur (also see Winn, 2004).

Another group of entrepreneurs that have been studied are 'copreneurs,' husband and wife teams sharing business ownership equally. Ironically, wives often take on the more traditional female roles of bookkeeping, secretarial work, and so on, while the husband takes on traditional male roles, such as financial planning, accounting, and so on (Marshack, 1994, cited in Moore, 1999, p. 385).

To sum up, women entrepreneurs face a number of challenges which men do not. Importantly, as well, women may view success differently from men. Moore (1999) said 'Women measure success differently, rating self-fulfillment and effectiveness highest, followed by profits, goal achievement, and employee satisfaction' (p. 385).

Brush (1992), Cuba et al. (1983) and Rosa et al. (1994) all find that women entrepreneurs tend to pursue intrinsic goals rather than financial goals. They are also concerned with customer satisfaction and social responsibility (Chaganti and Parasuraman, 1996). We now examine the research related to women in a number of professions.

Professional Women

Academics
A major early study of academic women (Bernard, 1966) found that there had been active discrimination against women, including famous women such as the anthropologists Ruth Benedict and Margaret Mead. Women who had received doctorates from prestigious universities tended to be

employed in low-status or low-prestige schools, compared with their male counterparts, and their rank and salary were lower. One example of the discriminatory treatment of women in the early 1960s was the holding of departmental meetings in male-only clubs (personal interview, October 1967).

Widespread changes have occurred since the 1960s, but women still encounter barriers in academia. For example, in 2003 in the USA, women held 44 per cent of doctoral degrees and a similar share of initial academic appointments, but they held only 33 per cent of the faculty positions and were slower to win tenure and full professorships (Krefting, 2003). They also receive lower salary benefits, including payoffs for academic achievements, relative to comparable men (Valian, 1998). Statistics Canada reports a gender-based faculty wage gap of 80 per cent for full-time tenured and tenure-track women professors and 70 per cent for women academics employed part time (www.fedcan.ca/english/issues/issues/wagegaps).

A study of law faculty members found that a high proportion (60 per cent) of the women was restricted to non-tenure track positions, compared with only 40 per cent of the men (McBrier, 2003). Another study found that 70 per cent of legal writing teachers and assistant deans were women but only 10 per cent of law school deans were women (Leavitt, 2001). Women served on more committees, especially committees concerned with student admission and support, and rarely served on the appointments committee (Leavitt, 2001). Experiences are also interpreted differently for women and men; for example, prosecutor experience is seen as an asset for men, but not for women (McBrier, 2003, p. 1243).

Studies have also shown that exit rates of women faculty from the natural sciences and engineering are double those from the social sciences (Preston, 2004). The reasons are similar to those stated of other male-dominated professions (lower earnings and advancement opportunities, dearth of mentoring, and the difficulty of combining family with a scientific career), but these women face greater barriers than those in other fields. Publication rates for women in science and engineering are almost equal to those for men (Xie and Shauman, 1998), but women make up a very small proportion of important academic leadership positions (Niemeier and Gonzalez, 2004).

Women faculty members at the Massachusetts Institute of Technology (MIT) began to meet to assess their treatment and found that women faculty members had lower pay than men, and were less likely to be in central positions in their department (Bailyn, 2003). The MIT study gave impetus to demands by women faculty at other universities for increased equity. As with other professions, academics complain that they are expected to follow the male model, without regard for differential demands during child-bearing years.

Women's accounts of their experiences in academia have three common concerns: authority and respect, isolation, and work–family balance (Krefting, 2003). Women interviewed by Krefting mentioned puzzling daily hassles (withholding information, subtle sexism, undermining, and so on) which became a burden that interfered with academic work (ibid., p. 265). Krefting's conclusion is that 'Neither the passage of time, evidence of women's competence, experience with competent women nor more women in the pipeline will necessarily change prescriptions that women should be likeable but not necessarily competent' (2003, p. 270).

Lawyers

Women in the legal profession face difficulties also. In 1963, when Barbara Allen Babcock (a noted Stanford law professor) graduated from Yale law school, only 4 per cent of the law students in the USA were women – clerkships were difficult to obtain, and there were barriers to participation in both civil and criminal litigation (Babcock, 2001). Many women entered law schools in the 1960s, and by 1970, 20 per cent of the law school students were women (Epstein, 1993). By 2001, 41.2 per cent of associates entering large firms were women, 15.2 per cent of partners in firms with over 250 lawyers were women, and women comprised 23 per cent of all lawyers (Epstein, 2001).

In spite of progress there are three barriers that have been recognized in the legal profession – the glass ceiling, exclusion from informal networks in the firm, and a lack of formal training and access to meaningful work assignments. The glass ceiling is still apparent in the legal profession (see Catalyst, 2001; Epstein, 2001; Rhode, 2001; Trei, 2002); Catalyst (2001) reported that women and men attend law schools for the same reasons and over 70 per cent of both begin their law careers with law firms (smaller percentages of minority women go into private practice according to the American Bar Association Commission on Women in the Profession, 1994). A study of job satisfaction among women lawyers in Canada and the USA found that women are less satisfied than their male counterparts (Chiu, 1998) because of a lack of influence and promotion opportunities. Chiu concluded that her results 'show that inequality in the workplace explains much more of women's dissatisfaction than wanting more time for the family or self' (Chiu, 1998, p. 534).

In terms of white men and women in the USA, over time their careers diverge (Catalyst, 2001); of those who graduated in the 1970s, twice as many women as men are currently in the education and corporate sectors, rather than in law firms. In 2001, women represented only 15.6 per cent of law partners 13.7 per cent of the general counsels of Fortune 500 companies.

The situation in Canada is similar to that of the USA. Career paths of women and men lawyers diverge after some years – women make more lateral movements, have more interruptions in their career and a greater likelihood of unemployment (Brockman, 2001; Kay et al., 1996; Wilson, 1993). There are fewer women lawyers in partnership positions, in comparison with the proportion of women in the legal profession, they are overrepresented in the public sector and are more likely to be working in marginal positions or leaving law altogether (Brockman, 2001; Hull and Nelson, 2000; Kay et al., 1996).

The reasons cited for the glass ceiling for women lawyers are similar to those for other professions – traditional stereotypes, inadequate access to mentoring, lack of opportunities for advancement and inflexible workplace structures (Brockman, 2001; Catalyst, 2001; Clanton, 2001; Epstein, 2001; Epstein et al., 1995; Kay et al., 1996; Rhode, 2001; Trei, 2002). For women lawyers, the most important barrier is the difficulty of reconciling their personal and family responsibilities with a career in law (Catalyst, 2001), because lawyers are expected to be on call 24 hours a day and seven days a week (Epstein, 2001), and firms do not truly support flexible workplace arrangements, with only 3–4 per cent of lawyers take advantage of them (Rhode, 2001). It was also noted that when women and men asked for modest time off for family reasons, the men were judged positively, but when women left for similar reasons, they were perceived as unreliable and uncommitted (Nossel and Westfall, 1998).

Difficulty finding a mentor and the exclusion from informal networks in law firms were also important considerations for women (Catalyst, 2001; Epstein, 2001; Krakauer and Chen, 2003). A study of female lawyers found that having a mentor appeared to be instrumental for career success in terms of earnings, promotional opportunities, procedural justice and social integration (Wallace, 2001). Men joining a law firm usually have a senior partner as a mentor, but the same may not be true for women.

A lack of formal training and access to meaningful work assignments was another issue for women in the legal profession (Catalyst, 2001; Clanton, 2001; Krakauer and Chen, 2003) and perceptions of women form a serious barrier to advancement – devaluing women's competence and accomplishments, perceiving less commitment on the part of women and women needing to live up to higher standards than their male counterparts (Krakauer and Chen, 2003; Rhode, 2001; Trei, 2002).

Physicians
The situation in medicine is similar to other professions. Research on women physicians has also shown skewed career advancement. Women work mainly in parts of the health care system and in specialties where

earnings are lower or prestige is less (see Cassell, 2000, Epstein, 1970; Hinze, 2000; Lorber, 1993; Riska, 2001). In medicine, as in other professions, we see patterns of gender segregation, and structural and developmental barriers, which result in women being in positions of lesser power, prestige and remuneration. There is a 'glass ceiling' here as well as elsewhere, impeding women's upward mobility (Lorber, 1993).

In 1970, Epstein noted that women medical students, relative to men, were less connected to a mentor and collegial network that aided socialization and provided necessary information for upward mobility. There are also differences in practice settings and types of specialties, creating inequities between women and men in medicine. For example, the median net income of male physicians in the USA was $177 000 and women's net income was 68 per cent of men's income – $120 000 (Moser, 1998). Men were found more in surgery and medical specialties, except for those involving childbirth and children, and pathology and psychiatry (Riska, 2001). Women are significantly more likely to be in part-time primary care positions than men (Simon and Alonzo, 2004).

Very few women physicians are employed in academia (20 per cent as of 1997 – Riska, 2001). Of those in academia, only 59 per cent had attained the rank of associate or full professor, compared with 83 per cent for the men, and the percentage of women achieving full professorship was only 5 per cent, compared to with 23 per cent for men. Even after productivity factors were adjusted for, women remained less likely to be promoted, compared with men (Tesch et al., 1995). Tesch et al. (1995) referred to the glass ceiling as more like a 'sticky floor'.

Engineers
Women engineers also face challenges. In 1965, only 4 per cent of the engineering students in the USA were female. This jumped to 14.8 per cent in 1985 and 19–20 per cent by 1995 (Blaisdell et al., 2002) but has not risen above 20 per cent since. In Canada, there has also been little change in the past years (Sherk, 2000). Female socialization has been cited as a reason for women not entering male-dominated professions; however, in management, law and medicine, women now comprise half of those trained in those fields. In common with other male-dominated professions, women engineers have typically been in less prestigious job assignments than men (McIlwee and Robinson, 1992).

In a study of two companies, it was found that in the one where the engineers had the most power, the culture was very masculine and unfriendly towards women, while in the second, which was more bureaucratic, with explicit job descriptions, career advancement policies, and so on, the atmosphere for women engineers was friendlier, and their mobility was greater (McIlwee and Robinson, 1992). It has also been assumed by the male engineers that women were more suitable for certain engineering fields than others, regardless of performance (Ismail, 2003; McIlwee and Robinson, 1992).

The atmosphere in most engineering firms appears to be even chillier than that for managers, lawyers and physicians, and the treatment of women as 'different' more overt (see McIlwee and Robinson, 1992; Miller, 2004; Sherk, 2000). The organizational culture is considered the most significant barrier to advancement for women engineers (Sherk, 2000); for example, in the petroleum industry in Alberta, daily interactions were characterized by informality and paternalism based on shared masculine interests that exclude women from power, division of work by gender and powerful symbols of the 'frontier myth and romanticized cowboy hero' (Miller, 2004, p. 49). Managerial and executive ranks are overwhelmingly male, compared with a more equal representation of women in other Calgary companies and general workforce (Miller, 2004).

A second major barrier for women engineers stems from the inflexibility of the profession, which often demands high mobility. Most engineers (male and female) are married and have at least one child (Ranson, 2000); however, 97 per cent of fathers were in full-time positions, while only 66 per cent of mothers were, and 92 per cent of the husbands of the women worked full time, compared with 25 per cent of the wives of the men (Ranson, 2000).

Exclusion from informal work-related networks and prestigious petroleum clubs (including clubs frequented by many men in the petroleum industry) was noted as hampering women in reaching influential-positions. In Canada, the influential petroleum club and ranchmen's club has only admitted women in recent years, even though in the early 1990s, ten out of 11 energy ministers in Canada were women (Miller, 2004).

Women engineers have reported several ways of coping with the juggling of their responsibilities. One was to work for a large organization with established maternity leave policies and precedents for part-time work and flextime schedules. A second was to do contractual or consulting work. The third way was to leave engineering (see Ranson, 2000, for a discussion of women engineers with children).

The following section looks briefly at background characteristics, focusing on the familial background of those who have been successful (note that culture and personality characteristics are included in Chapter 3).

Background Demographics

There are many aspects of a woman's background that can influence the likelihood of her achieving professional success. In this section we discuss some of those that have been considered most important.

There has been substantial research on the impact of childhood on successful women; research has included siblings, parent–child relationships and social economic status. It has been found that parent's expectations of their children are often based not only on gender but also on birth order (Manaster and Corsini, 1984). A general finding has been that firstborn children achieve more than do their siblings (Altus, 1966). One study found that 54 per cent of the successful women included were either firstborn or only children (White et al., 1997); further, that female only children have a high work ethic and a highly competitive profile (Snell et al., 1986). A study of eminent scientists, compared with non-eminent scientists, found that eminent scientists were firstborn and concluded that firstborns are higher in creativity and achievement orientation (Clark and Rice, 1982). The explanation is that firstborn children do not initially share their parents with siblings, and that only children never share them, encouraging more questioning and exploration. Firstborn children are often given responsibility for their siblings, and, thus, responsibility is learned early in life. White et al. (1997) found that the majority of successful women who were neither firstborn nor only children had older brothers (68 per cent), and the dyadic dynamics were characterized by competition (White et al., 1997). These women may imitate and identify with the older brother, and may develop masculine traits, such as achievement orientation. Falbo (1981) also noted that firstborns are more competitive than those born later. In terms of those who are later-born, they have been found to have more empathy (Stotland et al., 1971).

In terms of parental relationships, White et al. (1997) found that women divided between those who had a pleasant relationship with their parents (one-third of the sample) and those who had a difficult relationship, particularly with their mother, which contributed to a separate sense of identity, leading to a high need for achievement. The absence of strong mother love may aid in tolerance of frustration, decision-making and dealing with later-life stress (Kagan and Moss, cited in White et al., 1997, p. 29). The White et al. study (1997) a majority of respondents identified their fathers as more influential than their mothers; those who identified more strongly with the mother tended to have mothers who provided powerful feminine role models.

According to the White et al. (1997) study, the majority of successful women had middle-class origins (58 per cent), which may have contributed to their high career orientation and innovation. A large number of their mothers worked outside the home, in stark comparison with the proportion · of women in general during that time period (White et al., 1997).

Corporate culture has also had an impact on the career development of women. The corporate cultures of organizations have been characterized as a 'bureaucratic social order grounded in norms conventionally ascribed to men' by Maier (1999, p. 74), who observed that men who are subordinate to other men in organizations are perceived 'like women', just as women can come to act 'like men' (p. 75). Corporate cultures in most of the Americas are not only masculine cultures, but also white, masculine cultures. Women of color face particular challenges, hampered by stereotypes and others' lack of acceptance of them as authority figures (Giscombe and Mattis, 2002).

The next section looks at aspects of career development, such as training, mentoring and networking. These have been considered extremely important in predicting success, and are all areas where women feel hampered by characteristics of the corporate culture.

Career Development: Training, Mentoring, Networking

The typical barriers to advancement are structural barriers (glass walls and ceilings, lateral career ladders rather than linear ones, little support for dual careers) and career development barriers (lack of training, difficulty of finding mentors and being members of crucial networks). In this section we turn our attention to these second barriers.

Training, complemented by developmental job assignments, is very important in linear career development. Studies have found that there are differences between men and women in terms of the type and amount of training they receive and the relationship of this training to managerial success (see McQuarrie, 1994; Ohlott et al., 1994; Tharenou et al., 1994). Concerning developmental job assignments, McQuarrie (1994) suggested that male managers are less likely to assign challenging tasks to female subordinates, or to place women in highly visible or responsible positions. Another study found that women experienced 'greater developmental challenges stemming from obstacles they face in their job' (Ohlott et al., 1994, p. 46). Van Velsor and Hughes (1990) reported that women have fewer chances to turn around a business in trouble or to start something from scratch, two of the most important developmental experiences reported by men; however, a study by Ohlott et al. (1994) found the reverse, although their study revealed 'significant gender differences . . . relating to a high level of responsibility; high stakes; managing business diversity, and external pressure' (Ohlott et al., 1994, p. 61).

The difficulty women face because they are not assigned to jobs that provide the background and experience for high-level positions creates a cycle – if women are not given developmental job assignments, they will be perceived as less qualified than men and will not be considered for the next higher job, and so on (Wirth, 2001).

Mentoring appears to be another prerequisite for success in reaching high-level positions, and difficulties associated with finding mentors is the second most common barrier to success in both North American and other research (ILO, 2004b; Ragins et al., 1998; Wirth, 2001; Woody and Weiss, 1994).

Mentoring is described as the set of roles, such as coaching, teaching, supporting and sponsoring, undertaken by a mentor who recognizes potential in another (Kram, 1983; 1985; White, 1995). Mentoring has usually been conceptualized as a dyadic relationship, the mentor being higher in the organization than the mentee, or protégé. Recently, developmental networks have been stressed as relevant, especially in organizations operating in an evolving technological environment (Higgins and Kram, 2001; Thomas, 1990; 1993).

Mentoring has been divided into three distinct functions – career development, psychosocial support (Allen and Eby, 2004; Kram, 1983; 1985; Ragins, 1999; Wallace, 2001) and role-modelling (Scandura, 1992, Scandura and Viator, 1994; Wallace, 2001). Role-modelling and psychosocial support are often combined in the literature. Career functions include coaching, sponsorship, protection, exposure and visibility, and challenging assignments (Kram, 1985; O'Neill, 2002; Ragins, 1999) – these facilitate advancement in the organization. Psychosocial functions include counselling, acceptance, confirmation, friendship and role-modelling (Kram, 1985; O'Neill, 2002); these enhance feelings of competence, confidence, esteem and effectiveness. Male mentors often reported providing more career-related mentoring, whereas female mentors reported providing more psychosocial mentoring to their protégés, except where the female was the mentor and the male the protégé (Allen and Eby, 2004); however, there have been studies which have reported equal amounts of both for men and women or more career mentoring for women (O'Neill, 2002). Mentoring can also be examined from a career-stage perspective (Kram, 1985; Mainiero, 1994; Ragins et al., 1998). In the early career, mentoring accelerates rates of advancement (Noe, 1988; Whitly et al., 1991) and has a positive impact on the ability to engage in other mentoring relationships and intelligence networks (De Janasz et al., 2003; Whitly et al., 1991). A study of mid-career professional women found that mentoring was felt to be a key factor of success (Auster, 2001).

Mentoring relations are particularly important for women, especially in male-dominated professions, since they face gender-related obstacles to advancement (Kanter, 1977; Ragins, 1989; Ragins and Scandura, 1994; Wallace, 2001). Mentors can buffer women from discrimination and help them get on the 'fast track' to advancement (Wallace, 2001); however, women are handicapped by their difficulty in finding mentors, especially those well placed in the organization. Difficulties in finding mentors and not having women role models in senior positions hampers women in reaching higher-level positions (Fox and Schuhmann, 2001; Javidan et al., 1995; Kanter, 1977; Ragins, 1999; Ragins and Cotton, 1991).

There also appear to be differential outcomes depending upon the sex and race of the mentor. Dreher and Cox (1996) found that those with MBAs who had a mentor earned substantially higher salaries than others with MBAs; however, this was only true if the mentor were a white male. Ragins and Cotton (1991) found that protégés with a history of male mentors received higher compensation and more promotions than if mentors were women. Ragins and McFarlin (1990) found that same-sex mentors provided more role-modelling than cross-sex mentors, and social-izing was rare between cross-sex dyads.

In contrast with a mentoring relationship, a social network is a map of the relationships among individuals (see Barnes, 1954, who was the first to coin the term 'social network'). Social network theory views social rela-tionships in terms of nodes and ties; the nodes are the individual actors within the networks, and ties are the relationships between the actors. The shape of the social network helps determine the usefulness of the network to the individual; smaller, tighter networks are usually less useful than net-works with many loose connections, including individuals outside the main network. Kram (1985) suggested that individuals receive mentoring from a multitude of individuals along various points in time, and that networks include people not usually thought of as being mentors (family, senior col-leagues, friends, members of the community, and so on).

Exclusion from informal networks can hamper women in finding influential mentors, especially since most of those who are possible mentors are likely to be male. This exclusion also reduces women's access to infor-mation which is crucial to advancement in the organization (Woody and Weiss, 1994). Women do not differ markedly from men in their network-building; however, they formed more extra-organizational ties for the purpose of learning 'strategies for overcoming gender-related obstacles' (Ibarra, 1997, p. 94).

Structural characteristics, which are also rooted in the corporate culture, also have an impact on women's success in organizations. The following section outlines the impact of some of these characteristics.

Structural Characteristics and Success

A Catalyst study (2003a) concluded that structural barriers still exist relative to promotion to upper-level positions. The following discussion considers career ladders and the glass ceiling in organizations.

Career ladders

Longitudinal research has shown that males and female graduates from prestigious MBA programmes had contrasting organizational careers. Despite identical educational attainment, ambition and commitment to their careers, men progressed faster and ended in higher-status positions with substantially higher compensation (Olson et al., 1985; Wallace, 1982). Studies have portrayed managers climbing a ladder, meaningfully progressing through a series of related jobs, which predominantly reflects the male career experience (White, 1995; see also Mavin, 2001; O'Neil et al., 2003). This requires high commitment to work and continuous employment, with no breaks for family or other purposes. Research has shown, though, that women and men differ little in their organizational commitment (Stroh and Reilly, 1997; Van der Velde et al., 2003) but the perception remains that women are less committed. The job model 'has linked men's work attitudes and behaviour to their occupational experiences, while the "gender model," invoked only for women, links their employment relations to family experiences' (Mavin, 2001, p. 186).

Kelly and Marin (1998) found that corporations favour single women over married women for promotions. Since most organizations do not have more than one career ladder structure, women have found that they have to join the male paradigm of 'career' in order to progress in management (Burke and McKeen, 1994; Mavin, 2001; White, 1995). White (1995) found that successful women did not take career breaks and waited until their careers were well under way before having children, usually having only one child and taking a minimum maternity leave, or remaining childless. Some of these women later discovered that a glass ceiling was nevertheless impeding their career progress, and they changed organizations to gain promotion.

Glass barriers

Traditional practices in management, which used to be evident at all levels, have evolved into new, more subtle systems of bias for upper-level management positions. Women and minorities have been overlooked or ignored for managerial promotions and developmental opportunities. Top-level managers pick others who are like them, with whom they feel comfortable, as their replacements. According to Wernick (1994), most companies rely on informal practices and procedures that often use limited information to make selections, hence, making it easy to reinforce racial, ethnic and gender stereotypes and biases, and to limit the opportunity for advancement even of interested and educationally qualified employees.

This has been termed the 'glass ceiling' for women and the 'concrete ceiling' for black mangers. Organizations, thus, appear to have dual environments – one designed for white men, fostering their advancement, and one for women and other minorities, 'that presents subtle, but significant obstacles to their advancement' (Ragins et al., 1998, p. 37). The barrier most mentioned in interviews with women managers in the 1990s was differential access to assignments which would further the career of the middle manager (see Catalyst, 1993; Hollway and Mukurasi, 1994; Ohlott et al., 1994; Powell, 1999; Ragins et al., 1998; Wernick, 1994; Woody and Weiss, 1994). In a study conducted in 2002 of women executives in Canada, the major barriers mentioned remained structural and attitudinal (Women's Executive Network, 2002). Consistently, the most frequently mentioned barrier was the lack of comfort men experience in dealing with women on a professional level.

Another phenomenon experienced by women has been termed 'glass walls'. This refers to the segregation of women in functions not considered central to an organization's performance. In contrast, line positions, such as finance and manufacturing are male dominated. These glass walls reflect the wider societal characteristic of occupational segregation, which has remained more or less the same over the years in North America (see Andrew et al., 1994; Boyd et al., 1981; Catalyst, 1993; 2003b; 2004; Galinsky et al., 2003; Hamlin, 1994; ILO, 2004b; Malveaux, 1982; Wernick, 1994; Women's Executive Network, 2002).

Women are found disproportionately in staff positions, traditionally considered 'female' occupations, such as human resources and community and government relations, with less visible assignments than their male counterparts (Hollway and Mukurasi, 1994; Ohlott et al., 1994; Powell, 1999; Ragins et al., 1998; Wernick, 1994; Woody and Weiss, 1994). In order to advance to top-level management, managers need experience in functional areas that pertain to the organization's business, such as production, sales and marketing, engineering, accounting and finance, and few women are found in these positions.

One explanation for the small number of women at top levels is that objective criteria are less important in determining promotion to these ranks (Powell, 1999). The cognitive processes of decision-makers about top management positions can therefore reinforce the norm of male superiority. Decision-makers develop a schema or mental model about the attributes of job holders and this influences their hiring and promotion decisions (Powell, 1999, pp. 334–5). This is exacerbated by the fact that a lower proportion of women are groomed for top management positions by means of mentoring, developmental job assignments and experience in line positions. The 2004 International Labour Organization update to its 2003 report noted that it was still the case in 2004 that 'women who choose non-traditional jobs can face special constraints in the workplace, not least of which are isolation and] limited access to mentoring and female role models' (ILO, 2004a, p. 1). Further, the report noted that some employers did not see the promotion of women as beneficial to their organizations.

Recently some companies have tried to reduce barriers to women's advancement. For example, Galinsky et al. reported companies asking their own senior women to develop efforts to reduce barriers, and that these women's efforts 'become a powerful force in reducing stereotypes, in promoting more diverse developmental experiences for women, in opening up networks, and in providing more role models' (Galinsky et al., 2003, p. 49). They (Galinsky et al., 2003) stated that companies had realized that high turnover among scarce management talent (both male and female) is very costly for the organizations, and that if executives do not feel excluded from important networks, if they can see future opportunities in the firm, and if they have adequate sponsors and role models, they are less likely to leave. This has positive implications for women in the future – glass ceilings and walls may eventually be broken.

The apparent attempts to encourage the advancement of women into upper-level positions has had an unfortunate side effect. A new term has emerged recently to describe another barrier that women face in management. The new term is 'glass cliffs', and glass cliffs may also be seen as a new form of subtle discrimination against women. According to Ryan and Haslam (2005), women are often placed on a 'glass cliff', in the sense that they are appointed to leadership positions under problematic organizational circumstances that are associated with greater risk of failure and criticism. These high-risk jobs have a high chance of failure, and the women who take them on are closely scrutinized. The result being that, when women fail in these situations, their gender rather than the difficulty of the situation they faced is stressed. *The Times* (Judge, 2003) went so far as to say that the arrival of women in Britain's boardrooms had wreaked havoc on companies' performance and share prices. Ryan and Haslam (2005) argue that this apparent correlation can be attributed to the glass cliff phenomenon, where women are asked to take over when companies are experiencing poor performance and low share prices.

Another challenge for many women managers is that, in comparison with male managers, they receive less social support and their home environments reportedly are not as conducive to professional success. These issues are discussed in the next section.

Social Support

According to the International Labour Organization (2004), women are still mainly responsible for childcare and home management, and even women executives spend twice as much time on these activities as their spouses. At the same time, they are expected to adhere to the male model of the career being the most important aspect of their life. One consequence of this is the decision of some executive women not to have children.

In countries where servants are common, it is easier for those few women who reach upper-level management to have help with household management. In Mexico, for example, it is easier for upper-class women to pursue professional positions because they have domestic help for housework and childcare (Muller and Rowell, 1997). Nevertheless, 'negotiating the inherent contradictions in work and family roles requires skill and perseverance' (ibid., p. 431), since women holding positions outside the home violates important values of the patriarchal Mexican culture: some Mexican professional women choose to marry foreign men owing to their anticipation of problems with traditional male attitudes in Mexico (Muller and Rowell, 1997).

Mexico may be more extreme than Canada and the USA, but aspects of these attitudes are present in those countries too. Various studies (Barling and Sorensen, 1997; Bird et al., 1984; Greenhaus and Parasuraman, 1994; 1999; Paddock and Schwartz, 1986; Sekaran, 1986; Zedeck, 1992) have shown that there are distinct gender differences in the spillover between work and family roles. Husbands identify primarily with the breadwinner role and wives with the homemaker role. Since the career role is deemed most significant by the husband, he will tend to let the family time and space be intruded upon by work activities. Husbands more often than wives are likely to do office work at home or spend extra hours at the workplace after closing time. Wives who take on primary responsibility for the family role are more likely to allow family matters to intrude into the work sphere, as, for instance, taking care of an emergency at home or leaving the office early. These asymmetrical permeations of the home and work boundaries facilitate the husband's career progress but may cause the wife's career to stagnate.

Major challenges are faced by couples with young children, and these are often experienced when both partners are at important career stages. One major concern is the allocation of tasks or division of labour in the home. Wives in dual-work families spend almost twice the amount of time on family and children as do men, although men with wives in high-status occupations increase the amount of time spent on childcare, meal preparation and work roles (Bird et al., 1984). A second concern is that of competitive feelings that may occur if one partner, particularly the wife, has an edge over the other in terms of career progress.

Those studies discussed previously focused on dual-career couples, not necessarily those in upper-level positions. Due to the demands inherent in building their careers, many executive women have waited too late to have children (Hewlett, 2002). In a study of both executive women and men, it was found that men are more likely to have children than women, and they also have more children than the women who are not childless (Galinsky et al., 2003). It was also reported that the majority of these executive women are the major breadwinners in their family; however, they still have more responsibility than their spouses/partners in making childcare arrangements. There was a sharp contrast between the men and women in the sample – 94 per cent of the executive men had spouses/partners who take greater responsibility for making childcare arrangements compared with only 20 per cent of the women. Who takes care of the children during working hours? For the men it is the spouse/partner; for the women it is non-relative care, for example, a nanny.

What is the situation in Latin America? The International Labour Organization's 2004 update (ILO, 2004a), reported on an informal survey that indicated that when women began having children, many also began negotiating time off and flexible work schedules rather than wage increases and promotions. In line with the focus on family in Latin American cultures, childcare facilities were usually available, and this allowed women whose career was very important to them to continue focusing on their career. This same ILO update discussed an article in the European edition of *Fortune* (Sellers, 2003, pp. 58–65) on the most powerful women in the Fortune 50 firms in which the finding was that one-third of these women's spouses stayed at home. The presence of good social support is clearly conducive to career mobility for successful women. Some organizations do offer some flexibility in careers, but there still is not much change in organizational cultures, which would enable women and also men to take advantage of the policies that have been instituted by organizations (see Blair-Loy and Wharton, 2002; Burke, 2002; Gordon and Whelan-Berry, 2004; Lewis, 1997).

Blair-Loy and Wharton (2002) stressed the importance of social context in determining whether or not work–family policies will be taken advantage of by employees. Workgroup-level factors were very influential in that regard, especially the use of flexibility policies. Blair-Loy and Wharton conducted qualitative interviews, which lend support to the importance of 'supervisor and work group power in enabling the use of risky work–family policies' (ibid., p. 838). The prevailing organizational culture is most salient in ensuring that organizational programmes and benefits that are in place are actually used. If there are negative views present in the organization in terms of using these programmes and benefits, the results will be detrimental to those employees taking advantage of them (Gordon and Whelan-Berry, 2004). This is especially the case if the immediate supervisor does not see the value of these programmes. Training of supervisors and managers is an important way to ensure that these programmes are used effectively (Gordon and Whelan-Berry, 2004); equally important is top management's support for the programmes.

The next section considers leadership styles of women managers, and we discuss gender variations and the degree of participative leadership found among women managers.

Leadership Styles

There have been numerous studies comparing the leadership styles of men and women. Many researchers have asked 'is there actually a difference in the way men and women lead? If so, how are they different and what causes them to be different?' Various theories have been used to explain both objective and perceptual gender differences in leadership style, although many of the studies have not clearly identified differences in behaviour.

Much of the past research on leadership focused on identifying personality traits associated with effective leadership and understanding the impact of situational factors on the leadership process (Chemers and Ayman, 1993). The earliest theories were the trait, style and contingency theories. The earliest approach was the trait perspective, which compared the perceived attitudes, values and behaviours attributed to women with those attributed to men (see Brown, 1979, for a description of some of these studies). These differences were believed to be related to the different experiences that the two genders have in primary and secondary socialization (Ibarra and Daly, 1995); however, the results of these studies did not identify gender differences. Another approach focused on management/ leadership style. Most of these studies also indicated no significant differences between men and women (Bartol, 1974; Bartol and Butterfield, 1976). The third early approach was contingency theory, which considered the moderating effects of gender on leadership roles. Most studies looked at two dimensions of leadership behaviour – structuring and supporting. Women were found generally to be very similar to men in terms of leadership style, but were often higher on the supporting dimension. There are two proposed explanations for this: (1) women are socialized to be more supporting, and (2) people lacking ascribed status need to stress a supporting role in leading others.

Brown's review (1979) reported that half of the studies with student samples and half of those with managerial samples considered gender a significant contingency factor. Students considered gender a significant contingency factor for negative reasons, that is, women make inferior leaders. However, some managers considered women better in the supporting role; hence, for some managers, being female was positive in terms of leadership qualities. Some researchers (Jago and Vroom, 1982) have concluded that women, because of their emphasis on a supporting role, actually make better managers, and that the supporting skills are the ones that will be needed in the future. Loden (1985) argued persuasively regarding the importance of a supporting style of leadership.

In contrast, there may be a perception among some groups that structuring is more important than supporting, and that males are seen as more likely to focus on structure. Inderlied and Powell (1979) found that subjects (students and practising managers) registered a strong preference for a 'masculine team manager', and there was a positive relationship between masculine characteristics and structuring behaviour. Alternatively, one study showed that when leader performance information followed leader behaviour, women were rated as initiating more structure than men (Dobbins and Trahan, 1985). Clearly the studies are contradictory and inconclusive.

Other studies have looked at men and women in training groups and found that women were evaluated less favourably than men even when their decisions were more appropriate (Jago and Vroom, 1982). Studies have considered leadership emergence (Schneier and Bartol, 1980) and found that a female leader had to be high on self-monitoring in order to emerge – that is, she had to be concerned with whether or not her behaviour was appropriate to the situation and interpersonal relationships, and she needed to be task oriented and committed – but the same was not true for men.

Two related theories developed to explain the differences between women's performance as leaders are status characteristics theory (Berger et al., 1977) and social role theory (Eagly, 1987; 1997). Both of these theories suggest that women and men differ in their social position and these are the root cause of any leadership differences found between women and men and the perceptions of others concerning women and men in the exercise of leadership.

Men are believed to be more assertive, independent, competitive, and so on – characteristics seen as important for managers – while women are seen as more gentle, kind, supportive, and so on – characteristics not important for managers. These perceptions mean that women in management positions or typical 'male' professions have found that they have to perform better than their male counterparts to be considered equally competent (Carli and Eagly, 1999).

In the 1990s a new trend of leadership research emerged as organizations began to face major structural changes due to downsizing. Researchers began to focus on two contrasting management styles: transformational versus transactional (Bass, 1985; 1999; Burns, 1978). These are described by Bass: 'Whereas transformational leaders uplift the morale, motivation, and morals of their followers, transactional leaders cater to their followers' immediate self-interests. The transformational leader emphasizes what you can do for your country; the transactional leader, on what your country can do for you' (Bass, 1999, p. 9).

Managers who use the contingency reward leadership style devise work standards, communicate these standards to their subordinates and let them know the rewards they will receive if their performance is favourable (Bass, 1985). In contrast, transformational leadership moves the follower beyond immediate self-interests through 'idealized influence (charisma), inspiration, intellectual stimulation, or individualized consideration' (Bass, 1999, p. 11). Early research did not find support for the idea that women utilize different leadership styles than do men (see Bartol, 1978; Bartol and Butterfield, 1976; Bass, 1981; Eagly and Johnson, 1990; Powell, 1990; 1993); however, more recent studies contrasting transformational leadership style with transactional leadership have found gender differences (see Burke and Collins, 2001; Fagenson, 1993; Helgesen, 1990; Rosener, 1990). Rosener (1990) argued that women tend to encourage participation by making employees feel part of the organization, and ensuring that employees play a role in every aspect of the work. This has also been noted in a study of Mexican women managers (Muller and Rowell, 1997). Some advantages of participation for any organization include increased support (and decreased unexpected opposition) for decisions, as well as a reduction in risks associated with having a single person deal with a complicated situation. When a leader shares information and power with others in an organization, employees can feel more empowered since they are taking an active role in the major decisions of the firm. Additionally, loyalty is fostered among employees since it shows employees that they are trusted and that their input is valued. A study of business owners found that the women overwhelmingly preferred a transformational style (Stanford et al., 1995).

A study of Mexican woman managers, characterized their style as a 'feminine management approach', which is quite different from the autocratic and paternalistic Mexican management style of most Mexican males (Stephens and Greer, 1995, cited in Muller and Rowell, 1997). This style was described in the study as 'interactive, connective, and empowering of others', emphasizing support for employees' personal and professional problems, delegating, and prioritizing staff development (Muller and Rowell, 1997, p. 428).

In summary, there is little that we can say definitively about differences between men and women in terms of management/leadership styles, or about the predominant style used by women. It seems that women may be more supportive and participatory than men, but it is not clear whether this is really so or whether these results stem from perceptions about women.

CONCLUSION

This chapter examined women professionals, focusing on managers in the Americas, especially in the USA and Canada, owing to the limitations of research that has been conducted. Throughout the chapter we have attempted to identify the barriers that women face in advancing to the top, and to examine some of the reasons why there are relatively few women at the top. In spite of the barriers, we know that there are many women who do succeed. The purpose of this study is to examine some of these women in depth, to identify the characteristics and beliefs that these successful women share. The following chapter looks at national culture and personality characteristics, and their relationship to professional success. Later chapters focus on our findings in the Americas.

3. Culture and personal characteristics for professional success

Miguel R. Olivas-Luján and Betty Jane Punnett

If we go back 25 centuries, we find that Herodotus, the famed Greek historian of the fourth century BC, commented on the difficulties that King Darius faced because of the cultural differences between the Greeks and the Callatian Indians (Punnett and Ricks, 1997, p. 144). Today, we find books and articles that offer advice to both women and men on how to interact successfully with people from other cultures (Axtell, 1993; Axtell et al., 1997; Hall and Hall, 1990). Cultural differences and the issues engendered by such differences, are clearly not new or a modern phenomenon. However, cultural differences and their impact remain an ongoing area of concern, as noted by Punnett and Shenkar (2004, p. 7): 'we selected the topic of culture for its ongoing centrality in international management research and for the superficiality with which this subject is handled in other disciplines'.

We found in our study of successful women that even while they were quite similar in many ways, they often expressed values which distinguished one national group from another, as the following examples illustrate. We see these differences as reflecting their cultural backgrounds, while the similarities reflect the drives that led them to be successful, in spite of obstacles.

The women from Barbados, Jamaica and St Vincent in the English-speaking Caribbean all expressed a high need for achievement and early accomplishments, but the Jamaicans often said that their drive to be successful and the best was so that they could help the wider society. When this was reported to a group that included Jamaican women, the reaction was essentially, 'but, of course' – they felt this was a well-known and accepted aspect of the Jamaican society. This is interesting in a society that in many ways appears aggressive and sometimes violent. The St Vincent women were very internally motivated, as were the others, but they always mentioned the importance of God in their success and stressed their spirituality. Barbadian women, while also considering spirituality important, felt that they wanted to strive for accomplishment, much like Edmund Hillary climbing Everest, simply because of the challenge. One Barbadian said that achieving success for her was like Hannibal taking the elephants through the Alps.

Women from the USA had difficulty identifying great leaders, while in other places people like Churchill, Gandhi or Mandela were mentioned. In the USA, respondents were more likely to point to themselves as the best example of a good leader. It may be that in today's context, there are few, if any, 'great leaders' and that the respondents from the USA are reflecting this, but it may also be indicative of the culture of the USA – generally believed to be individualistic and nationalistic – which makes it unlikely that these respondents would identify leaders in other countries (nationalism) and would be willing to put themselves forward as examples (individualism). Canadians have sometimes been described as 'polite Americans' – they also had some difficulty naming great leaders and, interestingly, some also questioned the notion of a 'great leader'.

One Argentinean woman said, 'In the 70s, when I started my business, Argentinean women liked to be neat and well-dressed, and make-up was essential, (that) was part of the national culture at that time'. Another commented that in her country's context, 'you need to be very attentive, and that gives Argentineans unbelievable flexibility, and high speed reactions that few other countries have'. This was seen as an advantage, but also led to high levels of stress; she said, 'We go through events that others might believe would kill them'. One woman emphasized the European and male aspects of Argentina: 'We all feel ourselves as Europeans in some way or another. In general our culture had been very "machista" in Argentina, but it is changing.'

These examples are indicative of the important role that culture plays in construing success. In the following discussion we look at culture and personality, and the links between these two concepts.

WHAT IS CULTURE AND WHY IS IT IMPORTANT IN THIS STUDY?

Culture appears to be a fundamental aspect of behaviour, which needs to be addressed in almost any research project, particularly one where participants from several countries are involved. In the Successful Women project, we address cultural issues in terms of how culture interacts with the attributes that we expect to find among successful women.

This chapter examines issues associated with culture, and how culture can affect professional success. Culture is defined and explained, and a variety of cultural models are considered, including Trompenaars's, Kluckhohn and Strodtbeck's, Hall's, Triandis's and Hofstede's models. The cultural value model developed by Hofstede (1980a) is discussed in some depth, because this model is used in our current research. Scores on three of the Hofstede values are compared for more developed and developing countries, as well as for countries of the Americas included in his work.

We think culture is critical to understanding successful women and how they achieve success. To illustrate its importance and the reason for including culture in this study, consider the following comments from a few of the top scholars in the field of international business:

- 'culture is a powerful social construct' and 'touches all fields of study that are concerned with human behaviour' (Boyacigiller et al., 2004, p. 99).
- 'few constructs have gained broader acceptance in the international business literature than cultural distance' and 'measuring the extent to which different cultures are similar or different has been applied to most business administration disciplines' (Shenkar, 2004, p. 168).
- 'there has been a significant shift towards incorporating the role of cultural intricacies in our attempts to understand effectiveness of various activities dealing with globalizing the world' (Bhagat et al., 2004, p. 189).

Culture is a word that is familiar to most people. It is difficult, however, to specify what exactly is meant by the concept, and there is no commonly accepted academic concept of culture (Boyacigiller et al., 2004). For example, two anthropologists (Kroeber and Kluckhohn, 1952) catalogued 164 separate and distinct definitions of the word 'culture'. This issue is further complicated by the fact that the word 'culture' has several quite different meanings. Culture can refer to a shared, commonly held body of general beliefs and values that define what is right (or wrong) for one group (Kluckhohn and Strodtbeck, 1961; Lane and DiStefano, 1988), or sometimes to socially elitist concepts, such as refinement of mind, tastes and manners. The word apparently originates from the Latin *cultura* (to tend, take care of), which is related to *cultus*, which can be translated as cult or worship. Members of a cult believe in specific ways of doing things, and thus develop a culture, which enshrines those beliefs. For our purposes, culture is defined simply as 'the shared beliefs of a nation'; we are therefore looking at national culture. It is difficult to define culture and specify what the term means. It is even more difficult to measure cultural values. Over the past several decades, a number of models of cultural values have been identified, and these incorporate measures of the values described. In the following, we give the reader a brief taste of the most accepted models and measures of cultural values.

Recent interest in national cultural values was spurred by Hofstede's 1980 book, *Culture's Consequences: International Differences in Work-Related Values*, which reported on the cultural variations he had found around the world, in his landmark study of IBM subsidiaries. Hofstede's 1991 book *Cultures and Organizations: Software of the Mind* further developed his cultural value constructs. Hofstede's work has been praised, as a landmark in the national cultural literature, but it has also been criticized as lacking in academic rigour (Dorfman and Howell, 1988; Punnett and Withane, 1990 et al.). Nevertheless, the Hofstede value model has been used widely, since the publication of his first book; in fact, Earley and Singh (2000) suggest 'much of the research attention continues to be an extrapolation of Hofstede's values system' (p. 2). This may be because of the intuitive appeal of the cultural dimensions described by Hofstede. Management academics and practitioners seem to find his dimensions readily understandable, and the dimensions can easily be related to management approaches and practices. This model has been used quite frequently in other disciplines as well (Søndergaard, 1994).

Hofstede identified four cultural variables, in his original study. These are briefly outlined as follows:

1. Individualism/collectivism – the degree to which a society values individual contribution versus group contribution, and the degree to which individuals owe allegiance to their immediate family group versus the wider society. It should be noted that a collectivist culture tends to expect cooperation, harmony and group allegiance to members of its cultural in-group, but not necessarily to outsiders.
2. Uncertainty avoidance – the degree to which a society prefers certainty to ambiguity, and the degree of risk-taking that is considered acceptable by members of the society.
3. Power distance – the degree to which a society accepts differences in power as right and appropriate versus the belief in equality and the ability to rise to any level despite birth, status and so on.
4. Masculinity – the degree to which a society accepts 'traditional male' values of assertiveness, competitiveness and tangible rewards versus the 'traditional female' values of nurturance, care for the unfortunate and concern with the environment. Societies high in masculinity also tend to enforce stricter gender role differentiation.

With his colleague Michael Bond, Hofstede later identified a fifth value, Confucian dynamism (Chinese Culture Connection, 1987) in a study in the Far East. This dimension has also been called 'Long term/short term orientation' – a score high on Confucian dynamism indicates respect for social and status obligations within limits of thrift, perseverance and willingness to subordinate oneself for a purpose, while the reverse indicates a focus on immediate results.

The Kluckhohn and Strodtbeck value dimension framework has also been used relatively frequently: Kluckhohn and Strodtbeck's (1961) value framework provides a slightly different approach to understanding cultural values. These anthropologists developed a model of cultural variation, based on societies' reactions to the common problems that all societies face. This anthropological model was operationalized in the 1990s (Maznevski et al., 1997) and has been investigated in a number of recent studies (Kirkman and Shapiro, 2001; Lenartowicz and Roth, 2004; Olivas-Luján et al., 2004). This cultural model is appealing because it measures each cultural value independently, rather than using bi-polar scales. This model is also relatively easy to understand and interpret, but it has not been used as widely as the Hofstede model, perhaps because of the novelty of its psychometric operationalization.

Kluckhohn and Strodtbeck (1961) identified the following cultural variations:

- Relationships – societies can prefer group peer relationships, hierarchical relationships or individualistic relationships.
- Activity – societies can approach the world from a thinking, rational view, from a being, emotional view or from a doing, action view.
- Nature – societies can see the environment from a dominant perspective, from a subjugated perspective or from a harmony perspective.
- People – societies can see people as changeable or fixed, either good or bad.
- Time – societies can be past oriented, present oriented or future oriented.

Trompenaars and Hampden-Turner (1998) developed a practitioner-oriented framework that offers seven 'fundamental dimensions of culture' (p. 8), somewhat inspired by the paradigms above. The first five are based on Parsons's (1951) 'Relational orientations': universalism versus particularism, individualism versus communitarianism, neutral versus emotional, specific versus diffuse, and achievement versus ascription. In addition, attitudes towards time, and attitudes towards the environment are included as dimensions that differentiate world cultures.

The first of these dimensions, universalism/particularism has to do with the way people behave 'universally' following rules and regulations. Particularist cultures apply policies and conventions only under certain situations, but make exceptions in accordance with the way their own culture expects them to behave. In addition, universalist cultures espouse applying the same rules to everyone, while particularist cultures expect some leeway depending on personal relationships or social context. For example, in universalist cultures (such as Switzerland, Sweden and Canada), crossing the street when the light is red would be frowned upon, even when no traffic is present; in particularist cultures, on the other hand (such as Russia, Egypt and Venezuela), such behaviour would be accepted and would not make people feel uncomfortable. (An example of the measures used – 'You are riding in a car driven by a close friend. He hits a pedestrian. You know he was going at least 35 miles per hour in an area of the city where the maximum allowed speed is 20 miles per hour. There are no witnesses. His lawyer says that if you testify under oath that he was only driving 20 miles per hour it may save him from serious consequences'. Respondents are asked what right the friend has to expect protection.)

The second dimension, individualism/communitarianism is very similar to individualism/collectivism described previously.

The third dimension, neutral/emotional is related to how people show their emotions and their basic emotional tendencies (affectivity). 'Neutral' cultures (such as Ethiopia, Japan and Poland) keep their feelings carefully controlled and subdued. In contrast, 'emotional' cultures show their feelings plainly by laughing, smiling, grimacing, scowling, and gesturing, and they attempt to find immediate outlets for their feelings. Examples of emotional cultures include Kuwait, Spain and the Philippines.

The fourth dimension, specific/diffuse has to do with the way life roles 'cross over' to other areas. In specific cultures (such as Sweden, the Netherlands, Hungary and the UK) work and private life are sharply separated, and people would not expect that employer–employee relationship would extrapolate into personal life spheres. For example, an employee would be unlikely to help their employer paint his or her house, or run an errand for her or him, based on their boss–subordinate work roles. Diffuse cultures (such as China, Nepal, Nigeria or Venezuela) expect roles such as those related to employment or family relationships to cross over; in such places, it would be expected of an employee or a younger niece to help out with personal errands that the boss or aunt requested, even if they are not a part of the role or job description.

The fifth dimension, achievement/ascription dimension is defined as the way cultures attribute status. In achievement cultures (such as Norway, the USA, Australia or Ireland) status is obtained by accomplishments and results (frequently related to a Protestant work ethic). Ascription cultures (such as Egypt, Nepal, Uruguay or the Czech Republic) grant status based on factors such as family background, titles and seniority.

The other dimensions are attitudes towards time and the environment (or nature). In terms of time, at one extreme we find cultures that focus on the past and the present (such as the Philippines, Ireland, Brazil or India), and at the other those that focus on the future (such as Hong Kong, Israel, China or Sweden). In terms of attitudes towards the environment, or how we relate to nature, at one extreme we find cultures (such as Bahrain, Japan, Sweden and China) that believe that nature has its own course and we cannot influence this, and at the other extreme there are cultures (such as Uruguay, Israel, Norway and the USA) that believe it is important to try to control and harness external forces.

In addition to the previous dimensions of culture, some cultures have been described as high context, and others as low context (Hall, 1976; Hall and Hall, 1990). High-context cultures are those that focus on non-verbal communication and situational factors such as the relationship established between the parties, while low-context cultures focus on the explicit verbal content of the message. Some cultures have been described as polychronic, and other cultures as monochronic (Hall, 1983). Polychronic cultures view the world holistically and see time as a continuum (for example, Mexican and Mediterranean cultures), while monochronic cultures view the world in limited bits and bites and see time as sequential or compartmentalized (for example, Anglo and Nordic cultures).

Triandis (1995) also developed a model of cultural values based on different aspects of individualism-collectivism, which has been well received by academics, but not used extensively, perhaps owing mostly to the difficulty of measuring these variations reliably. Similarly, the Schwartz (1992) values model has been demonstrated as a valid model to represent cultures (Schwartz, 1999; Schwartz and Sagiv, 1995) but has not been used widely, perhaps because of a more complex operationalization than other paradigms.

This discussion of culture and cultural value models has illustrated the complexity of culture, and the difficulty of capturing the essence of culture in any research study. We believe that it is critical to this study to have a measure of culture, and this extensive review was needed to select the models and methodologies best suited to the needs of the study. Based on our review we decided which should be included in the Successful Women project.

WHAT IS PERSONALITY AND WHY IS IT IMPORTANT IN THIS STUDY?

Personality is often thought of as that special intangible something that makes each of us individual. We frequently describe people in terms of their personality – 'she's very outgoing', 'she's rather shy', and so on. In contrast to the cultural values, which are seen as shared with others, personality characteristics are seen as varying from person to person, and the sum of our various personality characteristics identifies each of us as unique. While each of us is unique in terms of personality, there are certain characteristics which we thought successful women were likely to share, and we believed that examining and measuring these characteristics would help us understand and describe successful professional women.

There are a wide variety of personal characteristics that have been studied as important in the workplace. We reviewed these and selected three that seemed likely to be shared by successful professional women. These are described in Chapter 1 and summarized here.

Self-efficacy

This is confidence in one's ability to perform successfully. Individuals with high self-efficacy tend to try harder to master challenging situations, persist in the face of obstacles and respond to negative feedback with increased effort. They demonstrate high levels of task-focus and motivation, set challenging goals, work harder and longer to achieve their goals (Bandura, 1997) and effectively use analytic strategies in managerial decision-making (Wood et al., 1990). Self-efficacy is further associated with decreased anxiety and self-defeating negative thinking (Bandura, 1997). Individuals with high self-efficacy are more likely to seek feedback and monitor their environments in order to improve role clarity and work performance (Brown et al., 2001). Although we found no prior research on national differences in this variable, it seems reasonable to expect that the emphasis on overcoming obstacles to achieve goals would make self-efficacy a crucial characteristic for women who break through the cultural and institutional barriers of their respective countries.

Locus of Control

This is the generalized expectancy about the extent to which one is in control of events in life. Individuals with an internal locus of control believe that success and failure are contingent upon their own actions or personal characteristics. Individuals with an external locus of control believe that success and failure are products of outside forces (fate, luck, deity or other people). Internals are more likely to engage in actions to improve or control their environment and place greater emphasis on striving for achievement; they are less alienated from the work environment and less likely to commit counterproductive behaviours in response to work frustration. While levels and manifestations of locus of control may vary from country to country, a study of 24 countries found that an internal work locus of control was universally associated with employee well-being and negatively associated with work stress and strain (Spector et al., 2002). We expect successful women, regardless of national origin, to have an internal locus of control.

Need for Achievement

This refers to a preference for challenging tasks and a willingness to work harder than required. Individuals with a high need for achievement are motivated to overcome barriers to success and they want specific feedback on how they are performing. Organizational research has linked need for achievement to job performance, prosocial behaviour in organizations (Baruch et al., 2004), and career commitment (Goulet and Singh, 2002). Punnett (2004b) points out that achievement motivation may differ from country to country, both in the language used to describe it and in its behavioural manifestations (for example, people seeking to achieve goals on their own or with their workgroups); nevertheless, it seems that women in all countries should exhibit a high need for achievement if they succeed in the face of barriers to success.

In the following section we link the cultural values that we measured to the personality characteristics. Table 3.1 summarizes the relationships that can be hypothesized regarding the two sets of variables.

RELATING CULTURAL VALUES TO PERSONALITY CHARACTERISTICS

We used the Hofstede model of cultural values for this study, including three of its cultural values. We did not include the masculinity/femininity dimension in this study because it has not been as widely accepted as the others, in fact it is the most controversial and least understood of Hofstede's paradigm. It was also less clear how this dimension would relate to the personality variables. In addition, in the Dorfman and Howell (1988) instrument the items measuring masculinity/femininity seem to relate more to male/female distinctions rather than to Hofstede's original meaning for this dimension.

The Hofstede model was easy to operationalize, because there was an existing instrument, which had acceptable psychometric properties (Dorfman and Howell, 1988) and which is intended to measure the dimensions at the individual level rather than at the cultural level. Most importantly, the three Hofstede variables were theoretically and conceptually linked to the personal variables we were going to examine (self-efficacy, locus of control and need for achievement), as the following section explains (see Table 3.1 for a summary of the expected relationships between cultural values and personal characteristics that lead to success).

Individualism/Collectivism

In more collective societies, the personal characteristics may be expressed more strongly in terms of working with others, in socially acceptable ways, and associated with group effort. Mentoring, on the other hand, could be acted out as a way to train the in-group members, or to increase their possibilities to succeed. In more individualistic societies, need for achievement, self-efficacy and internal locus of control may be expressed in terms of personal, individual ability, effort and hard work. Mentoring might be enacted as a personal strategy to improve chances for success (or as an organizational programme).

Uncertainty Avoidance

Where uncertainty avoidance is high, structure and rules are important. Need for achievement, self-efficacy and internal locus of control would all be expressed in terms of understanding the norms, and working within the context of the structure and rules. Mentoring is likely to be performed in more formal and structured ways, using specific objectives, procedures and schedules. Where uncertainty avoidance is low, freedom and flexibility are important, and people are more willing to take risks; consequently, these personal characteristics may be expressed in terms of being open to new opportunities, risks and so on. Mentoring is more likely to be unstructured and informal, perhaps with the implicit objective to develop judgement vicariously, in uncertain situations.

Power Distance

Where power distance is high, success depends on understanding what is allowable, given one's position. The personal characteristics may be expressed in terms of these constraints and one's position in society. Mentoring is more likely to take place among persons that have similar status, to ensure that the status quo remains, and favouring the most promising organizational members in the opinion of those in power. Where power distance is low, change in status is acceptable, and success will mean reaching a high level. Achievement, self-esteem and internal locus of control may be expressed in terms of ambitious goals and extra-ordinary achievements. Mentoring is more likely to be used as a strategy to address differences among members of different status, in an effort to equalize the standings.

Table 3.1 summarises the relationships between cultural and personal characteristics.

In the previous discussion, we reviewed the best known cultural value paradigms and our theoretical development linking success with the three personal characteristics that we chose for our Successful Women research programme. The following discussion considers comparisons of scores on the Hofstede variables across the Americas as well as between more developed and developing countries. The focus on development is included because the Americas include clear disparities in development.

COMPARATIVE SCORES ON HOFSTEDE'S VARIABLES

Hofstede, in his discussion of his findings, noted that there were fairly clear distinctions between more developed and developing countries. The Americas, as envisioned in the Free Trade of the Americas Agreement (FTAA) includes a complete range of countries in terms of economic development, ranging from among the richest and most developed (Canada and the USA) through middle-income countries, which score quite high on the United Nation's Human Development Index (Barbados and the Bahamas), to one of the poorest countries in the world (Haiti). It is interesting to consider how the Hofstede variables might differ because of levels of economic development. Figure 3.1 illustrates these contrasts on the three values included in our study.

There are two striking contrasts, as noted by Hofstede (1980) in his early work, and illustrated by these graphs:

- The developed countries are more individualistic and the developing countries more collective.
- The developed countries are relatively low on power distance and the developing countries relatively high.

One can argue in terms of individualism that in relatively poor countries (developing), it is necessary to rely on others to get by, therefore a relatively low score on individualism can be expected, whereas, as countries develop and become richer, people can afford to be more individualistic. In terms of power distance, one can argue that where most people are poor and only a few well off, those who are well off will have disproportionate power and

Table 3.1   Cultural dimensions/personal characteristics

Personal Cultural values	Relative value	High self-efficacy	Internal locus of control	High need for achievement
Individualism/ collectivism	High (collective)	Belief in group ability to get the job done and accomplish goals	Success depends on internal, individual effort but in concert with others, sense that 'we are in control'	Group effort needed to meet challenging group goals
	Low (individual)	Belief in personal ability to get the job done and accomplish goals	Individual hard work leads to success, with the sense that 'I am in control'	Individual effort needed to meet demanding goals
Uncertainty avoidance	High	Structure and rules, policies, procedures, expertise, norms assist in performance	Structure and rules contribute to internal sense of control	Structure and rules used to identify the best ways to meet demanding goals
	Low	Having freedom, flexibility contributes to high performance and results	Dislike structure, rules, see ambiguity as allowing internal control	Ambiguity, uncertainty accepted as giving freedom in working toward goals
Power distance	High	Performance defined in terms of what is allowable given one's position.	Internal control, within context of one's position and status	Strive to achieve goals appropriate to one's position and status
	Low	Performance and success based on one's ability not one's status	Indifferent to status; internal control based on individual ability and effort	Strive to achieve high goals and be the best you can be

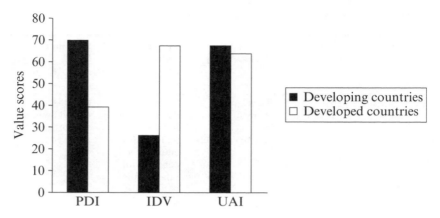

Figure 3.1   Comparison of scores on Hofstede variables

this will be accepted, whereas, as people become economically better off, they can feel freer to express greater equality.

Some contrasts in values between richer and poorer nations can be expected throughout the Americas, because of the range of economic conditions that prevail. Our project will help demonstrate what these differences are. These results, on their own, will be valuable to managers seeking to do business and manage effectively in this vast and diverse region.

While individualism and power distance differ quite clearly on an economic development basis, the same is not true of uncertainty avoidance. One can argue that people in developing countries prefer certainty (high uncertainty avoidance) while those in developed countries are more open to uncertainty and risk (low); however, the scores reported by Hofstede do not support this contention. Our research will provide additional evidence about the Americas on these variables.

SUMMARY OF SCORES FOR THE AMERICAS

Culture's Consequences: Comparing Values, Behaviours, Institutions and Organizations across Nations (Hofstede, 2001) updated the information from the first edition. The scores shown in Table 3.2 for countries in the America's are drawn from this source. Scores, ranging from 0 to 100 are reported, and we have categorized these scores into four quartiles, and they are also reported as high (H), moderately high (MH), moderately low (ML) and low (L).

Table 3.2   Scores on Hofstede values for countries in the Americas

	Power distance	Uncertainly avoidance	Individualism/ collectivism
Argentina	49 ML	86 H	46 ML
Brazil	69 MH	76 H	38 ML
Canada	39 ML	48 ML	80 H
Chile	63 MH	86 H	23 L
Colombia	67 MH	80 H	13 L
Costa Rica	35 ML	86 H	15 L
Ecuador	78 H	67 MH	8 L
Guatemala	95 H	101 H	6 L
Jamaica	45 ML	13 L	39 ML
Mexico	81 H	82 H	30 ML
Panama	95 H	86 H	11 L
Peru	64 MH	87 H	16 L
Salvador	66 MH	94 H	19 L
Uruguay	61 MH	100 H	36 ML
USA	40 ML	46 ML	91 H
Venezuela	81 H	76 H	12 L

Note: Scale 1 to 100 (1–25 = low – L, 26–50 = moderately low – ML, 51–75 = moderately high – MH, 76–100 = high – H).

The only two developed countries in the list, Canada and the USA, are clearly different from almost all of the others. Both Canada and the USA are high on individualism and relatively low on power distance and uncertainty avoidance, whereas the other countries, which are all less well off, are low on individualism and relatively high on power distance and uncertainty avoidance. Jamaica, which is moderately low on power distance and low on uncertainty avoidance, is the exception on these two values.

These contrasting profiles suggest that managers in the context of the Free Trade of the Americas concept will have to pay close attention to cross-cultural issues. Effective managers will need to be able to vary their styles and approaches to suit the varied cultural environments. If we surmise that much of the outward foreign direct investment (FDI) will originate from Canada and the USA, because they are well off and have capital to invest, and will flow into the other countries, we can see that the value profile of the investors is in stark contrast to those likely to receive the investment. If this is not carefully handled, the contrasts could potentially lead to conflicts, miscommunication and, even, mutual dislike.

EXPECTATIONS FOR THIS PROJECT

There has been much discussion in the business and research communities about the existence of unique personal and cultural characteristics that have an impact on professional success. Such characteristics may distinguish women from men, more successful from less successful individuals, individuals from different cultures and socio-economic classes, and individuals active in different industrial or occupational sectors. The purpose of this global research project is to focus on women, defined as 'successful', from a professional viewpoint, in order to identify the similarities and differences that successful women exhibit in different occupational contexts and different countries or regions of the world.

SUMMARY AND REVIEW OF OUR RESULTS ON CULTURE

Each of the upcoming chapters gives details of the results for individual countries and one region (the English-speaking Caribbean). These go into some detail regarding the findings on culture, and the cultural profile for the student populations measured, as well as for the successful women. In the following section, the cultural scores for the women in our study are summarized (Table 3.3) and briefly discussed.

We were struck by the similarity of the scores on the cultural values for the women from such an array of countries in the Americas. Although

Table 3.3   Scores on Successful Women survey for countries in the Americas

Country	I/C	PD	UA
Argentina	3.7	2.3	3.6
Brazil	3.6	2.0	3.7
Canada	3.3	1.9	3.6
Chile	3.6	2.1	3.6
Mexico	3.3	2.3	3.9
USA	3.2	2.1	3.5
West Indies	3.3	1.8	4.1

Notes:
I/C: individualism/collectivism 1 = individualistic, 5 = collective.
PD: power distance 1 = low, 5 = high.
UA: uncertainty avoidance 1 = low, 5 = high.

there are some statistically significant differences across the countries, we can say that, generally, the women were moderate on individualism and uncertainty avoidance, and low on power distance.

Women in the South American countries, Argentina, Brazil and Chile, were most collective, the West Indies and Canada had the lowest score on power distance, and the West Indies and Mexico were highest on uncertainty avoidance. Some of these results are contrary to popular beliefs as well as the literature reported previously. Women in the USA and Canada would have been expected to be high scorers on individualism, but they were not. Women in the West Indies and Latin American countries could have been expected to produce scores relatively high on power distance, but they were low. Women in the USA scored lowest on uncertainty avoidance, as was expected, but others had very similar scores – the West Indies high score was not surprising.

The scores on these cultural variables will be examined and discussed in more detail in upcoming chapters. This gives the reader some preparation for future chapters.

4. Beginning the research in a tropical breeze

Betty Jane Punnett and Lawrence Nurse

The research began in earnest in a tropical breeze, but of course the project began substantially before the data collection did. The birth of the project was actually somewhere between a tropical breeze and a polar wind, at the Academy of Management annual meeting in Chicago, Illinois. A professional development workshop was organized to consider a research agenda focusing on the Americas – it was called 'From polar winds to tropical breezes: developing research for the Americas'. At this workshop, Betty Jane Punnett put forward the idea that the attempt to develop a free trade area of the Americas was a more daring attempt at regional integration than had ever before been contemplated. The diversity contained within the Americas is literally staggering – from the very rich to the very poor, from the very large to the very small, from excellent to poor (in terms of education, health care, infrastructure and so on), from fragile to stable (in terms of economies, politics and so on). Some economies are agriculturally based, others service or manufacturing oriented, still others have a mixed economy. Some countries see the USA, the dominant proponent of the FTAA, as a neighbour and friend, others are wary and distrustful of the USA. There is an array of currencies, cultures, customs and languages through the region, as well as an array of climates – the region really does range from polar winds in the Arctic and Antarctic to tropical breezes in the well-known tourist attractions of Cozumel, Montego Bay or the Grenadines.

The need to understand the implications of the diversity that exists in the Americas is clear if there is to be a successful free trade agreement that benefits those at all extremes. There are hundreds of research projects that might have emerged from this workshop but, in fact, only one did – the project that has come to be called 'Successful Women Worldwide' (as we hope to expand from the Americas to the rest of the world) was born in 1999.

The project has spread and travelled, with meetings of the core group together, and with others, and conference presentations and papers. The project (or at least some of the people involved with the project) has travelled to Brussels and Ireland, Peru and Mexico, Concordia University in Quebec and Sam Houston State University in Texas – to mention only some of the places. We have experienced the cold of the north and heat of the tropics, the height of the Andes and the plains of Texas. Through this process we have developed an exciting and worthwhile project, which is now at a stage of completion that we can present it to a broader audience.

THE BEGINNINGS

Once the decision was made to proceed with the project on successful women in the Americas, it was necessary to design the project as rigorously as possible, so that, at the end of the project, we would be able to make statements about successful women, with confidence. Early on, we concluded that a pilot study was needed, to test the instruments we planned to use, and to get an early sense of how realistic the project would be. The pilot study was, in essence, to be a mini project that would represent the major project on a small scale.

For a variety of reasons, we decided to begin the project in a tropical breeze – the English-speaking Caribbean was selected as the locale for the pilot. Professor Punnett had been instrumental in getting the research group together, so the group supported the idea of doing the pilot in her region of research. She was already involved in projects which examined cross-cultural similarities and differences in the region, so this was a natural extension of her ongoing research. The English-speaking Caribbean also provided a locale where data could be collected from several different island nations, so that the pilot itself could begin to examine cross-national and cross-cultural variations.

The pilot study in the English-speaking Caribbean included mail surveys and interviews, as did the subsequent projects in the other countries. The pilot, however, also included some survey questions on certain cultural dimensions which were not included in the later projects. These cultural dimensions, and survey questions, were dropped from the final survey instrument because of the relatively low reliabilities, which were found in the pilot.[1] Part of the rationale for a pilot study in a major project, such as this, is to ensure that the instruments used are transferable across nations and cultures. It is difficult to ensure this, but through the use of statistical tests for reliability, we hoped at least to be comfortable that we were using the best instruments. Reliability estimates (Cronbach's alpha) refer to the internal consistency of responses to items in a questionnaire. Generally in research, reliabilities above 0.70 are considered acceptable – that is, this level of reliability suggests that respondents are answering in a consistent manner.

The pilot was carried out in the English-speaking Caribbean island countries of Barbados, Jamaica, and St Vincent and the Grenadines (SVG). These countries represent a fairly wide array in the English-speaking Caribbean. Jamaica is the most northern country, Barbados and SVG are among the most southern (Figure 4.1). Barbados and SVG are close neighbours (about 90 miles apart) but Barbados is much more economically developed than SVG. Barbados and Jamaica are both well-known tourist destinations, while SVG has very little tourism and no international airport.

The island states of the English-speaking Caribbean are small countries with developing economies; however, there is substantial variation among the islands in terms of per capita gross domestic product (GDP) and economic growth. The states were, until relatively recently, British colonies with a consequent British influence; but, with the exception of Barbados, they changed hands among the British, French and Spanish, and retain remnants of the influence of all three former colonial powers. A large percentage of the population in all the island states is of African origin, descendents of slaves brought to the West Indies to work the plantations; however, the ethnic mix varies from island to island, with larger Indian, Chinese or Syrian/Lebanese populations in some locations. These factors suggest that the English-speaking countries may share cultural values, related to shared influences, but also that there may be differences among the countries, owing to the variations.

The English-speaking Caribbean

Shared influences
All three countries are English speaking and democracies, with systems of education and law based on British systems. Christianity is the predominant religion. They have been independent since the 1960s/early 1970s and are classified by the United Nations as upper-level developing economies.

Variations
Barbados was never a French or Spanish colony, while both Jamaica and SVG have French and Spanish influences. The people in all three are predominantly of African origin (91 per cent in Jamaica, 80 per cent in Barbados, 98 per cent in SVG). Barbados has a slightly larger European population (4 per cent) than the other two (less than 1 per cent), Jamaica has more people of Chinese and Syrian or Lebanese descent. In 2004, Barbados' GDP/capita, adjusted for purchasing power parity (PPP) was estimated at US$16 400 compared with US$2900 for SVG and US$4100 in

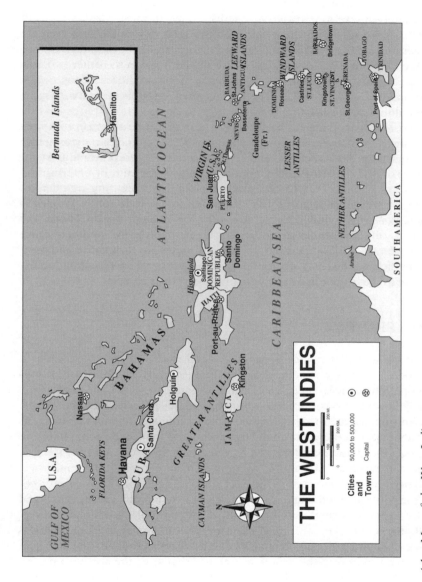

Figure 4.1   Map of the West Indies

79

Jamaica. Barbados has experienced economic growth of about 3 per cent in 2004 and up to 5 per cent in recent years, SVG only about 1 per cent in 2004, while Jamaica's economy grew by about 2 per cent in 2004 after declining for several years (CIA, 2005b).

Organizations in all three countries are relatively small, and even the larger ones, such as Grace Kennedy in Jamaica, would be classified as small in the USA. In SVG, organizations are smaller than in the other two, and would be classified as micro enterprises in larger countries. Many organizations are family owned, and even where they are publicly traded, they are often dominated by certain families.

In recent years there has been concern in the Caribbean region with what is termed 'the marginalization of young men'. More and more young men are dropping out of school, and few are continuing to university. At the University of the West Indies, approximately 80 per cent of entering students are female. This has naturally resulted in increasing numbers of women in responsible positions in the public and private sector. Women in the region remain underrepresented at the top levels of organizations, and there is still some gender stereotyping – for example, in the human resource field, women predominate, but the same is not true in the finance and operations fields. This may change in coming years when recent university graduates have the opportunity to advance in their careers.

THE PROJECT

As explained in Chapter 1, we had developed a specific definition of 'success'. Success was defined as 'reaching a relatively high level in one's occupation or profession'. Specifically, respondents were to be drawn from the following groups: middle- and upper-level managers in the private sector (managers of managers), university administrators and tenured full professors, entrepreneurs/small business owners in business more than two years, government ministers, and professionals, such as doctors or lawyers, who had evidenced substantial accomplishment in their profession.

These groups were used in the pilot study as well as in the other projects. In the pilot we found that it was relatively easy to identify professionals and entrepreneurs; a small number of university administrators and tenured, full professors and government ministers were also easy to identify; it was more difficult to identify 'managers of managers' because of the nature of the organizations in the region, as well as because of the apparent prevalence of male managers. Most organizations are small, therefore, in many, there are no 'managers of managers' – the levels in the organizations are limited, and there may be only employees and managers.

The small size of the states meant that our numbers were going to be small in the pilot study. A major concern initially was how it would be possible to identify successful women in any objective manner. We were fortunate to find some very helpful sources – in Barbados, the National Organization of Women provided a list of members that included information on employment status and roles; in SVG, the Ministry of Labour had prepared a booklet on successful women; in Jamaica, one of the local papers had done a series of profiles on successful women. All these sources provided a good beginning. We added to these by asking personal contacts to suggest women who fit our definition. The selection process is probably not very scientific, but we believe we covered a wide array of women in all three countries, and that their responses should be representative of the broader population of successful women.

Measures

As described in Chapter 1, various personal and cultural characteristics were measured in the pilot. The measures used are briefly reviewed below.

- *Self-efficacy* – the measure of self-efficacy used in the current study (Sherer et al., 1982) consists of 17 items, with five response choices ranging from 1 = 'strongly agree' to 5 = 'strongly disagree'.
- *Locus of control* – the measure of locus of control used in the current study (Spector, 1988) consists of 16 items, with six response choices, ranging from 1 = 'disagree very much' to 6 = 'agree very much'. High scores on the scale represent externality.
- *Need for achievement* – the measure of need for achievement used in the current study (Jackson, 1989) consists of 16 items, with responses of 'agree' or 'disagree'. Scores can range from 0 to 16, and the higher the score, the higher the need for achievement.

Mentoring also plays an important role in women's success, so we included an established measure (Tepper et al., 1996) consisting of 16 items measuring both psychosocial and career-oriented mentoring (the contributions of others to success from an emotional as well as a career perspective). We believed that successful women would all have been substantially influenced by mentors.

We also looked at cultural values in the pilot. The pilot included three cultural values based on Hofstede's (1984) model and measured by an instrument developed by Dorfman and Howell (1988). The cultural values are briefly described as follows:

- *Individualism/collectivism* is the extent to which the individual or the group is emphasized in decision-making and activities – some societies place more emphasis on the individual, others on group interactions.
- *Uncertainty avoidance* is the degree to which people are comfortable with a lack of certainty and seek security – some societies are more comfortable with certainty, others are comfortable with a higher degree of uncertainty.
- *Power distance* is the degree to which inequalities in power are acceptable – some societies accept inequalities as being appropriate, others prefer greater equality in power.

In addition, we designed an interview protocol to provide information that could be interpreted in the same terms as the questionnaire items, but that allowed for other important characteristics to be identified. An important part of the study was the use of both quantitative (the survey) and qualitative (the interview) measures. Quantitative measures like surveys allow the researcher to measure all respondents on the same questions with the same scales; however, these measures are limited to the particular items or variables the researchers have selected. There may be other items or variables that are very important that the researchers have not identified or selected. Qualitative measures, such as interviews, allow researchers to round out their information, by encouraging respondents to identify what the respondent believes is important. Qualitative measures provide additional information, as well as giving support to the findings of the quantitative aspects of a study such as this one. The interview protocol was designed to allow for interpretation of responses in terms of these cultural values as well as the variables discussed previously, and to capture additional cultural values that might be important in a particular location.

The mail survey allowed for responses from a relatively large number of respondents, and provided quantitative data, which could be statistically analysed to determine reliability and validity, and to examine similarities and differences across groups. The mail survey consisted of standardized questionnaires with well-established psychometric properties, which provide confidence in the results. These questionnaires focused on the personal characteristics previously identified. The limitation of the survey was that it included only those characteristics identified by the researchers. There may be other characteristics, potentially as important or more important, which would not be identified through a survey.

The interview overcame this limitation. The interview served two main purposes. One was to validate information obtained from the mail survey. The second was to gain insights into information that would not emerge from the survey. Interviews were designed so that responses could be interpreted in terms of the characteristics measured in the survey; however, they were also designed to be as open-ended as possible to allow for additional insights. Summaries of interview responses identify those related to concepts covered in the survey, as well as new concepts that emerge.

The combination of a quantitative approach (a large-scale survey with standardized measures) and a qualitative approach (an in-depth, open-ended interview) provides much richer information than either approach on its own. To the extent that the results support each other, one can be relatively comfortable in their validity. To the extent that they do not support each other, the need for further investigation is identified. In addition, the information from in-depth interviews broadens understanding of each situation, and provides additional insights.

The Pilot

The pilot study consisted of two phases:

1. A mail survey of women who conform to the operational definition of success.
2. Interviews with women who conform to the operational definition of success.

Data were collected from university students to provide scores on personal and cultural variables which could be compared with the scores for the successful women. The students completed the same instrument as the women, with the exception of the mentoring scale (this was not included because it assumes that respondents are working people). Students were selected as a comparison group because it seemed that this was a likely base from which successful women would emerge. Students themselves are likely to be relatively high on the personal characteristics identified; thus, if the women scored significantly higher than the students on these characteristics, it would be strong evidence of the importance of these characteristics in their success. The students and the successful women come from the same cultural backgrounds, and if the cultural measures are a valid representation, scores on these measures should not be significantly different for the women and the students.

The survey instrument and interview protocol were pre-tested with ten women who fitted the operational definition of success, to establish that respondents would be able to respond meaningfully and in a timely manner to both the mail survey and the interview questions. Based on the responses, minor modifications were made to the instruments.

In all three locations (Barbados, Jamaica and SVG) the list of women to be surveyed was developed by seeking existing lists of women, and by asking women identified as successful to identify additional women, based on the criteria discussed above. In St Vincent, the *Directory of Members of the SVG Chamber of Industry and Commerce* and the *Directory of Successful Women* prepared by the SVG Department of Labour served as the basis, in Barbados a listing of members of the National Organization of Women was used and, in Jamaica, a newspaper column on success-ful women and a book on Jamaican women (Simpson, 2000) provided names. A small number of women were selected, from the overall list, and interviewed.

- *St Vincent and the Grenadines* – a total of 75 women who fitted the research criteria were identified; ten of these were interviewed, all others were mailed surveys. Those interviewed were selected to represent several different categories – three respondents were well-known lawyers, five were owner-managers, two were top managers. Nine interviews were conducted by one of the principal researchers, and one was conducted by a research associate who was very famil-iar with the project. Thirty-six responses to the mail survey were received (a 47 per cent response rate).
- *Barbados* – surveys were mailed to 185 women and 90 responses were received (a 49 per cent response rate), and six women were interviewed.
- *Jamaica* – surveys were mailed to 100 women and 64 responses were received (a 64 per cent response rate), and 13 women were interviewed.

In total, 321 surveys were mailed and 190 responses received (a 60 per cent response rate). These response rates were considered 'high' by colleagues in the region, who indicated that response rates for mail surveys were gener-ally substantially lower.

RESULTS

The first phase of the project took place in St Vincent. The results from this study were used to make minor modifications to the instruments before administering them in Barbados and Jamaica. The results from the inter-views and surveys in St Vincent are reported in detail in the following section. The results from Barbados and Jamaica are reported in summary tables and compared with those from St Vincent.

Results of St Vincent Interviews

Several themes were identified in the SVG interviews. These are briefly described in the following:

1. All the women began by attributing their success to internal characteristics, and added external characteristics later or when specifically asked about them. Internal attribution was strong, and high need for achievement and self-efficacy were evident, in all the women interviewed. All the respondents described characteristics such as 'hard work', 'determination to be the best', 'ambition', 'confidence in ability' – thereby, demonstrating internal attribution and locus of control, need for achievement and a strong sense of self-efficacy.

2. Several women included their faith in God as an important contributor to their success (six out of ten respondents: 6/10). Some included a desire, interest in helping others as an important contributor to their success (3/10) – the importance of helping others was supported by the respondents' descriptions of the leadership roles they play outside normal work.

3. In terms of leadership roles, three out of ten specifically mentioned the importance of helping others, another three talked of working with community groups where they can have an impact, and an additional three identified the importance of helping those in the industry where they work. Only one respondent did not identify a leadership role for herself outside work.

4. The most important external contributors to success were family members – all the respondents referred to the importance of family support to their success. Family in general was cited by four respondents, children were also cited by four women, mothers were mentioned by three, and fathers, siblings, parents and husbands were specified by two each (respondents identified multiple family members, so numbers sum to more than ten). Other external contributors were 'being in the right place at the right time', 'luck', 'educational opportunities', 'discipline at school', 'access to resources' and 'need to provide for children/family'. None of these factors were a strong, common theme.

5. The most important mentors were also family, with three identifying their father and two identifying other family members, employers/managers were mentioned by three and other professionals/businesspeople by two, peers at work and a teacher were identified by one respondent each (respondents identified multiple family members, so numbers sum to more than ten).

6. Leadership style was described by most respondents (7/10) in terms of delegating, providing a role model, coaching, listening to input from subordinates and instilling a sense of pride. One respondent said she was perhaps considered dictatorial, another did not see herself as really engaged in management, and a third thought she was 'too soft' on subordinates.

7. Almost all of the respondents considered themselves successful from a work/professional point of view (9/10). The respondent, who did not agree, argued that she could have achieved so much more. Those who felt they were successful professionally, also generally felt there was more they wanted to achieve. Two business owners felt that their success was constrained by the business environment in SVG and that this was somewhat frustrating. Satisfaction with life as a whole was not as clear-cut, some felt that they were missing something in their personal lives (three) or that work took away from their personal lives (two).

8. Ethnicity was not seen as an issue (all but one of the respondents were women of colour). Some respondents said it might be elsewhere, but not in SVG – one respondent had experienced discrimination while in the USA and Canada. Most respondents viewed their ethnicity as a positive attribute.

9. Gender was largely described as positive or neutral. Positive statements about gender included 'women seek you out', 'women have special skills', 'women are determined and can make something out of nothing', 'women don't give up as easily as men', 'women can use their charm', 'women have more vision' and 'women can gain trust easier than men'. One respondent commented on the need to prove yourself to the men you work with, and another on discrimination on the part of lenders.

10. Great leaders included Nelson Mandela (two), Bill Clinton, John F. Kennedy, Pierre Elliott Trudeau, Eugenia Charles, Michael Manley, Sun Myung Moon, Mahatma Gandhi and one respondent's father, who she describes as her idol and a great businessman. The list was, thus, dominated by political leaders – seven respondents – followed by religious leaders – two respondents. The major reason for selecting someone as a great leader seemed to be their achievements, but particularly their achievements given a particular environment; for example overcoming great adversity (Mandela), a short time span (Kennedy), in the face of opposition (Gandhi), against the odds (Moon). Many respondents cited the importance of personal characteristics of their selected leader as well; for example, 'determined but humble and simple' (Gandhi), 'moderate, liberal thinker' (Trudeau),

'would not compromise' (Manley), 'independence and determination' (Charles), 'concern for family and God' (Clinton), 'determined to fulfil his responsibility' (Moon), 'achievement and humility' and 'understanding of humanity' (Mandela). These responses are varied, but may be summarized as respondents seeing great leaders as those who achieve much, often in the face of difficulty, and are both strong and humble, with an understanding of the needs of others. In many respects, their descriptions of their own success seem to mirror what they admire in others elsewhere.

Comparison with Barbados and Jamaica

There were many similarities in responses to the interviews. In all three countries, women were high in terms of their beliefs in their own ability to accomplish the tasks they undertook (self-efficacy and internal attribution) and all had a high need for achievement, often discussed in terms of setting difficult goals for themselves. The choice and descriptions of leaders were very similar in all countries. Mentoring varied in importance from individual to individual, and mentors came from a variety of groups. Jamaicans mentioned teachers as mentors more often than the other two groups, and parents and family were most important mentors in Barbados. Some differences that surfaced were:

- a greater emphasis on spirituality and the role of God in St Vincent
- a greater emphasis on the importance of family in Barbados
- a greater emphasis on helping others in Jamaica.

One Barbadian woman likened achieving success to Hannibal taking his elephants over the Alps; a comment that particularly resonated with the interviewer.

These themes were present in all locations, but the emphasis and importance was somewhat different in the different locations.

Results of the SVG Mail Surveys

The mail surveys used standardized tests to measure a variety of personal characteristics. What follows is a description of each characteristic, the reliabilities for this sample and a brief discussion of the scores in our survey. These are the results of the questionnaire survey in SVG only.

1. The first set of questions measured self-efficacy. This measures the degree to which people believe they are capable of doing what they set

out to do. At work high self-efficacy generally shows up in people's acceptance of responsibility, and high performance. We expect, generally, that successful women will score relatively highly in terms of self-efficacy. Scores can range from 1 to 5, 1 being low and 5 being high. Our sample of SVG women scored, on average, 4.14. This score suggests that these women do have a high sense of self-efficacy and believe that they can accomplish their objectives.

2. The second set of questions measured internal versus external locus of control. This measures the degree to which someone believes that results come from themselves, or are because of external forces. At work, an internal locus of control generally shows up with people explaining success or failure as based on their own actions; an external locus of control shows up with people using factors around them (co-workers, superiors, subordinates, luck, the weather, and so on) to explain success or failure. We expect, generally, that successful women will exhibit an internal locus of control and believe that they are responsible for results. Scores can range from 1 to 6, 1 representing an internal locus of control and 6 representing an external locus of control. Our sample of SVG women scored, on average, 2.38. This score suggests that these women do have an internal locus of control.

3. The third set of questions dealt with mentoring – both the psychological importance and the career-oriented importance. We expect, generally, that successful women will have been substantially influenced by mentors, and will score highly on the mentoring scales. Scores can range from 1 to 5 – 1 is a low score and five a high score. The SVG women scored, on average, 2.9 on the psychological aspect and 3.38 on the career-related aspect. These scores suggest that mentoring has not been particularly important in the SVG context.

4. The fourth set of questions measured three cultural characteristics – individualism/collectivism, power distance and uncertainty avoidance. Individualism/collectivism refers to the degree to which the individual is important relative to the group, power distance refers to the degree to which differences in power (associated with birth, education, and so on) are accepted, and uncertainty avoidance refers to the degree to which people accept or avoid uncertainty. Scores can range from 1 to 5. One indicates that the cultural characteristic is low in importance; 5 indicates that it is high in importance. Our sample of SVG women scored as follows:

– uncertainty avoidance   4.12 (high)
– individualism/collectivism   3.05 (moderate)
– power distance   2.17 (low)

These scores suggest that our sample prefers certainty to uncertainty (although the relatively low reliability suggests caution in interpreting this score[2]), is neither strongly individualistic nor collective, and is low on accepting of differences in power.

5. The last set of questions measured need for achievement. This is the degree to which someone wants to accomplish difficult goals. At work, a high need for achievement generally shows up with acceptance of challenging goals, and hard work to accomplish these goals. We expect, generally, that successful women will have a high need for achievement. Scores can range from 0 to 16, 0 being lowest on need for achievement, and 16 highest. Our sample of SVG women scored, on average, 12.36. This score suggests that these women have a high need for achievement.

The results of the SVG survey support the results of the interviews in terms of personal characteristics. Successful women in SVG have a high sense of being able to accomplish what they set out to accomplish, they are internally motivated and attribute accomplishments to their own activities, and they want to accomplish difficult goals.

In terms of mentoring, the mail survey also supports the results of the interviews. Mentoring is not currently seen as a critical aspect of success for women in the SVG context.

The cultural profile that emerges from the mail questionnaire suggests that successful women in SVG like to co-operate and work with others but that they are also independent, they believe in equality and do not see an authoritarian leadership style as positive, and would prefer to work in an environment that is relatively stable and certain. This cultural profile is consistent with the results of the interviews.

These results support our general hypotheses on personal characteristics, but do not support the hypothesis regarding mentoring.

When the study in St Vincent was complete and we had reviewed the reliabilities and the results, we made the decision to modify the mail survey instrument. We eliminated one cultural measure (Triandis, 1995) because the reliabilities of these scales were felt to be unacceptably low, and we did not believe the results could be interpreted meaningfully. We also decided to add a measure of satisfaction to our questionnaire for the next stage of the pilot. We agreed that the other reliabilities were acceptable for a pilot study, and that the results were very interesting, so that we would continue the study in two other English-speaking countries, Jamaica and Barbados. This would complete the pilot. In many ways this was a critical point in the development of the project. While all the core group were committed to the project, up to this point, we were ready to abandon it, or modify it substantially, if the results from St Vincent were disappointing. In the next section of the chapter, the means for the three countries are presented and compared.

COMPARISON OF MEANS

Means for each sample on each measure were calculated and compared, using Analysis of Variance (ANOVA) followed by t-tests, where the ANOVAs were significant. In all cases, the cut-off for significance was 0.05. Table 4.1 presents the means on the personal characteristics, psychosocial and career mentoring, and the dimensions of culture.

Respondents from all three countries exhibit a high level of self-efficacy, an internal locus of control and a high need for achievement. The scores

Table 4.1   Comparison of scores in the Caribbean countries

	Personality characteristics		
	SE	LoC	Ach
St Vincent	4.14	2.33	12.38
Jamaica	3.97	1.93	13.66
Barbados	4.27	2.10	14.08
Notes:	1 = low	1 = internal	0 = low
	5 = high	6 = external	16 = high

	Mentoring career	Psych
St Vincent	2.91	3.34
Jamaica	3.38	3.94
Barbados	3.01	2.84

Note: 1 = unimportant to 5 = important.

	Cultural values		
	I/C	UA	PD
St Vincent	3.03	4.13	2.14
Jamaica	3.27	4.29	1.82
Barbados	3.30	4.33	2.05

Note: 1 = low to 5 = high.

from the three countries are quite similar (although there are some significant differences, at the 0.05 level, which are discussed later). This supports the interview findings that these women felt confident of their abilities, responsible for their own actions and successes, and that achievement was important to them.

Mentoring scores from all three countries are essentially 'neutral' – neither important nor unimportant. This supports the interview findings, which indicated that mentoring was not a process that was common in these locations. Mentoring is somewhat more important for Jamaican respondents than for respondents from the other two countries.

Responses from all three countries are moderate on individualism/collectivism, moderately high on uncertainty avoidance, and moderately low on power distance. Again, this supports the interview findings. In the interviews:

- respondents described themselves as valuing independence and individual action as well as finding teamwork and social support systems important
- respondents were entrepreneurial in spirit, but they did not describe themselves as risk-takers and appeared to be more comfortable with a degree of certainty and security
- respondents strongly supported equality and stressed their beliefs in power sharing.

Overall Profile

Considering the profiles from the three countries, we find that they are very similar – correlations of 0.99 for all pairings. This is a very high correlation and essentially indicates that the profile for the three countries is identical. There are some differences in absolute scores on specific variables which are identified later in the chapter.

Comparison with student responses

Student responses were first analysed to see if there were significant differences between female and male students. As there were no significant differences, the mean scores for the successful women were compared with the mean scores for all the students. The women and the students are similar on the culture measures and the personal characteristics measures (significant differences are discussed in the next section) – correlations of 0.99 – but the successful women were higher in terms of self-esteem, internal locus of control and need for achievement, as Table 4.1 illustrates.

Country and Population Differences

There were some significant differences between the successful women in the three countries, and between the successful women and the students, as the following outlines.

Barbadian women were statistically significantly higher on self-efficacy than Jamaican (the relatively low reliability in Jamaica for self-efficacy means this result is questionable).

Jamaican women were statistically significantly higher on internal locus of control than the other two, and Barbadian women were significantly more internal than those from SVG.

Barbadian and Jamaican women were statistically significantly higher on need for achievement than those from SVG (the low reliability in Jamaica for need for achievement means that the Jamaican result is questionable).

Mentoring was statistically significantly more important in Jamaica than in the other two.

Barbados was statistically significantly higher on collectivism and uncertainty avoidance than SVG (the low reliability in SVG for uncertainty avoidance means that the result relative to uncertainty avoidance is questionable).

Jamaica was statistically significantly lower on power distance than the other two (the low reliabilities in Barbados and Jamaica on this variable mean that this result is questionable).

Women/student comparisons showed some interesting results. The successful women sample scores statistically significantly higher on uncertainty avoidance, but not on the other two cultural variables. The successful women sample also scores statistically significantly higher on self-efficacy, internal locus of control and need for achievement. These results provide some support for the hypotheses that guide this project. Successful women do appear to be high on the personal characteristics that we expected to influence success – and they are significantly different from the student population on these variables. Mentoring, which we believed would play and important role in success, did not appear to be of special value to our samples. This also supports our hypothesis that the importance of mentoring may differ from location to location. The women were similar to the student population in terms of collectivism and power distance, suggesting a sharing of cultural values, but they were higher in terms of uncertainty avoidance, suggesting that there may also be value differences, perhaps based on age and life experiences.

The scales used in the survey have a variety of scoring ranges, and this makes it difficult to compare them visually. The graph in Figure 4.2 has

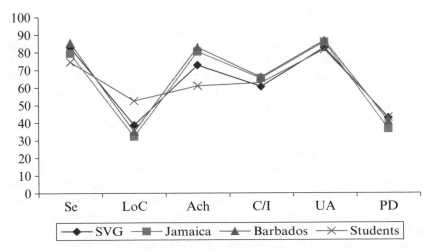

Figure 4.2   Comparison of successful women and students

standardized the scores, so that they are all based on a score from 1 to 100. This standardization allows a better visualization of the comparative scores among variables, countries, and populations.

Figure 4.2 illustrates the similarity in scores on the cultural variables (collectivism, uncertainty avoidance and power distance) for all groups, and the relative difference on the personal characteristics (self-efficacy, locus of control and need for achievement) between the successful women and the students.

DISCUSSION

This first phase of the Successful Women Worldwide project provided a valuable beginning for the project. The profile of the women from three English-speaking countries in the Caribbean supports the hypotheses that successful women will be high on self-efficacy, internal locus of control and need for achievement. Especially interesting is that the successful women were significantly higher on these measures than were the university students. This finding supports the researchers' belief that these personal characteristics may be supportive of success for women. The results do not support the importance of mentoring to women's success – it may be that the concept of mentoring is better developed in the North American and European contexts, and it will be interesting to see if this is borne out by further results.

The cultural profile that emerges from the women as well as the sample of university students is low on power distance, moderate on collectivism/individualism and relatively high on uncertainty avoidance. The cultural value commonalities across the three countries, as well as across women and students, suggests that this cultural profile is indicative of the cultural values in the region, at least among the more educated and more success-ful in the region. Understanding the value profile in the region may be valu-able in examining management practices, and their effectiveness in the region.

The results from this study illustrate the value of combining quantitative and qualitative research methods. The interview and survey results support each other and give us confidence in the validity of these results. At the same time, the interviews uncovered themes that were not covered in the survey – for example, the importance of the spiritual context, the special role of the family and the need to give back to society. These are themes that would have been missed without interviews. The first phase of the Successful Women Worldwide research project provides encouragement for the continuation of the project.

From the perspective of organizations competing in a global environ-ment, the profile of successful women in the three countries in the English-speaking Caribbean is a profile that should be considered very attractive. The respondents are self-confident, internally motivated and they have high goals. These are the attributes that one associates with excellence in organizations. These are also attributes that are needed to compete in today's global environment. Organizations from the region should be able to draw on the talents of women such as these to succeed internationally. Multinational organizations operating in the region should find this group a valuable resource.

These results do not allow us to compare successful women with suc-cessful men. It is quite likely that successful men will similarly exhibit high self-esteem, internal locus of control and need for achievement. The study was not designed to investigate this, although it would be an interesting comparison. It does allow us to say, with some conviction, that successful women in the region exhibit this profile and that, in terms of these charac-teristics, they are significantly different from the norm of university stu-dents. A concern in the region has been the decreasing number of young men completing high school and attending university, and the consequent marginalization of these young men. It would be interesting to look at these and similar characteristics, to see if those young men that do complete school and attend university are in some ways different from those who do not.

SUMMARY

The results of this study support the hypotheses that professionally successful women will be high on need for achievement and self-efficacy, and have an internal locus of control. The results did not support the contention that mentoring would be especially important for these women. The scores on the cultural characteristics for the women were similar to those for the broader population, represented by a sample of students. The cultural profile is moderate on individualism, high on uncertainty avoidance and low on power distance.

Other researchers can build on the results of this research in a variety of ways. We hope that colleagues around the world will use these results to develop other projects that help us understand culture, women and the world of work. The upcoming chapters in this book give results from a variety of counties in the Americas, as well as identifying similarities across countries and professions, and differences. These comparisons help us to understand how to address women in the world of work in the Americas.

Before we turn attention to the detailed results for each of the countries in the study, we give readers an overview of 'what our women said' in the following chapters. These chapters look at the results relating to personality, management style, leadership, professional and life experiences, mentoring and social support, across the group of countries. In Chapters 5 and 6 we highlight both the similarities across countries as well as the distinctions that we encountered.

NOTES

1. The reliabilities for many of the scales were quite acceptable for cross-cultural research. The measures or personal characteristics were generally better than those for cultural characteristics. The lowest on personal characteristics was need for achievement at 0.732, and this is considered acceptable in such research. The Dorfman measures of culture had mixed reliabilities. The individualism/collectivism and power distance dimensions were acceptable, but the uncertainty avoidance dimension was not. The reliability of the uncertainty avoidance dimension can be increased from 0.33 to 0.53 by using only three questions, but this is still unacceptably low. This does suggest that there is a cultural bias to this particular dimension. Because two of the three dimensions proved to be reliable, we included this measure in our further research.

   The table overleaf compares the results of the surveys in Barbados (B'dos), Jamaica (Ja.) and St Vincent (StV.). Reliabilities were compared for the three samples.

   Reliabilities of 0.60 are generally considered acceptable in cross-cultural research. Using this base, most of the reliabilities are acceptable. There are notable exceptions – reliability in St Vincent was unacceptable on uncertainty avoidance, Jamaica was unacceptable on achievement and marginal on self-efficacy, and Barbados was unacceptable on power distance. The scores on these dimensions should, therefore, be interpreted with caution.

	SE	LoC	MC	MP	I/C	UA	PD	Ach
StV.	0.78	0.82	0.92	0.90	0.74	0.33	0.72	0.73
Ja.	0.55	0.75	0.84	0.82	0.62	0.79	0.57	0.42
B'dos	0.75	0.77	0.86	0.83	0.68	0.69	0.39	0.65

Note: self-efficacy (SE), locus of control (LoC), mentoring – career (MC), psychological (MP), culture – individualism/collectivism (I/C), uncertainty avoidance (UA), power distance (PD), achievement orientation (Ach).

2. Appendix D gives details of the reliabilities for all the variables measured, for each of the countries.

5. Personality, management/leadership styles and views on great leadership

Suzy Fox and Ann Gregory

One of the oldest debates in the study of human behaviour is whether people's successes and failures can be attributed to factors within the individuals themselves or to factors in their external situations (Heider, 1958). Accordingly, a key question underlying this Successful Women of the Americas project was the extent to which the women we studied attributed their own success to internal or external factors. As we shall see, there were differences in perceptions and emphasis. Yet virtually all the women we interviewed were aware of both characteristics within themselves (personality, style, values and beliefs) and characteristics of their environments and life experiences (opportunities, education, support systems and discrimination) that helped or hindered their efforts to achieve professional success.

In this chapter, we listen to our women describing themselves – their own words about their personality characteristics and the management/ leadership styles to which they attribute their success. To hone in on their leadership beliefs and values, we also asked them to name the individuals they saw as great leaders, and to identify the qualities these great leaders possess. We look for systematic differences between women of different national cultures, and also seek fundamental commonalities among successful women, regardless of country.

In Chapter 6, we examine the women's descriptions of demographic and family factors, external situational factors, barriers and support systems they have experienced that they feel have contributed substantially to the successes and challenges in their professional careers. Again, we will look for differences and similarities among women across national borders.

Tables 5.1, 5.2, and 5.3 summarize the key internal themes that emerged from our conversations with the successful women of each country, in the order of most to fewest respondents mentioning each theme. Table 5.1 presents personality characteristics, Table 5.2 presents management and leadership styles and Table 5.3 presents the women's choices of great leaders and the qualities that make for great leadership. These tables provide compelling evidence of deep similarities among successful women across the hemisphere; they also highlight a few intriguing cultural differences. We now proceed to a discussion of these key themes, illustrated by examples from our conversations.

PERSONALITY AND OTHER INTERNAL FACTORS

In analysing the interviews in terms of internal factors, it is quite evident that these successful women from various countries and cultures shared several of the attributes that were measured in the written survey, such as high self-efficacy, a high internal locus of control, and a high need for achievement.

> I think that my self-confidence, leadership skills, drive and ambition all contribute to where I am today and where I am going. I don't believe in chance. I believe in hard work, opportunity, the ability to take risks and timing; people often confuse those factors with luck. (Canada)

A few specific characteristics seemed to resonate with women across the Americas, as we can see from Table 5.1.

Hard Work, Achievement Orientation, Persistence

The factors behind success most frequently cited by our women were hard work, desire to succeed/excel and persistence. Women in different countries used different terms, with somewhat different emphases, but an overall, universal picture emerged of extraordinary achievement motivation – what could be called 'fire in the belly'!

> I am a professionally successful woman, because I worked hard. (Argentina)

> Willpower and perseverance. I wanted to be an executive woman and I struggled in every way to reach my objective. (Brazil)

> I am very tunnel-minded and when I want to do something, I do it. My motto is 'Where there is a will there is a way'. If you want to get anywhere you cannot be timid. I have been called a bulldozer. I do my own thing and do it the best way I can. I'm still around and I'm still fighting. (Canada)

> I pursued success – asked for promotions, aggressive career planning, worked very, very, very hard. (USA)

> I am a hard-working person, obsessive, determined. Not so tidy, but my obsession and my hard-working style compensate for my untidiness. Being an

Table 5.1   Personality and other internal factors

Country	Themes
Argentina	Hard work, dedication Persistence, tenacity Positive view of life
Brazil	Persistent, determined, focused Willpower Competitiveness Desire to be successful, independent, the best Decisive Conscientious, thorough Collaborative See opportunities Courageous Goal driven, 'fire in belly'
Canada	Risk-taking Desire to be successful, independent, the best Self-confident, self-directed Not intimidated Motivated to learn, engage Goal driven, 'fire in belly' Hard-working Inventive Persistent, determined, focused
Newfoundland	Hard work Set realistic goals, perfectionist Organized Tenacious, focused Outgoing, people oriented, want to help, empathetic Desire to be successful, the best, achieve, compete Open-minded, innovative, love learning new things Self-confident, self-directed
USA	Desire to be successful, achieve Hard work Person skills See opportunities, future Optimistic, open attitude Self-confident Thinking competencies Risk-taking

Table 5.1   (continued)

Country	Themes
Chile	Hard work
	Happy
	Passionate, enthusiastic, love what I do
	Perseverance
	Find opportunities, overcome difficult situations, learn from failures
	Disciplined, studious, balanced, serious, committed
Mexico	Personal motivation, drive to succeed
	Tenacity, dedication, perseverance
St Vincent	Hard work (all)
	Determined to be the best, ambitious (all)
	Confidence in ability (all)
	Faith in God
	Desire to help others
Barbados	Drive to improve self, overcome fears
	Can-do attitude, self-confidence
	Desire to make a difference
	Strong sense of purpose

influential woman requires having a strong character. People are attracted to the mix of fragility and strength. (Chile)

The next time I put the bar up, I raise the stakes. I have to improve. Actually, when you challenge me that is when I am going to get hard-nosed. (Barbados)

Perseverance and persistence. It doesn't matter at all if something seems like a difficult challenge, because in fact, the more I determine to face a challenge, the more interesting it becomes. (Brazil)

The above quotes are all illustrations of a high need for achievement, and these quotes of the successful women echoed those of the larger survey sample in terms of the results of the achievement motivation scale (see Appendix D for detailed survey results). All the successful women, no matter from which country, evidenced a high need for achievement. Their emphasis on striving for achievement also indicated an internal locus of control; again, this was reflected in the larger sample of successful women.

Self-confidence

A second set of themes included self-confidence and the belief that one could succeed. One aspect of self-efficacy, as described in Chapter 3, is confidence in one's ability to perform successfully, which is a part of leadership self-efficacy. There was also some evidence of creative self-efficacy, though leadership self-efficacy was a stronger theme and more common.

Women who were self-confident also expressed a sense of being self-directed. In some ways, this was also reflected in comments about optimism and a positive view of life.

> Very, very strong work ethic, very strong conviction of who I am – very confident and secure in my management style and my abilities to do my job and do it well. (USA)

> I have always been a person who never thought that a task was too difficult to achieve. I always believed that you can break things down and you can achieve things and you must put in an effort, you must try. I don't think I have a defeatist attitude. I think that I have an attitude that says I can get it done and there has to be a way and a means to do it. (Barbados)

> I can deal with ambiguity and uncertainty; I don't have much need for stability. I'm . . . open, positive about solutions . . . confident, comfortable with my abilities. (USA)

> Not being put off by challenges. Just do it and worry about it later. I'm optimistic and again, I keep going. Things will work out you will get there. Always putting one foot in front of the other. (Canada)

Conscientiousness, Disciplined Approach to Work Tasks and Learning

A third set of themes that emerged had to do with general approaches to work tasks that contributed to these women's success. These included qualities of conscientiousness, thoroughness, discipline and decisiveness, as well as analytical or innovative approaches to problem-solving and decision-making and an orientation to continuous learning. These themes are related to creative self-efficacy and leadership self-efficacy. These themes were especially pronounced in the statements of women from Brazil, Canada, Chile and the USA.

> In my opinion, my core competencies include exceptional organizational skills, the ability to network and to communicate. I also have good analytical skills, which are essential in this field. (Canada)

> I'm goal oriented and organized. My husband says I'm obsessive. I have never been late for a paper or a project. (Canada)

> I love learning and following my nose. I listen, I hear and I see things. (Canada)

> Stick-to-itness. Being determined, not to give up. Sticking to the end. (USA)

People Orientation, People Skills

Some of the respondents among the women of the USA, Canada and the West Indies emphasized their caring orientation, empathy, people skills and desire to help others.

> I am very open, warm, outgoing . . . able to put people at ease. (USA)

> I have a truly authentic desire to make a diffierence with people who are sick. That sounds very altruistic, but it's what's so for me. So building empires has never been my motivation. I do think that when you are doing the right thing that it makes a diffierence for people, people can see that. (Canada)

> [I have qualities of] social sensitivity, social dynamics, empathy. [They] seem to be more developed in women and I use that stuff all the time. (USA)

Passion and Happiness

One of the most interesting cultural differences was a unique emphasis of the women of Chile on happiness, passion, enthusiasm and love of what they do.

> I am a successful person because I am passionate about 90 per cent of what I get to do. I feel that day after day I move a single grain of sand . . . and this has to do with success. I try to be happy and optimistic in my work . . . I transmit enthusiasm and [faith] that barriers can be pulled down. (Chile)

> I think the game is looking at what the environment has to offier, and trying to match our own motives with the opportunities we get. Sometimes opportunities appear, but disguised, not exactly what we are searching for. I think I have the ability to assume tasks that, perhaps, are not what I would have loved to do, and I change them into something I really am interested in doing. (Chile)

> I am happy, a hard worker, I work hard, hard, hard . . . I enjoy having new projects on my mind. I think everything is done with love. When you love something very much, you will obtain what you desire. [Success is] to be in love with my projects. (Chile)

Faith and Sense of Purpose

Finally, a characteristic discussed primarily by the women of the West Indies was a sense of purpose, a desire to make a positive difference in people's lives, and faith. Even within the West Indies, differences emerged. The women of St Vincent were more likely to cite their faith in God as well as desire to help others, while the women of Barbados emphasized their own strong sense of purpose and desire to make a difference.

Contrasting with the women from St Vincent, in Newfoundland the Catholic religion was cited by quite a few of the women to be counterproductive in terms of encouraging women to become successful in their careers (there was only denominational schooling in Newfoundland until 1997, and women who went through the Catholic school system were steered towards marriage and children; thus only three of the 22 women interviewed were Catholic). The one woman from Newfoundland who saw religion as an asset was with the Salvation Army and she felt that women and men were equal in the church.

The dominant themes of hard work, perseverance in the face of obstacles, achievement orientation, self-confidence and agency resounded throughout the interviews across the Americas. They were also echoed in the results of the written surveys. As we can see in Appendix D, the successful women scored higher than the comparison student samples on the personal characteristic of self-efficacy in every country surveyed. This difference was statistically significant in every sample except for Brazil. As highlighted in Chapter 3, high self-efficacy, or confidence in one's ability to perform successfully, has been shown to predict effective leadership, persistence in the face of obstacles, and successful strategies for goal attainment and decision-making.

Similarly, the successful women scored higher than the comparison students on need for achievement in every country we surveyed. The difference was statistically significant for each country except Chile. This characteristic, which indicates a willingness to work harder than required and a preference for challenging but achievable tasks, has been associated with high motivation to overcome barriers to success. As we have seen, this is of paramount importance to the successful women in our study.

The third personal characteristic in the survey, locus of control, was expected to demonstrate a decided tendency towards internal attributions. Contrary to expectations, only the women of Brazil and Canada reported a statistically significantly greater internal locus of control than the comparison student sample. Perhaps the higher than expected external tendency is consistent with the keen awareness, demonstrated by so many of the women we interviewed, of the powerful external forces they have had to face along their roads to success.

MANAGEMENT AND LEADERSHIP STYLES

Today it is common in the academic, business and popular presses to attempt to distinguish between management and leadership. However, both historically (see Bass, 1990, for the classic guide to management and leadership theory) and in the words of our successful women, these terms are often used interchangeably, and the descriptions are often overlapping. We do not distinguish between the two in this chapter.

When asked to describe their own management and leadership styles, the most frequent answer of the women in every country of our study, with the exception of the USA, was 'participative' (Table 5.2). The women used a number of terms for participative, including collaborative, consulta- tive, inclusive, consensus-building, collective and horizontal. Among the women of the USA, the most frequent style cited was a 'people skills' approach. In a sense, 'people skills' in management may be closely related to participation; both would be included on the people side of the typical theoretical dichotomy of people orientation (also named 'consideration', 'concern for people' and 'relationship behaviour') versus task orientation (also named 'initiating structure', 'concern for results' and 'task behav- iour'). Bass (1990) highlights this in his summary of the work of the Ohio State Leadership Studies and subsequent research of Blake and Mouton, Fiedler, Hersey and Blanchard, and others.

> I am proud of my management style. I am very inclusive and very much into con- sensus building. I have a great ability to recognize and engage the people that I need to do the things I want to do. (Canada)

> I would say very much, I believe in participation. I believe that people have to buy into anything, any project, any goal, anything that they have got to achieve. So I don't like to tell people 'just do this'. I want to talk it through with them, what is it that we are trying to achieve, and see if they can take ownership of it. Because at the end of the day, I think the reality of life is that you can't do people's jobs for them, so they have got to take ownership. (Barbados)

> To lead a team, [you need] vision, participation, balance between reason and sen- sibility, to know how to delegate tasks, to share knowledge and to inspire trust. (Brazil)

> When working with my team, I feel I am a peer. I think there are so many things I don't know, that I can't handle well enough, that I have to learn – many things that my team knows – I would be a blind person if I didn't see the potentialities on my team. The project is 'our project', not mine. (Chile)

> I am more inclusive than not. I lay the groundwork and then get people on side by letting them believe that it was their idea. People don't like the unknown.

Table 5.2   Management and leadership styles

Country	Themes
Argentina	Participative Consults Teamwork Obsessive, orderly Delegates, but maintains own responsibility
Brazil	Participative, collaborative Teamwork, brings right people together Consults, communicates Encourages others to develop, supportive, motivating Flexible Teaching
Canada	Participative, collaborative, collective Team work, brings right people together Consults, communicates Encourages others to develop, supportive, motivating
Newfoundland	Participative, collaborative, inclusive, consensus-building Authoritarian, gets things done, takes charge, autocratic, directive Teamwork, brings right people together Communicates, explains, listens Sets goals, clarifies roles, monitors results Delegates Requires prompt results, quality
USA	Action, takes initiative People skills, nurturing Vision, strategy Empowers, collaborates Integrity, values
Chile	Participative, horizontal Hears suggestions, then makes decisions and takes responsibility Teamwork Develops and supports subordinates, concerned that people are ok, have balance between work and personal life Consults, communicates Rigorous, defines and achieves goals, clarifies roles Delegates

Table 5.2   (continued)

Country	Themes
	Without a controversial or combative attitude ('gringa style') Authority based on credibility, builds truthful environment
Mexico	Democratic-participative
St Vincent	Delegates, provides a role model, coaches, listens to input from subordinates, and instils a sense of pride Importance of helping others Having impact on community or industry
Barbados	Listen to people, communicate Participative Develops, encourages people Autocratic Different styles in different circumstances Leads by example Does not court the limelight

> They will oppose change. Thus you need to make them feel it was their idea. (Canada)

Do we sense gender differences in leadership style?

> I am very participative . . . But in management style in general I think women are more participative. (Argentina)

Another Argentinean women echoed this sentiment:

> Women are more able to manage situations using peaceful coexistence. I believe that males are more authoritarian and more aggressive.

Two of the successful Newfoundland women commented that women tend to look at the larger picture, at the organization as a whole when they make recommendations and exercise leadership.

> Men tend to be more self-centred, while women tend to look at the organization as a whole. (Canada)

A related theme that was emphasized by the women of nearly every country was the importance of communicating and listening.

I try to foster a sound environment where ideas are welcome and communication is encouraged. I think we all have to learn from each other but I do exert my leadership skills when it is essential to do so. (Canada)

I should say more a talking style than an authoritarian one . . . not so much hierarchical and formal. I think [my management style] is by interaction. I like to define the objectives, and talk about them, define the goals, and talk about them . . . very dialectical. (Chile)

Clearly, a participative style was not viewed as abdication of responsibility. A resounding theme was that after thorough discussions with one's subordinates, the ultimate responsibility of the decision rested with the leader herself.

My office doors are always open. I always hear suggestions, but I make my own decisions and assume the consequences. (Chile)

I need as much information I can get, within reason, to make the better decision. If problems exist within a specific programme area, I will ask a person in this area for the pros and cons. I guess I'm consultative – you must have people involved – I try to get buy-in. (Canada)

I believe very much in consultation and trying to work together collectively to come to decisions. Recognizing that there are going to be times when you are going to have to go contrary to what people would like. But I like to engage people in the process of achieving a task and then providing them with the support to facilitate their achievement. (Canada)

I'm very collaborative until we're in trouble, then very dictatorial. I'll try to get consensus, work as a team. If it's the last day of the quarter, I'll say you do this you do that. I expect the best of the team. I pull individuals aside and tell them what they need to do. People know where they stand. But I'm very fair, very supportive. (USA)

In research applying contingency theory in leadership (discussed in Chapter 2), it has been found that women are similar to men in their leadership style, but higher in the supporting role, mainly owing to women's socialization to be more supporting and lower in status, hence needing to stress a supporting role in leading others. What has been evident in the interviews with successful women from most of the eight countries is their transformational style. Common themes as you saw in the quotes is the emphasis upon participation, the sharing of power and information, enhancing the self-worth of others and being able to energize others (see Rosener, 1990).

Overall, the tone of many of the women from the USA and Mexico was more discipline and results oriented than we heard in the comments of women of other countries (in Newfoundland some women also commented that, owing to the traditional authoritarian culture, they sometimes had to fall back on an authoritarian mode, especially with workers).

> I take the idea that I'm not their mother. I try to macromanage as well as I can . . . if they can do their jobs. I don't care when they do things. However, some may need to be micromanaged. To me it's 'Do you do the job? I don't care how you get there'. (USA)

> I make no bones about it: I am a demanding leader and manager. I set goals for both myself and my organization, which I think are stretched in nature. I like to be explicit and clear with people in terms of my expectations for them. And then I try to give people a lot of freedom about how they go about meeting the objectives as long as it is within the company's guiding business principles, the law and etc., so there are boundaries. I try very hard not to be directive, but I am not afraid to do so when other methods of trying to coach and help a subordinate to meet objectives are failing. I'm very results focused. (USA)

> I am a 'Management by walking around' person. I am a high accountability person. So I am usually good at setting goals for people, checking in with them and seeing where they are at and holding them accountable for getting there. My people say I am very approachable. My people say I am very easy to work with until they don't deliver and then they don't think I am very nice at all. (USA)

> Authoritarian! [laughter] I am an authoritarian leader. Of course we have meetings . . . about every two weeks, you see. This is to see how the employees are feeling; we have participation because we deffinitely depend upon them, don't we? And we also want that they are comfortable working with us . . . Still, I am the one in command [laughter] whether they like it or not [laughter]. And many times men . . . don't like a woman giving them orders, right? But that is my position and it is my work and my obligation. (Mexico)

Although Mexico and the USA are far apart as societies on Hofstede's power distance scale, in the USA business organizations were organized on a hierarchical basis with a more downward flow of communication than would be surmised by its placement on Hofstede's scale. Mexican managers traditionally were also fairly paternalistic and authoritarian.

GREAT LEADERS

We have seen how our interview participants described their own management and leadership styles. But to really understand leadership as they understand it, and perhaps aspire to, we asked them to name one or more individuals (living or dead, public figures or personal acquaintances) whom they considered to be great leaders. We probed their answers, to learn what specific qualities and characteristics they thought these individuals possessed that made them great leaders (Table 5.3).

As Table 5.3 highlights, this was one of the questions for which striking national differences emerged. While some women in all eight countries named world icons such as Gandhi, Nelson Mandela and Jesus, the respondents from Canada (except for Newfoundland) and South America were more likely to name local and national political figures or individuals with whom they have close personal ties.

The Brazilian women named several Brazilian politicians, but also their own teachers, professors, friends and mothers. The Canadian women named Canadian political leaders, but also their bosses, colleagues and teachers. Within Canada, the Newfoundland sub-sample emphasized Mandela and Gandhi, distantly followed by national Canadian and local political leaders. Chilean women cited Chilean political and religious leaders, with a strong emphasis on social and political activists. The women of Argentina and the USA had a difficult time coming up with examples of great leaders – as evidenced by long pauses, the comment that this was a difficult question and, in many cases, admitting there was no one they could think of. A special twist was that among the USA women, two finally answered 'me'. They considered themselves to be the best examples of great leaders!

Across the eight countries, the most popular answers were Nelson Mandela, Mahatma Gandhi, Jesus, Winston Churchill, Bill Clinton, Margaret Thatcher, Mother Theresa and John F. Kennedy. The only country in which Mandela and Gandhi were not mentioned was the USA. Jesus was listed in the USA, Chile and Mexico. Interestingly, the women in St Vincent stressed their faith in God as an important contributor in their success, but did not include Jesus as a great leader. Clinton was not mentioned in the USA and also not in Mexico. Margaret Thatcher was only mentioned in Canada (three times) and Mother Theresa only in Canada and the USA. John F. Kennedy was not mentioned in the USA, but in Canada and St Vincent.

Most of the traits attributed to great leaders clustered around three themes: (1) vision and wisdom, (2) ability to guide and motivate people to follow them, and (3) courage and perseverance in the face of personal hardship. Other themes included principles and integrity, simplicity and genuineness, effectiveness and impact, compassion, ability to resolve conflict, determination, courage, charisma, open-mindedness, passion and commitment.

It is interesting how these themes reflect the personal management/ leadership styles attributed by the women to themselves – or a Rorschach

Table 5.3   Great leaders

Country	Leaders names	Characteristics of great leaders
Argentina	Jesus Moses Pope John Paul Mahatma Gandhi President Alfonsin	Vision Ability to solve conflict between other people Modelled life of peace Rebuilt democracy
Brazil	Jesus Henrique Cardoso (ex-president of Brazil) Commandant Rolin (Brazilian leader) Ruth Cardoso Zulae Cobra (Brazilian deputy) Silvio Santos (entrepreneur) Norberto Bobbio (Italian teacher) Professor Neusa MBF Santos (SWW member) Bernardinho (athlete) My mother My friend Lincoln Gandhi Thatcher	Wisdom Power to lead, guide, motivate Simplicity, compassion Little education but high motivation High level of education, multi disciplinary and a woman Does not give up Values and moral foundations Courageous, bold, combative Determination, intelligence, social and political vision
Canada	Local businessman Thomas Jefferson Mahatma Gandhi Mother Theresa My boss My colleague My teacher, professor Pierre Trudeau Dalai Lama	Courage, charisma Leads by example, open- minded, quiet leader, smart decisions, well travelled, well spoken, embraces cultures No nonsense, straightforward, down-to-earth Not afraid to be himself Public agenda Good person, moral, inspiring
Newfoundland	Nelson Mandela Mahatma Gandhi Pierre Trudeau Winston Churchill Bill Clinton	Vision, principles, good heart Passion, commitment Longevity, keeps on going Respect, credibility Helping and teaching

Table 5.3   *(continued)*

Country	Leaders names	Characteristics of great leaders
	Margaret Thatcher Indira Gandhi John F Kennedy Adolf Hitler Mother Theresa Billy Graham William the Conqueror Adrienne Clarkson, our Governor General Robert Kennedy Queen Elizabeth Socrates Florence Nightingale Marie Curie Prime Minister Mulroony Premier Clyde Wells Bruton and Ahern (Irish leaders)	Motivate and move people Personal sacrifice Style Principled and popular Inspirational Not afraid of conflict Put aside partisanship Far-reaching thinking Administer well
USA	Mother Theresa Eleanor Roosevelt Mayor Daley (Chicago) Sargent Shriver Jesus Lao Tsu Hippocrates Abraham Lincoln Rudolph Guillani (Mayor of New York) Winston Churchill My CEO My mother Me	Worked for people, humanity Great impact, change Values, integrity and vision Achieve, effective
Chile	My parents Lagos (Chilean president) Chilean women Mario Zañartu, a priest Cardinal Silva Henriquez Soledad Alvear, Michelle Bachellet, Maria Errazuriz,	Integrity, consistency between words and actions Changed people, get people to follow for higher good, peace Brave, strong, vigorous Lived simply, worked without resources

Table 5.3   *(continued)*

Country	Leaders names	Characteristics of great leaders
	Esperanza Cueto (political leaders and candidates) My work colleague Jesus Pope John Paul Bill Clinton Indira Gandhi Mahatma Gandhi	Participated in historical social movement
Mexico	Mahatma Gandhi Jesus Local authorities (governors or mayors) Mother Theresa	Congruency in public and private life Commitment to cause Self-effacing, sacrificing Principled, ideal-based actions
St Vincent	Nelson Mandela Bill Clinton John F. Kennedy Pierre Trudeau Eugenia Charles Michael Manley Sun Myung Moon Mahatma Gandhi My father	Achievements Overcoming adverse environment, opposition, short time span Determined but humble Moderate, liberal thinker Uncompromising, determined Concern for family and God
Barbados	Martin Luther King Nelson Mandela Gandhi Errol Barrow (father of independence)	Endure great hardships, come out from prison: forgiving, work for good of country great accomplishments but also great flaws Articulate vision Persistence Non-violence

image of the styles to which they aspire. The women's concern with the well-being and involvement of others in the achievement of broad and visionary goals comes through in their descriptions of both themselves and the great leaders they admire.

SUMMING UP

In this chapter we have seen that the successful women from eight countries are internally motivated and feel that the contributions to their success have primarily come from within themselves, such as a high need for achievement, persistence, hard work, high self-confidence and a very disciplined approach to work tasks and learning. Some also stressed their skills in terms of working with others. These are in line with previous research findings, as well as with the results of our written survey (see Appendix D). The women's descriptions of their styles are also consistent with the research literature. In Chapter 2, transformational leadership was stressed as the type of leadership which is in evidence at present, especially in a time of the restructuring of organizations. Finally, there were some commonalities in terms of great leaders. It is interesting that the two leaders who were mentioned the highest number of times in the most countries could be associated with transformational leadership, Nelson Mandela and Mahatma Gandhi. It was also noted that neither of these two were mentioned by any of the successful women in the USA.

In this chapter we explored what the successful professional woman said about the role of personality and leadership/management style. In the following chapter the discussion is on what they said about professional and life experiences, especially barriers they faced and the social support that they were given to help ameliorate and deal with those barriers.

6. What the successful women said about professional and life experiences: barriers, social support and mentors

Terri R. Lituchy and Jo Ann Duffy

What do successful women say about their professional lives or careers? What do they say about their home or family lives? Which of their personal and professional experiences have contributed to their success, and what barriers have they had to overcome? Did they have social support, role models or mentors?

> I always had people who helped me . . . who gave me advice, who guided me. (Chile)

This Chilean woman echoes the responses of the successful women throughout the Americas to the interview question: 'Have there been others in your life that have contributed substantially to your success?' The successful women in the Americas were quick to recognize that other people had supported and influenced their lives.

> I was supported by a lot of people, the network we develop . . . my parents, who supported me. (Argentina)

> I believe that it has to be family, husband and friends, people that surround us, the 'circles' we set up . . . (USA)

> Starting in high school people helped me have confidence in myself, and instilled in me knowledge that you can achieve but while achieving you need to have a humble spirit. (USA)

In Chapter 5, we looked at personality, management and leadership styles, and views about great leaders. However, there are a number of demographic factors and life experiences that may have a positive or negative influence on women's success, such as ethnic background and religion,

Table 6.1   Demographic factors

Country	Themes
Argentina	Family upbringing
	Gender
Brazil	Family upbringing
	Environment
	Early experiences (childhood, education)
	Culture/race
	Religion
	Economic status
Canada	Family upbringing
	Environment (language, culture, religion, nationality, ethnicity)
	Gender
	Age
Mexico	Family upbringing
	Education
USA	Family upbringing
	Education
	Ethnicity
	Gender

family upbringing, birth order and number of siblings. We examine these factors for the successful women of the Americas in this chapter.

Beyond the individual woman and her personal life experiences, a number of external factors must be considered. If you look back at the concentric influences model (Figure 1.1) presented in Chapter 1, departmental, organizational and environmental factors could all affect a woman's success. In this chapter we examine a number of external factors such as education and opportunity, as well as factors that have served as barriers to women's educational and professional aspirations. More specifically, Figure 1.2 showed that support plays a major role in people's careers. Support can come from within the workgroup, department or organization, or from non-work sources such as family or friends, social or religious institutions, or professional associations. Support may be formal (such as formal mentoring programmes) or informal (such as social networks). In this chapter, we focus on support: external social support from family and friends as well as internal organizational support, specifically, mentoring.

Tables 6.1 and 6.2 summarize the key demographic and other external factors that affected the successful women. Sometimes these variables had a positive effect on their success; sometimes they were seen as barriers or challenges.

Table 6.2   External factors

Country	Themes
Argentina	Luck
	Opportunity
	Education
Brazil	Luck
	Opportunity
	Education
Canada	Luck
	Opportunity
	Education
Mexico	Education
USA	Luck
	Opportunity
	Education

DEMOGRAPHIC FACTORS

Demographic variables may also affect one's success. As stated in Chapter 2, family upbringing, including being the firstborn or oldest child is one such factor. Other demographic variables include ethnic and religious background, and economic status. What do the successful women of the Americas say about these variables?

In our study, 46 per cent of the successful women surveyed were either the only child or eldest child. Of the women with siblings, 60 per cent had both brothers and sisters; this is inconsistent with the study by White et al. (1997) (see Chapter 2) who said that successful women, who were not only children, were more likely to have only brothers.

The literature states that starting off as middle class also increased the chances of becoming successful. Some of the women in this study agreed with this, as the following quotes illustrate:

> Being born where I was born. I had a high social and economic status that allowed me to attend a private school and go to the university. (Chile)

> To be born in a family that has a good economic status . . . education options . . . (Chile)

While not a major theme, some women mentioned culture, language, ethnic background or religion as having an effect on there success, sometimes positive, sometimes negative:

Being an Anglophone [in Quebec] hindered my professional progress. (Canada)

. . . as a child . . . having an immigrant parent, my mother was highly inspirational . . . I had a fire in my belly to move out of my current status to something better . . . because of the ethnicity issue. (Canada)

It's . . . a patriarchal society. (USA)

Brazil is . . . still machismo . . . despite this; the women in the family (my grandmothers and my mother) were always part of a matriarchy. (Brazil)

Machismo was always present . . . (Mexico)

Religion was mentioned by all of the women from Brazil. Here are some examples of whether or not it impacted on their success:

Practising it helped me to establish relationship approaches and norms of conduct. (Brazil)

I come from a Christian family that taught me values, Christian ethics, which permeates my life and my professional life. (Brazil)

I am not practising, but everything I do is with faith and trust in God. Always staying calm and having deep faith in reaching my objectives. (Brazil)

Religion did not affect my career . . . the companies that I worked for never cared about my religion. (Brazil)

In our survey of successful women in the Americas, almost 60 per cent of our sample were married and had children. They were most likely to have bachelor's (39 per cent) or master's degrees (29 per cent). How did external factors, such as education and family support affect these women? Next we review the external factors that the successful women of the Americas said had a significant impact on their success.

EXTERNAL FACTORS

In priority order, I would say that opportunity is a fundamental factor related to success, along with knowledge of influential people in prominent positions . . . Education is also important. (Brazil)

This comment from a Brazilian woman summarizes the key external factors related to success by the women interviewed. The only external factor connected with success in all countries was education. Opportunity or luck was an important theme in all countries except Mexico.

First, social support, role models and mentors are discussed.

No (Wo)Man Is an Island: Where Does the Successful Woman Find Support?

For the successful women of the Americas, support came from informal and formal sources. The primary informal support group was the woman's birth family. This was a major theme in the interview data across all countries.

My parents always taught me there exists no difficulty that cannot be surpassed, since we have willpower and determination. (Brazil)

Family . . . extended family . . . was great role models; they left me feeling I could do anything I wanted. (USA)

In my family, my parents were the origin of my personality, and my grandparents. (Argentina)

Without the constant encouragement of my family, I do not think I would be as self-confident and ambitious. (Canada)

My family's support; my parents and four brothers. Attitude, if we ever have a clue you need something, you'll get it. (USA)

My parents didn't see gender roles. So they never discouraged me. (USA)

My parents are adventurous and instilled good values. (Canada)

Without the constant encouragement of my family I do not think I would be as self-confident and ambitious. (Canada)

My parents were an example, a life example. My father was very focused on his work, and my mother, my sweet mother . . . so I got a family education that allowed me to develop inside. (Chile)

My education, my family – they have been an integral part of my education. So I would say that the two of them rank first and foremost. I think that I came from a family where you had to have a university education, you had to have higher education and it was ideal if you could end up in an independent-type profession. (Caribbean)

My mother has been living with us [a family of three children, wife and husband] almost since I got married, and well, she really is the housewife. (Mexico)

My grandmother who is about 80 years old . . . she is a woman that always blazed the trail . . . as a woman that read, a woman that shared and taught us to read . . . [She gave us an] example that for women there are no limits but those that we imposed upon ourselves and we were educated like that at home too . . . that you impose limits upon yourself . . . (Mexico)

The woman's father rather than mother was most frequently mentioned as the primary source of support and mentoring in all countries except Brazil where there was no distinction between support from mother and father.

I was never made to feel I was too small, too young to give an opinion . . . I remember my father and I, we just used to sit sometimes in the gallery as you call it in Trinidad, chatting and what not. I remember one day he told me, we were talking about what it is you wanted to be and all that and I was a little worried . . . He said to me, 'don't worry but whatever you do remember that you can conquer the world. Regardless of what you choose to do, you can conquer the world'. That remained with me. (Caribbean)

My father to a great extend inspired me to enter public service. He was a civil servant and became executive director of the children's hospital here. It was the way he performed his job. I absorbed it. It was more behavioural, I guess. I was able to see the value of public service. (Canada)

My dad very consciously undertook to prepare me for my career. (He) taught me logic, statistics, research design and methodology. (He) built sense of confidence. (USA)

My father moved me. He died when I was 16, but I travelled to Buenos Aires with him since I was 8. I enjoyed talking with him about marketing. (Argentina)

My parents, but more particularly, my father. He was the model and the ideal to be realized by me. I didn't have difficulty in finding a mentor. It turned me into a better human being, it guided me in my life and career and he knew how to seek protection in the difficult moments. Without my father, I would not be the successful professional that I am now. (Brazil)

The thing with me is that I wanted to be as good a professional as my father who was an M.D. because I identified with his ideals but, at the same time this was a very ambitious standard, am I clear? I had very educated parents, I could not expect to do less than they. (Mexico)

Later in their lives these successful women found other sources of male support. The woman's husband emerges as a significant source of support in all countries studied.

My husband. I don't think – maybe I could have done it without him. Both his support emotionally and in the home too. Someone that wishes you well is just thrilled; I have been very lucky and had complete support from my husband. My husband was willing to take on much of the burden of raising the children while I went to school. Without that type of support, I definitely could have done it, but it would have been much more difficult. (USA)

My husband's wonderful. He helps me a lot – he's made it possible to be successful. Since I've been with him it's been a complete change. He picks up the slack. I'm far more successful than before I met my husband. (USA)

My husband. With certainty, his support was fundamental for my growth, because, we shared all our activities in relation to administration of the home and our children's education, which allowed me, in a certain way, also to be devoted to my career. (Brazil)

I think my ex-husband contributed a lot. He supported me very much when my kids were very little; I was very tempted to 'throw' all things away. He helped me so I was able to finish my studies. He allowed me to do that, because he took care of the children, gave me the freedom and support so I could go on with my studies. By that time we had a very intensive social life, and my children, and my studies, all of this was an effort for me and he helped me a lot. What is obvious is family is a great permanent helper for us. (Chile)

My second husband also helped me a lot. Particularly when the kids were little, I was afraid of leaving them to work outside the home, and he gave me his support. (Argentina)

A husband who was very supportive at all stages of my career, who did not feel either threatened by or constrained by the fact that I was moving ahead; who sometimes had to suffer from things like not having his meals ready when he may have wanted them or those kinds of domestic things that some men expect but he was very understanding in that area. (Caribbean)

Support from children was also a theme in the responses from the Argentine women.

My children. I have an excellent dialogue with them, and feel their support.

Few women listed teachers as sources of support. However, friends and colleagues were also frequently found to be supportive.

I had a friend to whom I owe a great deal. (Argentina)

My colleagues, some at first had been my own students, and then became researchers, five of them in particular, who contributed a lot in helping us continue in our careers. (Argentina)

A great friend that I had supported me and it motivated me to look for success and to win my place in the job market. This friend also works in the same profession as I do, and is managing a computer science company. (Brazil)

I have a friends and important colleagues, generous people, valuable, that are my every day's adrenaline. I've been fine, that is why I feel myself to be successful. (Chile)

Yes, I have had mentors different ones along the way. Usually I would find someone that I respected, whom I felt deserved to be where are and I would talk to them. There was one woman where I worked in Toronto that influenced me. I used to work a lot of overtime and when I was thinking of returning home I felt I couldn't leave because who could possible replace me. She told me to think of the organization as a pool of water. When we take you out, as important as you are, the pool will close. Someone else will do your work. Make the best decision for yourself. She taught me balance. That analogy had a great impact and I pass it on. (Canada)

Mentoring is described as a set of roles and activities such as coaching, teaching, supporting and sponsoring an individual in whom the mentor recognizes their potential (Kram, 1983; 1985; White, 1995; 1997). Mentoring can be psychosocial and/or career related.

As discussed in Chapter 2, career-related mentoring includes coaching, exposure, and challenging assignments (Kram, 1985; O'Neill, 2002; Ragins, 1999). Psychosocial mentoring functions include counselling, acceptance, confirmation, and friendship.

The survey data indicate that the successful American women did not have particularly high mean scores on either the psychological mentoring or career mentoring scales (3.6 and 3.5 out of 5.0 respectively). They were only mildly in agreement that their mentors or role models had been encouraging or helpful in providing assignments that would advance their careers. On the psychological support scale the means ranged from 3.4 to 3.9, with the West Indies women having a significantly lower mean score and the USA were significantly lower (3.4) than Mexico (3.8). The mean scores for all the countries were not significantly different from each other. (See Appendix D.)

In our interviews, the term 'mentor' was not defined. This may explain why the women interviewed did not really perceive that they had received mentoring.

I don't have a mentor. It is very difficult finding one and it did not affect my career. (Brazil)

There was, however, some evidence of support from someone at work. Many of them reported that their bosses had supported them.

He took a real shine to me. He was very impressed with the amount of knowledge that I had and so I was given the opportunity to work on really interesting projects . . . He was always interested in the data and what we were finding and how the projects were moving along. He is managing the exploration budget so the future direction of the company was based on what we were doing – huge and hands-on . . . He was instrumental to make sure I got interesting projects to work on. (Canada)

I really believe in the organization – Society of Women Engineers. That's where my mentoring support network came from. Outside of that, I can only point to one time in my career that I had a mentor – An older man, boss. I was a fairly new engineering major; he took me under his wing. He had quite a bit of experience – a good 15 years of engineering management and really saw what leadership was, where it was important. Lots of good lessons like that. (USA)

[What contributed to my success was education] . . . together with my boss who has always supported me so I can continue growing within his companies. (Mexico)

There was a senior lawyer in the firm that first hired me. He was instrumental in me getting hired. We became very good friends and now that he is involved with a corporation and I have my own practice, he sends business my way. I still consult with him when I have doubts or questions I need to discuss. (Canada)

An analysis of the survey data on formal mentoring reveals that the majority (54 per cent) of the women said that the person who was most influential in their career was not part of a formal programme. Two-thirds of the women reported that the influential person tended to be in the same organization; 58 per cent said the person was a man. Seventy-eight per cent had a mentor who was older than they were, while 18 per cent had a mentor their own age. Over one-third of the women reported having two mentors during their career, 26 per cent had three mentors and 17 per cent had one mentor during their career. The number of mentors did not differ significantly across the countries studied.

My mentors have been about 50:50 men and women. Women I have found to be more open, they talk more. Men put up a little bit of a front. (Canada)

I had the opportunity to know two mentors in my professional life that guided me and they opened some opportunities in the workplace. [One of them] guided me and it helped me to tread my professional career. (Brazil)

I always wanted to have a mentor, because it facilitates the growth of one's professional career a lot, but unhappily, the men are macho and they confuse the mentoring with sexual favours – that ends up complicating the professional relationship. (Brazil)

The analysis of the interview data failed to show a pattern of responses supporting formal mentoring. However, it should be noted that very few organizations offer formal mentoring programmes to develop their talent pool. This is consistent with Ragins and Cotton (1991) who found that women perceived the presence of more barriers than men in accessing mentors. Fox and Schuhmann (2001) also indicated that women see fewer opportunities than men to find same-sex role models.

Most of my bosses were close to my age or a few years older. Mentoring – I've never thought of them as mentoring me. But I always got along well with them. (USA)

No one played a mentoring role for me – I found my own people who gave me directions for individual goals. I never had any real mentor who made a significant impact on my life. (USA)

I had to have access to people that I trusted that really knew what to do. And I had gathered up people like that in my life. I intended to do that. I've never really had one mentor. I had people who I admired in this area, some of them I admired in this area, some of them I talk to, some of them I don't – I just observe what they do. (Canada)

No, No, and I'll tell you most of the women I know would say the same thing, that they haven't had a mentor. I've had people who at different times have helped me but I would say part of that is exploiting of an opportunity. I would see someone who could be in a position to help me and would be willing to go and say I need your help with this. I would network with a lot of senior professional women and a group of us were together and went out to dinner and had a pretty heated discussion about this. How many of you actually had a mentor? And it was stunning that all of us said the same thing. We are being asked to mentor now and we are still waiting for someone to mentor us. We benefited from direct intervention from individuals, which I personally think of as very different from mentoring. (USA)

I had difficulty in finding one. It didn't affect my career, because from very early on, I had to grow and to look for my own ideals. (Brazil)

I didn't have a mentor at the beginning of my career [Would you like to have one?] Yes, of course, I think it should be fine to have someone conducting me and giving me advice, and trying to show me the road instead facing it alone. (Chile)

I think it could be . . . is always easier if you have a mentor that contributes by opening up opportunities, but I don't think this (the lack of mentor) was critical. Perhaps in professional life, but as that part was in the United States . . . maybe in Chile it would be different. (Chile)

Other research has stated that informal mentoring works better than formal, organizational-sponsored mentoring programmes; that women prefer informal mentors; and that mentors can come from all levels of the organization as well as outside the organization (Eby, 1997; Lankau and Scandura, 2002), as our study also supports.

Burke et al. (1993) suggest that women develop mentoring relationships differently than men – that women are more relational and may see their mentoring relations more akin to friendships. This is consistent with the results of our survey which showed women were more likely to receive psychosocial mentoring than career-related mentoring, as stated above. One US woman described the difference between mentors and sponsors and attributed success only to the latter.

> I think it is more important that a mentor is actually a sponsor.

> The difference in my mind is a mentor is somebody who can be a role model, and show you the ropes so to speak, how things work around here. But they aren't necessarily in a position to promote your career and they don't necessarily put themselves on the line for you. Whereas a sponsor is someone who is willing to put their own reputation on the line and recommend you for positions that further your development and in most cases also further your positions in the hierarchy.

> . . . I think mentoring is a good thing and I am not against it in any way, but if a mentor isn't in a position to really do the other piece, which is to put their personal and professional reputation on the line, it's not nearly as powerful – Particularly in creating key opportunities for development and advancement. (USA)

These successful women acknowledge having received help, but ultimately attribute success to their own efforts. This may be a result of the women's high sense of self-efficacy and internal locus of control.

> There were no mentors as such. I did what I wanted to do because of myself. (Canada)

> I could name hundreds of people in hundreds of ways. But it comes down to me – the work I've put in and my vision couldn't have come from anyone else. (USA)

> No, I got a little help, but I feel that perhaps I didn't need a mentor. (Chile)

Consistent with theoretical perspectives, such a social role theory and gender studies, male mentors often reported providing more career-related mentoring, whereas female mentors reported providing more psychosocial mentoring to their protégés, except in the case where the female was the mentor and the male the protégé (Allen and Eby, 2004).

Education

'Well, I think education basically, right?' said one Mexican women when asked about success. Education was found to be important to success across countries. For example, based on the interviews, in Argentina it was mentioned by four out of ten women, and in Brazil six out of 17. In Canada education was mentioned by nine out of 31 women and in the USA by seven out of 15.

Sometimes formal education was specified:

My education, my formal education, the university . . . (Argentina)

An expectation that now that we're Americans we'll get an education. (USA)

Education had nothing to do with promotion, but it got my foot in the door. (Chile)

Several of the Argentinean and Chilean women mentioned studying abroad, 'I received an excellent education, at private schools and abroad'. Other times, the women mentioned informal or on-the-job education:

Education options, to be able to finish your studies, to travel, and to learn from interesting people and on the job . . . (Chile)

However, when I refer to education I don't necessarily mean school. Although my education was important, the lessons learned from others and on my own were far more influential. (Canada)

Constant investment in education to stay updated in my profession. (Canada)

Luck

Not only was education important to these women but also luck. One-third of all the Canadian women mentioned opportunity, luck or being in the right place at the right time. Four out of 10 women from Argentina, four out of ten from Brazil and five out of 15 from the USA also mentioned luck. Here are a few examples of what the successful women said:

Education is vital . . . but also luck. (Argentina)

Beyond education, luck. (Chile)

Sheer blind luck. Had a counsellor, upon seeing math scores, said I should be an engineer, not a secretary . . . I started to take those classes. (USA)

Luck . . . being in the right place at the right time (knowledge and skills are prerequisites but there must also be opportunity there to work on challenging projects) (USA)

I was very lucky. I was really, really lucky. (Canada)

But things worked, I was a lucky person and I feel myself successful. (Chile)

Luck. It's very important. Anybody who denies it is lying. (Canada)

This is not inconsistent with our survey results that showed women in all countries had a higher internal locus of control (see Chapter 5). Only one woman from Canada actually mentioned that she did not believe in luck. 'I don't believe in chance. I believe in hard work, opportunity, the ability to take risks and timing, people often confuse those factors with luck.' As demonstrated by the preceding quote, many women perceived that the external factor behind their success was not luck but, rather, opportunity.

Opportunity

In priority order, I would say that the opportunity is a fundamental factor the conquest of the success . . . (Brazil)

I look to take advantage of opportunities that are appearing . . . Opportunities are very important . . . (Brazil)

Circumstance equals coincidence. Meeting the right persons. Seeing an opportunity that happens to be there at the time. All sorts of coincidences – having read something and suddenly there's an opportunity to learn more about it by moving in that direction. It really is luck. (Canada)

Exploiting of an opportunity I would see someone who could be in a position to help me and would be willing to go and say I need your help with this. (USA)

Being in the right place at the right time. (West Indies)

The literature (see Chapter 2) and the results of our large-scale survey (see Appendix D) show that an internal locus of control is related to success. Luck emerged as a theme in most countries based on the women we interviewed, this is inconsistent with our survey results and the literature. However, the successful women interviewed were also very internal. As shown above many of the women believed they were uniquely able to find and seize opportunities – even when there were barriers, they were able to make lemonade out of lemons.

Barriers

External factors were viewed not only as positive influences on success but also as negative influences. Some external factors act as barriers to women's success and satisfaction in the beginning of their career, while other barriers are associated with the present – during a time when they are in positions of power and near the top of their professions. Barriers differed also in terms of specificity and subtlety: some are obvious and irrefutable, others vague and difficult to pin down.

Early career
In the beginning, barriers appeared in the women's higher education experience when professors underestimated their potential, and in their first jobs when bosses' prejudices influenced the types of job and salaries they received.

> There were definite gender barriers in school . . . in junior college there was surprisingly a specific teacher who was difficult – known to be a big chauvinist. He used to give women in calculus classes difficulty about how they were dressed. The point for me in his class was to be as competitive as possible. A true triumph for me was he had to give me an A – he hated that, but of course I had to really work to get an A. At graduation he said, 'Where are you going?' I said I'm going to be an engineer. He said [she wouldn't make it.] He was the guiding reason for me to get through some tough times at UIC – the idea of shoving my diploma in his face. (USA)

Some women found that age and gender were barriers.

> I also have faced some challenges because of my age. People have a hard time taking you seriously when you're significantly younger than they are. (Canada)

> When I first graduated men used to always think the female lawyers were secretaries. When we would tell them we were lawyers they'd turn around a walk the other way. Men are still surprised when I tell them I'm a partner and have been practising for 12 years. (Canada)

> It took longer to come to peoples' attention because of my gender. For the longest time I was the only woman in this sector (agriculture). And you know the old saying, as a woman you have to work twice as hard as a man to be noticed, but fortunately that's not hard . . . The culture has shifted to include more women. There was a levelling of the playing field. If you were good enough you didn't have to wait for the last man to be appointed to advance. (Canada)

> I was welcomed by the [men], but at the same time you feel somewhat alienated, excluded from certain other conversations the guys felt I should be kept out. (USA).

> Men in the organization would complain if I were put on assignment with them. I put up with a lot of grief that I probably shouldn't have. I worked hard to be as good as or better than anyone else . . . they could get me at a low salary! . . . I later got a huge inequity raise. (USA)

I only remember a 'company boss' that harmed me in the position and way for being a woman and who told me clearly that was my wages and functional positions were smaller than my friend's for that reason. (Brazil)

Present barriers

At the present time, although they are established in their professions, barriers are still evident.

I didn't perceive any barriers starting out . . . Feeling this more now than when I started. [It's] abstract. I'm not taken as seriously. I can't say 'This situation, this is what happened'. (USA)

Today it's harder to get past barriers than then. Then blatant – pornography on walls, off-colour jokes. But when people say, 'we're all for diversity', but don't deal with the fact that our organizations are not very diverse, we don't have women rising in management. (Canada)

Many times, actually I say you know probably this man doesn't like dealing with women. It might hit me afterwards . . . It only registers in little things that in the sense that if I go with two of my managers to a meeting, males, you will find that they . . . will be looking at [the other males] when they are making points. (West Indies)

Sometimes . . . I do believe there is an old boys' network. It's there. I feel I have to work my way either through it or around it. It happens and pops up. I feel I have to be more aggressive. (USA)

Sometime working as a public manager . . . a man would invite you to talk about a job and tell you things like 'you are so nice, very pretty' . . . and this becomes uncomfortable . . . or in other sense we make these disadvantageous situations for women, because we continue in this cultural situation . . . these things are sometimes expectations that we have to discard about ourselves so we don't repeat the patterns that culture itself imposes upon us. (Mexico)

Now working with diversity elements in business, the support is now here. But I'm not sure the message gets down to lower-level managers. Biggest obstacle women face today: the men they are dealing with do not see themselves as discriminating, but they behave in ways that discriminate against women and minorities. They don't get it. (USA)

Some women did not identify specific barriers. This tendency is often related to the fact that the women perceive the present barriers to be subtle and nebulous and therefore difficult to challenge.

It doesn't matter how much it can seem a difficult challenge, because while I make every effort to face it, the more interesting it becomes. I have to say that is a characteristic in my sign, Taurus. (Brazil)

I think the obstacles today are a bit harder. As you rise in the organization, it's harder to say [it's due to gender, because there are fewer positions at that level]. It feels like you have to fight twice as hard to get what you want . . . (Canada)

Most businesses are run by men, and although they use women as their visible face, the leadership belongs to them. (Argentina)

It is important to note that many women were able to turn barriers into opportunities as illustrated in the following remarks:

In most political parties [in Mexico], specifically in . . . the one that I represent, we, women were second-in-command, we would do all [the groundwork] and then men would take the credit . . . But just as that was a barrier (not for me, but I have seen it) this has created a situation for helping . . . a space whereby we, the women' have held each other's hand and created space for ourselves, and this has contributed to our success. (Mexico)

Machismo was always present; I think that has let us, women, advance very little, and precisely whatever small achievements we have made are because we have snatched it away, or, insisted upon, with more maturity. (Mexico)

I believe my gender perhaps has made some things difficult, when the environment is mainly masculine, but that is just at the beginning, because you later forget that this is a factor and then we are simply working on the task and what becomes important there is the competitiveness you have to offer. (Mexico)

Positive Effects of Being a Woman

In the preceding sections it became obvious that being a woman often translates into a barrier for advancement. However, it is important to note that many women recognized gender as a positive factor in their success.

Besides, I think many times it is not true that [being a woman] gives you problems; sometimes it gives you great advantages. For example, in my experience as a consultant for top managers, I have been with state secretaries, company CEOs, top-level managers – and the interesting thing is that it is possible to create learning environments with more openness than if I were a man . . . I am perceived more . . . perhaps like a Jewish mother, with great respect, but . . . not so much as a rival. (Mexico)

Others like this successful woman view gender as both a barrier and an aid in career advancement.

I think [being a woman] has done both [contribute positively and negatively to my success]. In some ways it has kept me back and in some ways it has propelled me. Sometimes when you apply for something, they are looking for a black woman, to say they have employed a black woman . . . In other ways when you are in certain jobs and you are female, as well as black, it can hold you back because we still live in Barbados and there is still a certain amount of colour prejudice and there is always the old boys' network that look out for each other, so if you are a woman, you tend not to be included. They are in your company and they crack all kinds of dirty jokes to make you feel uncomfortable; you can' do anything about it because they are the people in charge, so you don't object. The old boys' network is very strong, they fend for each other. (West Indies)

SUMMARY AND CONCLUSION

The demographic factors that the successful women from every country in our study mentioned as affecting their success were gender, family upbringing and education – sometimes a barrier, at other times, an opportunity. Other factors differed depending on country – religion, ethnicity, culture or race, and language.

Social support was important for all the women in our study. This is consistent with the literature presented in Chapter 2. Where the support came from – parents, teachers, spouse, friends, children, co-workers – differed slightly depending on which country the women were from. Many women said that they had support or informal mentors or role models at work, but not necessarily a formal mentor that provided career-related mentoring. In Canada and the USA, mentoring that the women received was often not part of a formal programme; this differed from the three Spanish-speaking countries (Mexico, Argentina and Chile) where mentoring was part of a formal programme.

While women mentioned other external factors such as education, luck or opportunity, most of the women said that they found their own opportunities, that they were responsible for their success. When surveyed on whether they were satisfied with their lives and their jobs, all the women (n = 1110) were extremely satisfied; there were no differences between countries. This is what makes these women successful – no matter what barriers or limitations they had to overcome, they were overwhelmingly happy with both their work and home lives.

7. Successful women in the polar winds of Canada

Terri R. Lituchy, Ann Gregory, Joan Dewling and Robert Oppenheimer

Canada, the country of 'polar winds', is the northernmost country in our study. The ten provinces and three territories span the northern portion of North America from ocean to ocean to ocean (the Atlantic, Arctic and Pacific). Although Canada is the second largest country in the world, 90 per cent of its 32.5 million people live within 100 miles of the US border. Here are some voices of successful Canadian women.

> I do think I'm successful. I do something I love every day. Not everyone enjoys that luxury. I have earned the respect of my peers and I'm happy with my professional growth. Also, I am proud of what I've accomplished though it's only the beginning of a long journey.

> Somehow in business I land on my feet. I don't know how or why but I do – at the end of the day, I might understand why. It is interesting with a whole background in arts I made it.

> Yes, I have a long marriage, I have happy children, successful children, I earn a good living, I travel and am well educated. I am still learning, when I have decisions to make, I make them.

As shown in these quotes, the Canadian women thought they were successful in their careers as well as their lives. Before we go into the details of the study conducted in Canada, the following provides a brief description of Canada, its culture and its women.

CANADA: LANGUAGE, ETHNICITY, REGIONALISM AND GENDER

Canada has been described as a mosaic (Bowman, 2000), encompassing various ethnic groups and diverse regions with differing historical experiences; this is in contrast to the idea of the 'melting pot' of American

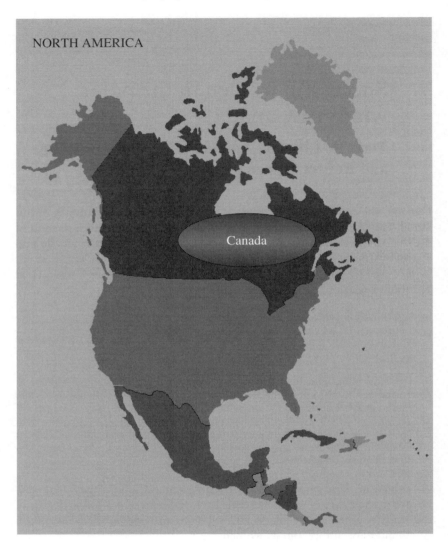

Figure 7.1   Location of Canada

ideology. Regional diversity is also illustrated by drastic differences in average earnings and unemployment rates of the population. The
overall earnings for Canada as a whole were C$31 757 in 2001, with
regional differences ranging from a high of C$35 185 in Ontario, C$29 385
in Quebec to a low of C$24 165 in Newfoundland and Labrador (the
above figures are taken from www40.statscan.ca/01/cst01/labor 50b.htm).

Unemployment rates also show vast regional differences. In May 2005 the average unemployment rate for Canada as a whole was 6.8 per cent. The lowest was in Alberta (4.6 per cent); Ontario had 6.9 per cent, and Quebec 8.5 per cent. However, Newfoundland and Labrador had a high of 15.2 per cent, which has been average to low over the past several decades (see www40.statscan.ca/01/cst01/labor 07a.htm).

One of the most important books describing Canadian society, influencing research for years afterward, was *The Vertical Mosaic* by John Porter (1965). In this book, Porter added to the concept of mosaic by stressing the hierarchical relationship between Canada's many cultural groups; it was clear to Porter that Canadians of British origin 'had remained within the elite structure of the society . . . and that in some institutional settings the French have been admitted as a co-charter group [with the British] whereas in others they have not' (Porter, 1965, pp. xii–xiii). A lot of change has occurred in the relations between ethnic groups in Canada and between these groups and the institutions of society since *The Vertical Mosaic* was published. The non-dominant groups in society changed in terms of their educational achievement and socio-economic circumstances, as did their 'self-conceptions, aspirations, and expectations' (Breton, 1998, p. 60).

Ethnicity in Canada

Ethnically, Canada has been made up of British and French. However, there have been changes over the years, lessening the dominance of the English and French. For example, the percentage of the population that considers themselves British decreased from 33.6 per cent in 1986 to 28.1 per cent in 1991, while non-British or French increased from 24.9 per cent to 30.9 per cent during that time (Kalbach and Kalbach, 1999).

In 2001, the census contained a new category, 'Canadian', thus making it very difficult to be precise in terms of ethnicity; 39 per cent identified with that category. Canadians of Asian origin make up 10 per cent of Canada's total population (Asia Pacific Foundation, 2003). The proportion of the foreign-born in the Canadian population has also increased; within ten years (1991–2001), the percentage rose from 16.1 per cent to 18.4 per cent (Statistics Canada, 2005). Finally, First Nations peoples (Aboriginals, North American Indian, Metis and Inuit), make up 6 per cent of the Canadian population.

Regionalism

Canada is a nation of distinct regional and provincial cultures, and various researchers have described these differences (Berry, 1999; Hui et al., 1997;

Li, 1999; Ueltschy et al., 2004). The provinces span from Newfoundland and Labrador in the east to British Columbia in the West. Ontario accounts for 30 per cent of Canada's population, and is considered the economic centre of Canada; the political capital of Canada is also in Ontario (Ottawa). Going west from Ontario are the agricultural prairie provinces of Manitoba and Saskatchewan; continuing west is the oil-rich province of Alberta and the forestry and mineral-rich west coast province of British Columbia.

Going east from Ontario, there is Quebec, the maritime provinces of Nova Scotia, New Brunswick and Prince Edward Island. Furthest east is Newfoundland and Labrador. The remaining landmass of the country is composed of the geographically large, but sparsely populated three northern territories (Yukon Territory, the Northwest Territory and Nunavut). The three northern territories are considered to be culturally unique (Delaney et al., 2001). Although our successful women study was a national survey, the women interviewed are from Ontario, Quebec and Newfoundland (none lived in Labrador). These provinces will be described in more detail below.

Quebec accounts for one-quarter of Canada's population. French is the mother tongue of more than 80 per cent of Quebecois. As noted above, there have been changes in the relationship between the French and English, especially in the province of Quebec. In the past, the English of Quebec had both political and economic power, and even imposed their language on the much more numerous French Canadians (Denis, 1999). The Quebecois not only considered themselves culturally different from Canada, but felt that their language and culture were threatened by English Canada. This led to in what was termed the 'Quiet Revolution' during the last part of the twentieth century, which resulted in an increase in power of the Quebecois in terms of the economy, society and politics (Breton, 1998). One outcome was the institution of provincial laws specifying French as the official language of Quebec, requiring all external signs to be only in French and the children of those who had not been educated in English to go to French schools.

Newfoundland and Labrador joined Canada in 1949 after two referenda were held, results of which are still questioned today, and occasionally calls for separation are still heard (see Leuprecht and McCreery, 2002). Public sentiment can be gauged by the waves of 'Republic of Newfoundland' t-shirts being worn there and the flying of the old Republic of Newfoundland flag! The island enjoyed 80 years of independence (until 1933 when it went bankrupt and England took over receivership). This experience with independence has fuelled the occasional demands for separation.

The cultures of Quebec and Newfoundland can be considered to be the most distinctive in Canada. Until the last half-century, the island of Newfoundland was isolated from both without and within, owing to the limited network of roads. Newfoundlanders have all the hallmarks of comprising an ethnic group, including common ancestry, mainly from southwest England and Ireland. One cannot become a Newfoundlander through residence; you are born into the group, whether or not you reside in the province. The characteristics of the island, which still have an impact today to a greater or lesser extent (influencing the composition and attitudes of the successful women) are the following: the psychological impact of recent experiences of colonial rule; the economic and social dichotomy between St John's and the rest of the island; the intensity of the Protestant–Catholic divide in all parts of life until very recently; a rather rigid social stratification system; and the strict separation of roles for women, with the Catholic Church notably vocal in their support of the traditional role for women; and the exclusiveness of the culture (see Dewling, 2003; Forestell, 1995; McCann, 1988; Murray, 1979; Rowe, 1980). A final distinction is the absence of racial differences traditionally in Newfoundland; hence the society differentiated more strongly in subdivisions of class, religious affiliation and gender within the Newfoundland group (McCann, 1988).

The capital of Canada, Ottawa, is located in Ontario is the largest province in Canada. Toronto, also located in Ontario is the most populated city and is the financial and industrial centre of Canada. According to the World Economic Forum, Canada is in the top ten countries in terms of narrowing the gender gap (World Economic Forum, 2005).

Language

Canada has two official languages, English, which is the first language of 59.3 per cent of the population and French, which is the first language of 23.2 per cent, most of whom live in the province of Quebec. The balance, 17.5 per cent is indicative of the mosaic nature of Canada (CIA, 2005a).

Culture

Hofstede's study of culture was conducted at the national level. According to Hofstede (1984), Canada is low on collectivism. That is, Canada is highly individualistic, ranking the fourth highest among the nations he studied. In Hofstede's research, Canada is low on power distance, scoring slightly lower on power distance than the USA. Again, Hofstede (1984) found a relatively low uncertainty avoidance score for Canada. Canada is also medium on masculinity.

Gender

Since the mid-1960s, women's participation in the labour force has grown rapidly, as has their participation in post-secondary education. Those years saw government action in terms of easing some of the discriminatory treatment of women in the workforce, for example gradual imposition of at least some job equity, as was discussed in Chapter 2.

Women in Canada make up 46.2 per cent of the labour force (Little, 2002) and just below 50 per cent of the 15 to 64 age group of the population (CIA, 2005a). However, women comprise only 32 per cent of the managerial roles, 12 per cent of senior management and 7.5 per cent of directorships. Half of Canada's companies do not have any women in their senior ranks, even though 57 per cent of those holding graduate degrees are women. In academic institutions, women comprise less than 30 per cent of full-time faculty members, and their wages are only 90 per cent of their counterparts (CFHSS-FCSH, 2002). On a more positive note for women, they are starting businesses at a rate three to four times more than men (Snyder et al., 1999).

The present study assesses characteristics of successful Canadian women. Information was obtained by using interviews and surveys.

A STUDY OF SUCCESSFUL CANADIAN WOMEN

Researchers in Ontario, Quebec, and Newfoundland conducted surveys and interviews of women who were defined as those who were successful in management, government, their own business, or their profession.

Survey

The survey was pre-tested in a Canadian context by administering it to MBA students at Concordia University in Montreal, Quebec.

Of the 199 women who responded to the survey, 120 were recruited nationally and 79 are from Newfoundland. The position or professional breakdown of these women is as follows:

- executives (53 per cent) and professionals (13 per cent)
- university professors (9.5 per cent)
- entrepreneurs/small business owners (16 per cent)
- public officials (9 per cent)

Women included in our study were identified in different ways. Full professors were identified through university calendars and directories. The contact information for women managers, entrepreneurs and small business owners was obtained from the Canadian Association of Professional and Entrepreneurial Women. Surveys were mailed or e-mailed to the successful women and returned to the researchers by mail, fax or e-mail.

We sent questionnaires to 143 successful women in Newfoundland. The response rate was 55 per cent, and was roughly proportionate to the division of professions in the population. Because of the way data was collected in our study, we have information on Newfoundland separate from the rest of Canada. For those interested in the Newfoundland results, see the note at end of the chapter.[1]

The survey was also administered to undergraduate students at Memorial University of Newfoundland and Concordia University in Montreal to use as a comparison to our successful women. As will be seen below, there were significant differences between the undergraduates and the successful women.

As presented in Chapters 5–7 the characteristics we identified as most likely to vary from country to country and which also were likely to contribute to high levels of professional success, included:

- national/cultural: collectivism/individualism, power distance, and uncertainty avoidance
- personal: self-efficacy, locus of control, and need for achievement
- social-experiential: mentoring.

Demographic questions addressed income, ethnicity, marital status, age, birth order, educational level and parents' educational level.

Data collection

The 199 successful women ranged in age from 23 to 66, with a mean age of 47 years old. Most of the successful women were in executive positions (52.8 per cent) or were entrepreneurs (16.1 per cent) or had professional careers such as doctors, lawyers or accountants (12.6 per cent). In the Newfoundland portion of the survey the largest number was in governmental positions, understandable owing to the prominence of government in terms of overall employment in this province. The highest number of full professors was also based in Newfoundland, again, understandable owing to the size of the university in this small city. Half the women were the oldest of their siblings (49.7 per cent), had university degrees (nearly 90 per cent) and were married (69.7 per cent).

Successful women were compared with undergraduates (93 male and female students with no work experience) and the MBA students (with work experience). The comparative groups included 26 MBA students, ranging in age from 23 to 39, with a mean age of 30 years old, and 93 under-graduates, ranging in age from 18 to 39, with a mean age of 25 years old from Concordia University and Memorial University of Newfoundland. These students, by definition, would not yet be as successful as those that have obtained a certain level of success in their profession.

Results of the survey
Our research is consistent with Hofstede; the successful Canadian women surveyed were moderately high on individualism (mean = 3.29), fairly low on uncertainty avoidance (mean = 3.64) and very low on power distance (mean = 1.94).

In analysing the results of the surveys it was determined that the successful women had a significantly greater self-efficacy (mean = 4.23), internal locus of control (mean = 2.04), need for achievement (score = 12.75) and were more satisfied (mean = 6.23) than the undergraduates (see Appendix D). The successful women also had significantly greater self-efficacy and satisfaction than the MBAs (both men and women) and a significantly greater internal locus of control than the male MBAs.

Mentoring was important to the successful women. They had a high score on psychosocial mentoring (mean = 3.57) and career-related mentoring (mean = 3.37) than both the female and male MBAs, regardless of the extent of the work experience the MBAs had. Forty-five per cent of the successful women reported that they were part of a formal mentoring programme. A majority of those who had mentors had male mentors (60.4 per cent); that is understandable owing to the low percentage of women in positions in which the occupants could serve as mentors. The mentors were significantly older than the mentees (82.4 per cent).

The average number of mentors for the successful Canadian women was 2.59, ranging from a low of none to a high of ten mentors. Although a majority of the mentors were in the same organization as the successful woman (53.9 per cent), there were many mentors in a different organization (46.1 per cent). The trend for women to look for mentors outside the organization was noted in Chapter 2. A small majority of successful women are themselves mentors (51.5 per cent), and are about equally likely to mentor in the same organization where they work, (45.4 per cent), as compared to outside their organization (47.4 per cent); a small percentage have mentees both inside and outside their organization (7.2 per cent). Again, this is in line with studies in the literature concerning the usage of mentors and networks outside the woman's organization. They also mentor those who are younger than they are (52.6 per cent) rather than those who are older (21.6 per cent).

Interviews

Participants and research protocol

Thirty-one successful women were interviewed: 22 were from Newfoundland (71 per cent) and nine were from Ontario and Quebec (29 per cent). The interviews consisted of open-ended questions designed to provide more in-depth information than could be interpreted from the questionnaire items. They helped to uncover other perceived important characteristics of success, and also ascertain what were the barriers the women faced in achieving success. We first look at demographic variables that were considered important in influencing the success of these women, followed by internal and external aspects related to success. To what extent the successful Canadian women interviewed in this study face the barriers discussed in Chapter 2 is also explored.

Demography: gender and ethnicity/regional background

Gender   The successful Canadian women mentioned that gender was neutral to their success. However, they also said gender played either a positive (nine of the 31 women) or a negative role (16/31) in their success. The following quote was fairly representative of most of the women interviewed. 'I never felt that I either got or lost business because of being a woman.' However, in conversation several could recall some event where gender had played a negative but not necessarily a detrimental role. One woman, who had gone into a male-dominated field many years ago (construction), had a different opinion from the others, probably owing to the time period in which she became active. She stated, 'You cannot be timid; you have to play hardball'. She went on to say:

> Gender has not helped me in any way. Being the only woman in construction in the early years, I was therefore the only female member of the Builders Association.

An interesting finding is that, whereas a majority of women regarded their gender as playing a neutral role in their success, they usually discussed difficulties they had faced or sometimes were still facing. Some examples of what these women said are:

> It took longer to come to peoples' attention because of my gender and you know the old saying that as a woman you have to work twice as hard as a man to be noticed.

> When I went for promotion for full professor, I was held back twice by the head of my department . . . I had pages and pages of publications – far more than he did . . .

There were those who only saw the negative aspects of gender. The example below is a remark by a lawyer:

> Women tend not to be as successful. Women end up doing a lot of family law . . . In the larger firms it is the women who are doing the family law; the men won't do it. There are dorky men doing big deals and you know they couldn't find their way out of a paper bag. Yet they get the best work, because they're male.

As a group, the women lawyers did find their gender to be a hindrance to their success. They spoke of the culture of practice and its underpinning that billed hours measure success. Professions such as law that are based on this culture lose women at a rapid rate. One lawyer remarked:

> In the informal culture some men still think that you are not as good a lawyer if you cut hours to be with your family.

The majority of women interviewed did emphasize the necessity of being extremely good at what they did. Women need to rely upon expertise, not upon networks, to be promoted and to be successful. Several women who had cited gender as being essentially neutral did also comment that they had to change their approach in order to deal effectively with men, for example:

> You had to change the way you speak in order to be heard.

Several mentioned a positive aspect of their gender, although it was not always appreciated! They stated that women in organizations tend to look at the whole, while men are more individualistic or self-centred.

> One must be sensitive and not too overbearing, being careful not to step on the male ego.

In general, the interviewees in Newfoundland were more expressive about the negative effects of being a woman. A common statement was: 'being a woman makes things more difficult and has not been a help to me; it is hard to get your opinion heard'. The woman went on to say that, 'in Newfoundland we are penalized for being women'. This was not the case for the women from Ontario or Quebec; they had either a positive or neutral view of the effects of gender on their success.

Age, ethnic and regional background   Age or ethnic background was also seen as positive by eight of the Canadian women, while it was seen as negative to 13 of them. Here are some examples of what they said:

I also have faced some challenges because of my age. People have a hard time taking you seriously when you're significantly younger than they are. However, woman, young whatever the case, once you prove yourself, even the ignorant, look past their initial hang-ups. I don't believe it's a handicap; at the very most I see it as a fun little challenge to be a woman in the workforce today.

I think again that that my ethnicity combined with my gender have both helped create opportunity and take it away.

All the women from Newfoundland discussed the negative image and/or stigma associated with being a Newfoundlander. One responded that she was so influenced by the prejudice associated with the negative image of Newfoundlanders that it influenced her choice of university. Another remarked that within her organization (a federal government one) there is a penalty associated with being a Newfoundlander:

I feel the implications of the Newfoundland culture more now as a director at the national table. As a Newfoundlander you always have to try harder. They don't understand much about us. We are penalized – it is harder.

Several interviewees remarked about struggling daily with the colonial mind-set. For additional quotes from Newfoundland on ethnicity, see endnote.

In addition to issues of gender, age and ethnic background, internal and external aspects relating to success and motivation were addressed in the interviews.

Aspects related to success
The interviews began with a question ascertaining how they defined success and to what they attributed their success. They were asked how they defined success and what made them successful. We were probing to see whether or not they attributed success to internal or to external characteristics, such as luck or through the help of some other individual (see Chapter 2 for a discussion of the attributes of success).

Internal factors Unlike many of the studies (for example, see Deaux and Emswiller, 1974; Deaux and Farris, 1977) which have shown that women tend to attribute their success more to external factors, the group of women that were interviewed spoke more of internal factors:

The reason for my success is definitely internal. I'm like a dog with a bone; I will go at something until it is completed. I am a fighter. I am very tenacious. Doing what has to be done. Keep going. I guess the major factors are internal. Not being put off by challenges. Just do it and worry about it later.

My determination – a willingness to take a chance and to fight for what I believe.

Personality and internal motivation   Most of the interviewees discussed how hard they work, their strong motivation and drive, and a clear vision of what they wanted to do. Eight of the 31 women interviewed stressed internal factors; they were goal driven, full of aspiration, took the initiative and were highly ambitious.

> I think that my self-confidence, leadership skills, drive and ambition all con-tribute to where I am today and where I am going.

> I guess I've always had pretty high self-worth. I don't want to say self-confidence because it's a lot of time that I lack confidence . . . But I have a high self-worth. I am not quite sure what is the difference between self-worth and self-esteem but I know there is a difference. Esteem implies comparing myself to somebody else, that's not me. I didn't compare (myself) to anybody.

Eight women also mentioned that they were hard-working. One woman mentioned that she works for a 'very complex organization'. She said:

> [I] need to have skills in managing ambiguity, integration and rapid perspective and relationship-building skills extraordinaire. It is a very tough job.

Four women also mentioned that they were very high-risk-takers. This suc-cessful woman nicely summed up her internal attributes:

> I don't believe in chance. I believe in hard work, opportunity, the ability to take risks and timing. People often confuse those factors with luck.

Management and leadership style   In describing their management and leadership styles, the successful women clearly fit Bass's transformational model, as described in Chapter 2. The successful women said their man-agement or leadership style was consultative (16/31). They used terms such as 'consulting', 'frequent communications', 'encourages others', 'suppor-tive' and 'motivating'. They also stated that they were 'participative', 'col-laborative' and 'team oriented' (15/31). Reflecting the lower power distance score evidenced in the survey, the interviewees also regarded subordinates and superiors in an egalitarian way and valued individual achievement and action as well as teamwork and group decision-making. Most real-ized that in certain situations one needed to be authoritarian (a gentle authoritarianism) and directive.

> I let them know where I want us to go. I set the goals but I don't dictate the path. I tell people to express their own style. I like to teach people to use what they have.

Others remarked:

> I think that, without a doubt, I see myself as a participative leader. I try to foster a sound environment where ideas are welcome and communication is encouraged. I think we all have to learn from each other but I do exert my leadership skills when it is essential to do so.

> I manage people on a long rope . . . [I have] high expectations, with frequent communications. I hope others find me encouraging. I encourage others to develop, [I am] team oriented, and supportive.

One woman in the provincial government elaborated in detail concerning her management and leadership styles:

> I don't follow a theoretical model. It is important to surround yourself with good people. I am at a senior level with directors reporting to me. I mentor and maintain an open-door policy. I delegate: we set objectives and monitor the progress. I guess you could call [my style] participative and mentoring. I consult, not excessively as we can have endless consultation, but if it were appropriate, such as situations where I don't have the skills or knowledge needed to make the decision [I do consult].

Although she does not consider herself to be following a transformational model, this quote does fit within the rubric of the model. Another woman described her approach, which would fit into the contingency model, stating, 'The style really depends on the situation'.

There occasionally is resistance at the bottom of the organization to participation. An executive for a private firm spoke about how she has tried to involve the front-line people but, owing to the traditional authoritarian Newfoundland culture, it is difficult to achieve. '[The people] don't want it; we [Newfoundlanders] are socialized not to question.' So she has had to adjust to that and have more of a top-down approach.

External factors related to success
In terms of the attributes for success, although the stress was on internal factors, most of the women did point out that there were some external factors which were also important, such as social support, education, luck, role models and mentors.

Social support   In terms of social support, the women mentioned their families or upbringing (12 of the 31), especially their fathers and their husbands. One successful woman stated, 'Without the constant encouragement of my family I do not think I would be as self-confident and ambitious'. Another woman said, 'One of the questions in the survey is to what do I attribute to my success – it is the support I have in the background. Be it my parents, husband, family or kids.'

Several women mentioned the important role their husband had in serving as a mentor. One woman mentioned that her husband helped her cope with the male management culture.

> He told me to look at this as a game and that you don't always know the rules, but look at what the others are doing and you'll catch on.

Others spoke of the difficulty in juggling work and family, and keeping everything in balance.

> I did feel pressure to raise my children: not to miss a hockey game and to boost my daughter's spirits by spending some special time together.

As found in studies of dual-career couples (Falkenberg and Rychel, 1985; Marshall, 1984; Schneer, 1985), these women still had more responsibility for the house and children than their husbands and often their career is slowed down because of these responsibilities. One woman made a conscious choice not to aim for partnership in her law firm at the same speed as her male colleagues owing to her desire to have a child, and she ended up on the 'slow track'. A couple of the interviewees solved this problem by marrying 'stay at home' husbands; this situation is not yet common.

Education   While some of the successful Canadian women (9/31) said that their education helped them succeed, one person said it was not necessarily formal education: 'However, when I refer to education I don't necessarily mean school. Although my education was important, the lessons learned from others and on my own were far more influential.'

Luck   Another external factor that emerged from these interviews was luck. Ten of the 31 women mentioned things like 'luck', 'circumstance', 'coincidence', 'opportunity', 'chance' or 'A great deal of being in the right place at the right time'. Several of those interviewed referred to luck or timing as being a critical element in their achievements: 'Being in the right place at the right time.' These remarks were mentioned primarily by women in the age group of late forties to mid-fifties and most remarks were made with reference to being 'on the cusp of attitudinal and social change for women', for example, being already within the government organization when gender equity initiatives were being put into place to facilitate female mobility to the executive level.

This may indicate that some of these women had an external locus of control; however, many said that their own efforts, as well as being in the right place at the right time contributed to their success. When asked if gender or age affected her success, one woman stated:

No . . . right place right time . . . on the leading edge of the women's movement . . . it being acceptable for women to be working. I always had choices.

Role models and mentors   The scores from mentoring from the survey, which indicated that it played a moderate role in their success, were supported from the interview data, especially the interviewees based in Newfoundland. In terms of role models or mentors, the most frequently cited were fathers (10/31) and colleagues (9/31).

My dad to some extent . . . he had a great enthusiasm for so many different things and the aspect of the business. I think I certainly caught that from him.

Some cited women as mentors. One woman remarked:

Usually I would find someone that I respected, whom I felt deserved to be where they are and I would talk to them. There was one woman where I worked in Toronto that influenced me. She taught me balance . . . Women are more open; they talk more.

One of the interviewees spoke at length about the influence her mentors had upon her.

The first one (a woman) hounded me until I did my doctorate. The second mentor [a man] was the medical director at the hospital who encouraged me to pursue the MBA. He told me I had more talent and ability than to be just the director of pharmacy. He told me I had senior management potential . . . I think that once you've had that kind of experience and you've had that confidence expressed in your abilities, you begin to look differently at what the world has to offer. As a result I have tried to play a mentoring role whenever possible.

Are they successful?
Finally when we asked the Canadian women if they thought that they were successful, 22 out of 31 said they were professionally successful while 19 out of 31 said they were successful in life and 25 out of 31 said they were successful in general.

Sometimes it's scary the degree to which I am succeeding. It's a great deal of work. You are always 'on'. You must always be careful that something you say isn't taken out of context or believed to be the stance of the organization that you represent. With each success comes responsibility and a significant package of work.

Yes, I have a long marriage, I have happy children, successful children, I earn a good living, I travel and am well educated. I am still learning, when I have decisions to make, I make them.

Yes, I am very happy with my life. As most people I am still searching for the optimal balance. I do try to balance work with an active social life, travel, family, hobbies, personal life etc. . . . To me, it's important to be well rounded . . . I do think I'm successful. I do something I love every day. Not everyone enjoys that luxury. I have earned the respect of my peers and I'm happy with my professional growth. Also, I am proud of what I've accomplished, though it's only the beginning of a long journey.

RELATIONSHIP TO THEORY AND RESEARCH STUDIES

As discussed in the second chapter, women who are the token women in their organizations tend to experience stereotyping and find that everything they do is attributed to their gender (Kanter, 1977). Several of the Newfoundland women interviewed mentioned the difficulty of being tokens in their organization or particular industry sector, or at one point during their career. They mentioned the difficulty in being heard when they were placed in a token situation.

Most of the successful Canadian women believed they became successful on their own, without a formal mentor or organizational support. The feeling often is: 'I've done it on my own; why should they need help?' The following quote is illustrative of this pattern:

In the public sector there are more women in higher positions. I can see there are some senior women who have difficulty relating to and being supportive of other women. It probably has to do with insecurity and identifying themselves more with men.

According to the gender context theory (Falkenberg and Rychel, 1985; Marshall, 1984; Schneer, 1985), women have to work hard in order to be accepted, and they need to be careful in projecting an image of being politely assertive, and not aggressive.

Some of the successful women remarked about the culture of their organizations and the barriers this placed in front of them, often necessitating that they aim for success in a way quite different from that of the men. The gender divide was most prominent among the lawyers.

I think I did it a different way than I would have had I been a man. I chose a different route. In our business there are the 'rainmakers', the ones who bring in a lot of money. They have built networks . . . Women don't have that. Then there are those people who build up expertise and become a draw and build a network that way . . .

You can network within women's groups and get clients, but the big difference still is that women do not hold the power and the money. You cannot build a practice without clients. Physiologically my gender has hampered my career and also it limits the ability to get into those inner circles.

There is difficulty getting into the inner circle. This is where there is a difference in the career path.

In Chapter 2, research on social support mentions the difficulty women have in pursuing their careers, and taking care of the home and children. Prominent in the interviews with the Newfoundland women who were married, were illustrations of the challenge and the difficulty in doing both and the sacrifices that have to be made.

I remember a woman at one of our firm's retreats who completely fell apart. She had a 16 month old and she felt she didn't know her children.

I know this other female lawyer who was about to present a case in Supreme Court. Her baby had to be rushed to the Children's Hospital over that weekend and her case was due on Monday. She worked Sunday because she felt asking for an extension would be frowned upon.

The women also mentioned the many hours they work – far more than their husbands, since they are more responsible for the home and children than are their husbands.

It has been said that now women work 40 hours a week outside the home too. This is in addition to the 40 hours of household work.

They felt that there had been changes, but there was still a long way to go:

There is no doubt there still exists a gender divide. The boys and girls go out separately; the guys still eye the secretaries. It is better but the problems are not solved. And I don't know what it will take.

SUMMARY AND CONCLUSION

The successful women in this survey scored high on internal locus of control, need for achievement and self-efficacy. These findings are supported by other researchers (Brush, 1992; Buttner, 1999; Lituchy and

Reavley, 2003; Lituchy et al., 2003; Reavley et al., 2005, Schein et al., 1996). This is an important finding for policy-makers and educators interested in harnessing the benefits of women professionals and entrepreneurs to stimulate economic growth and employment. These attributes can be taught and/or enhanced. Ideally, children, both girls and boys, should be encouraged to set high goals, strive to accomplish them and be provided with positive reinforcement.

These results should be important to educators, governments and non-governmental organizations (NGOs) that are interested in supporting the success of women in managerial, entrepreneurial and other professional roles. There are several implications of this research both for academics and practitioners. Theory on successful men in various countries or cultures cannot be assumed to apply to women. Although there were significant similarities between the successful Canadian women in this study, there were also some differences. To be successful and have an impact on the economy of their country, women entrepreneurs need to have the appropriate characteristics and competencies as well as social support such as role models and/or mentors.

NOTE

1. Reflecting the traditional dichotomy of the division between St John's and other parts of Newfoundland, of the successful women interviewed who are Newfoundlanders, 60 per cent were born in St John's, a city which has 20 per cent of Newfoundland's population. The university, though, has had a levelling influence, which is probably a factor why not more than 60 per cent of students came from St John's. Their parents were far more educated than was the case in Newfoundland; the largest group had fathers who were professionals and 15 of them were in business. Quite a few of them had mothers who were professionals (18 out of 79), again, unusual considering the fact that in Newfoundland in 1949 there was a literacy rate of 60 per cent.

   Concerning the colonial mind-set, which several interviewees talked about, one remarked: 'Yes, I want to go higher . . . but there is a part of me that is still a Newfoundlander that says, "I can't do that".' Many discussed the image that anyone not from Newfoundland is better than a Newfoundlander. Others discussed impressions of 'mainlanders' resulting from the perpetuation of a stereotype associating modern-day Newfoundland with the Newfoundland of 1949. For example, a professor from Newfoundland who had taught in Ottawa remarked: 'I found that the students had an image of what they thought Newfoundlanders were like and they seemed to have difficulty reconciling that with this person with a PhD from Oxford.' Several also remarked that it would be difficult for a non-Newfoundlander to succeed in Newfoundland, unless she were a university professor, due to the 'traditional suspicion of mainlanders'.

8. Successful women of the United States of America

Jo Ann Duffy, Suzy Fox and John Miller

Many people view the USA as the birthplace of modern feminism. The first women's rights convention, held in 1848 in Seneca Falls, New York, set the agenda for the struggle for domestic, political and economic equality for women. The history of the USA is peppered with the stories of strong, out-spoken courageous women – women who were very much the exceptions for their cultures and their times. From Abigail Adams (first lady of one president and mother of another, who spoke out for the rights of women in early revolutionary America) to Eleanor Roosevelt and Hilary Clinton, women have gone beyond their expected roles to speak out for participation and progress. From the great Abolitionists Sojourner Truth and Elizabeth Cady Stanton to Rosa Parks, symbol of the modern civil rights movement, women have emerged as leaders of the struggle for equal opportunity for all.

Paradoxically, women in the USA lag behind much of the rest of the world in their participation in leadership at the upper echelons of politics and industry. Countries as disparate as the UK, Pakistan, Israel, Sri Lanka, India, Portugal, Norway, Finland, Lithuania, Bangladesh, France, Poland, Turkey, Rwanda, New Zealand, Mozambique, Mongolia, Iceland, San Marino, the Philippines, Ireland, Yugoslavia and the Ukraine across the great oceans, and Canada, Haiti, Guyana, Peru, Argentina, Bolivia, Nicaragua and Panama in the Americas, have had women heads of state over the past 50 years (Women World Leaders, 2005) – but never the USA. In the legislative branch, as of 2005, women held 14 per cent of the seats in the US Senate, and 15 per cent of the seats in Congress. Eight out of 50 state governors were women (Center for American Women and Politics, 2005).

In the domain of economic leadership in the USA, women do not fare much better. According to the US Census (2002), women made up 52 per cent of the resident population 25 years and older. However, in a 2002 study of Fortune 500 companies by Catalyst, an institute that studies the progress of women and works with business and professional leaders to expand opportunities for women (Catalyst, 2005b), fewer than 16 per cent of corporate officer positions and fewer than 8 per cent of the highest officer titles

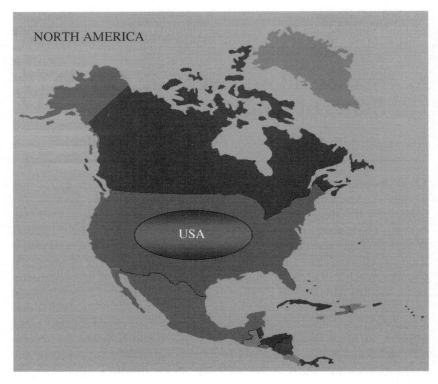

Figure 8.1   Location of the USA

were held by women (Catalyst, 2002). The US Census (2002) demonstrates that women fare somewhat better as entrepreneurs in the USA, and make up about 26.5 per cent of business owners (21.4 per cent of majority interest owners).

While it is commonly assumed that the status of women in the upper levels of politics and business is more favorable in the USA than in many of the 'less developed' countries of the Americas, this is one of the many ways in which our work on the Successful Women of the Americas research project has been an eye-opener. Starting with the recognition that the USA shares with its neighbours a very modest base rate of highly successful women in the domains of professions, politics, and business, we turn to our key research question: what is it that distinguishes those exceptional women who manage to succeed in spite of the barriers they encounter? To begin answering that question, we first reflect on how the US women who participated in our study feel about themselves.

[I'm] absolutely [satisfied]. Probably 250 per cent satisfied with my work and my life. There has not been a day when I said to myself: I don't want to go to work today.

My husband said to me last night: you're working so hard and you're so happy.

[I'm motivated by] inner satisfaction. Find yourself that you feel good about what you're doing –fulfilled enriched. You're reaching your own capabilities.

I am basically very satisfied . . . but I have to say there is always a certain amount of dissatisfaction that creates an energy to kind of go to the next step or do the next thing.

STUDYING SUCCESSFUL WOMEN IN THE USA

Data on successful US women were collected from 126 respondents to a survey and from 15 interviewees. Initially a variety of professional sources – the *Women's Yellow Pages*, Marquis' *Who's Who in America*, women's networking organizations and listserves, attendees at conferences and workshops addressing issues of concern to businesswomen, and listings of female, tenured professors at a private Midwestern university and a public Southwestern university – were used to identify women who met the criteria for success. This convenience sample was drawn primarily from the West, South and Midwest. The snowball or chain referral approach, in which participants are asked to recommend other prospective participants, was subsequently used as a method of identifying more successful women. Although this was a sample of convenience, there is no reason to suspect that these women who fit the criteria for successful women are not representative of the broader population of successful women. In addition, 128 undergraduate business students were surveyed so we could compare their responses with the successful women. We anticipated that the successful women would tend to be similar to the students on the cultural indices but higher on the personality variables related to success. By and large, these expectations were met (see Appendix D).

The survey consisted of seven scales measuring satisfaction, personality, cultural assumptions, and mentoring experiences. These have been more fully described in Chapters 2, 3 and 6. In particular, self-efficacy (the extent to which a person believes she is able to accomplish what she wishes to accomplish) and need for achievement (how much a person wants to accomplish objectives she sees as representing something worthwhile) have been positively related to performance. People who have a high need for achievement work hard towards goals, and therefore perform well, and individuals with high self-efficacy have the self-confidence to pursue challenging goals. Both need for achievement and self-efficacy have been associated with overcoming barriers or initial obstacles to success.

Locus of control (the attribution of what happens to either internal or external influences) was another measure on the survey. An internal locus of control has been positively related to performance – people who believe that results depend on their own performance tend to work hard and perform well. In the literature, mentoring has been linked to success. For that reason both psychosocial and career mentoring scales were included in the survey.

An interest in how successful women compare across the Americas meant that measures of cultural dimensions were needed. Chapter 3 described in detail three culture indices that were included in the survey: individualism/collectivism, the extent to which the individual or the group is emphasized in decision-making and activities; uncertainty avoidance, the degree to which people tolerate a lack of certainty and seek security; and power distance, the degree to which inequalities in status or power are acceptable. In the original Hofstede (1980a) study, the USA tended to be individualistic, tolerant of uncertainty and low on power distance, indicating a preference for equality.

The interview protocol composed of open-ended questions was designed to provide information that could be interpreted in the same terms as the questionnaire items and to uncover other perceived important characteristics of success. In the following sections we link the results of the 15 face-to-face interviews with successful USA women and results from the survey.

RESULTS

Successful US women express delight with their careers. Of the 126 women we surveyed and the 15 women we interviewed, the average age of the survey respondents was 53 years old and of the women we interviewed was 49. The majority of our survey respondents (94 per cent) and all our interviewees have graduate degrees. Most are married (66 per cent of those surveyed), but 67 per cent of our interviewees and 31 per cent of our survey respondents have no children. Contrary to popular literature on birth order and success (Toman, 1993), the US successful women are just as likely to be the oldest (40 per cent), middle (30 per cent), or youngest (24 per cent) child in their families. However very few (about 6 per cent of the survey respondents and none of the interviewees) are only children. Over 40 per cent of them have both brothers and sisters, while 26 per cent have only brothers and 25 per cent have only sisters.

Attributions of Success

What were the main causes to which our women attributed their success?

> I'd say first my parents, their upbringing and instilling values, the value of hard work and education, their support. I'd say it is following through on hard work and education. And blessed with some good genes.

The women were divided in the extent to which they cited internal or external sources of success. Many of our interviewees emphasized internal attributes and approaches, such as hard work, persistence, personality, openness, optimism, self-confidence, people skills, management/leadership styles, aggressive career management, and the ability to recognize and seize opportunities. In contrast, some of the key external sources of success were family support, mentoring, education, affirmative action programmes or preferences, internships and leadership development programmes.

Internal sources: personality
The previous quote along with the mean scores from the survey scales indicate that successful US women tend to have an internal locus of control and high self-efficacy.

> I could name hundreds of people in hundreds of ways. But it comes down to me – the work I've put in and my vision couldn't have come from anyone else.

> [I'm] Confident, comfortable with my abilities.

> I was raised to believe I could do anything I set my mind to. I've really believed that.

> Very, very strong work ethic, very strong conviction of who I am – very confident and secure in my management style and my abilities to do my job and do it well.

These expressions of self-efficacy and confidence were confirmed by the written survey data. The successful women scored significantly higher on the measure of self-efficacy than the comparison student group (mean scores of 4.22 and 3.82, respectively on a scale from 1 to 5); see Appendix D.

This pattern was also evident for the personality trait of need for achievement. In the interviews women spoke frequently of their success/achievement orientation in terms such as 'ambitious', and 'motivated', even 'aggressive'. One woman describes how she pursued success – asked for promotions, aggressive career planning, worked very, very, very hard.

The survey data confirmed the importance of achievement orientation for successful women. On a scale from 0 to 16, the successful women (score: 12.57) scored significantly higher on need for achievement than the comparison student group (score: 11.23).

Similarly, seven of the 15 interviewees cited their persistent, determined personality as a reason for their success. More that half of the interviewees reported that their 'hard work' ethic was important. Another internal characteristic that emerged as a major theme in the interviews was the ability to think, expressed in terms such as 'independent thinker', 'intuition' and 'quick-witted'. Over a quarter of the woman highlighted their 'self-confidence' and the same number mentioned their 'optimism' and 'positive attitudes'.

Internal sources: people skills

Very open, warm, outgoing . . . Able to put people at ease.

Open and honest with people. Most people appreciate that.

Ability to empathize . . . listening skills . . . ability to face conflict.

Caring for people, investing in people, helping others to achieve.

Five of the interviewees said that their personal skills contributed to their success. This is further reflected in the next section on the management and leadership styles of our successful women.

Management/leadership styles

All but one interviewee mentioned her management style as being a source of their success. When they were asked to describe their management style, 11 of the 15 used the terms 'empower' or 'collaborate'. They also noted their 'supportive' people skills in such terms as 'approachable', 'give them what they need', 'guide', 'appreciative'. Another major theme that emerged was the achievement goal and result focus of their management style. When they responded to a question about their leadership style, there was a similar pattern to their responses along with an additional theme, which could be captured by the term 'vision'. Many of them expressed quite complex styles, and highlighted the struggle to balance goal orientation with prototypically feminine people-oriented approaches.

I have no problems speaking my mind. If I had my way, I'd be quite auto-cratic. But never really have been. Not pure consensus, but want to hear from all members, make certain I hear from quiet members. Try to steer in the best way.

I really cared, had a loyal team, I cared about their careers, success. Because my attitude towards teams meant I had loyal members and [my teams were success-ful]. Interpersonal skills are not unique to women, but part of their success – very collaborative until we're in trouble, then very dictatorial. I'll try to get con-sensus, work as a team. If it's the last day of the quarter, I'll say you do this you do that. I expect the best of the team. I pull individuals aside and tell them what they need to do. People know where they stand. Very fair, very supportive. Praise publicly, beat up privately. I really like to challenge people. Yes. I'm very collab-orative. I think the collaborative is much more important today.

Internal sources: approach to external opportunity

Locus of control reflects the extent to which people attribute what happens to them to internal causes (their own actions and characteristics) or exter-nal causes (luck, fate, other people, God). In the written survey, one of the most surprising findings was how relatively externally the women from the USA scored on the measure of locus of control (2.32). Successful women were not significantly different from the comparison student group (2.40). Even more surprisingly, the successful women scored more externally than women in any of our other country samples, with the exception of Argentina and Brazil. At first sight it appears from the interview data that many of the successful American women are not internals because they link luck, chance, having opportunities with their success. However, closer examination reveals that the women juxtapose the external attribution with an internal ability to exploit opportunities:

I guess I put a lot of faith in the fact that I was lucky enough to have opportuni-ties, so there is some element of luck involved. Being in the right place at the right time. When something that might have unusual opportunities or implications attached to it became available.

an ability to exploit a lucky opportunity, because what I've seen is a lot of people who have . . . worked as hard as I have, maybe had some of the same breaks as I have, but haven't been quite as focused on how do I make sure I use that break as a break . . . I have an ability to see when something is going to be big before other people see that it's going to be big.

It appears that they believe that they are responsible for 'grabbing hold' of the opportunities that come their way. They spoke of being 'futuristic', 'entrepreneurial', able 'to see opportunities', being a 'strategic thinker'. These comments indicate that they do see themselves as being in charge of their own destiny (internal locus of control) although the opportunity might be a matter of luck (external).

External sources: family support

The support and encouragement from family and others, and the luck to be where an opportunity presented itself were the main external factors influencing success. These external opportunities might have been education, sponsorship, or specific organizational programmes such as affirmative action, internships and leadership development.

All but two women reported a great deal of support from their birth families, especially from their fathers. Husbands were also seen as a major source of support by 40 per cent of our respondents.

> My parents, especially my Dad, have had extremely high expectations of me. I had to live up to them . . . My dad very consciously undertook to prepare me for my career. Taught me logic, statistics, research design and methodology. Built sense of confidence. Attitude: something being hard is no big deal.

> My husband's wonderful. He helps me a lot – he's made it possible to be successful. Since I've been with him it's been a complete change. He picks up the slack I'm far more successful than before I met my husband.

External sources: education

All the women attributed their success to education. The majority of them reported having a Master's or PhD degree. This is interesting in light of the fact that 95 per cent of their fathers and 98 per cent of their mothers had a Bachelor degree or less.

External sources: support of mentors

Over two-thirds of the US women reported that the one person most influential in their career was not part of a formal programme but did work in the same organization. Fifty-five per cent identified the most influential person as male; more than a third said this person was the same age, while the remainder said that the person was older. Of those who did have mentors more than a quarter reported having had two influential people in their lives; another quarter had three people who positively impacted on their career advancement. An overwhelming proportion (86 per cent) of them act as mentors for someone younger who works in the same organization.

When the women identified mentors, they tended to be professors, academic advisers or bosses. However, most of the interviewees did not perceive mentors as important to their success. This was reinforced by the results of the written survey, in which the psychosocial and career mentoring mean scores (3.5 and 3.4/5.0 respectively) were not as high as might be expected from the literature on mentoring. Overall, the following comment reflects the mentoring experiences of successful women in the entire study, as discussed in Chapter 6.

> No one played a mentoring role for me – I found my own people who gave me directions for individual goals. I never had any real mentor who made a significant impact on my life.

> I think more important than a mentor is actually a sponsor . . . The difference in my mind is a mentor is somebody who can be a role model, and show you the ropes so to speak. How do things work around here? But they aren't necessarily in a position to promote your career and they don't necessarily put themselves on the line for you. Whereas a sponsor is someone who is willing to put their own reputation on the line and recommend you for positions that further your development and in most cases also further your positions in the hierarchy.

Additional sources of support

Success was infrequently related to God (only two women mentioned God or faith). Ethnicity was seldom a factor. However, being an American was mentioned by three women.

> Just an old USA American. I grew up living in Arkansas. In high school self-sufficiency and self-determination were very highly valued, ability to take care of your own life. Lesson when you live close to the land: what you get comes from what you put into it. Taught me to put heart and soul into your work.

> Being an American even more than being the gender. In fact interestingly enough if you look at the most senior people, the women in my company, most of them are American. And it's because women in the US in our company have tended to get more opportunities for higher positions which aided their development, which put them in a position to be considered for senior jobs overseas which when we look to diversify our leadership, essentially American women, were the only women that were available.

Gender-related issues

When the interviewees were asked how being a woman impacted on their success, their reaction was positive more frequently than negative. Nine of the 15 women interviewed said that being a woman gave them an advantage in terms of being more caring and compassionate.

> Qualities [of] social sensitivity, social dynamics, empathy seem to be more developed in women and I use that stuff all the time.

> As women, [we take on a] nurturing role, compared to men. More to give. Not so much territorial, don't charge as much, not always looking for what I am getting back.

I have to think though women have a side to their personalities . . . an ability to be disarmingly honest, to view life and work and people's place with a kinder, gentler attitude. More valiant . . . not entirely motivated by power and money.

Gender barriers

Gender barriers to success were encountered at the start of their careers and at the present time. Family was never mentioned as a barrier to success. Men, especially college teachers, however, were frequently labelled as obstacles to early success.

> There were definite gender barriers in school. There wasn't so much at graduate school. In junior college there was surprisingly a specific teacher who was difficult. Known to be a big chauvinist. He used to give women in calculus classes difficulty about how they were dressed. The point for me in his class was to be as competitive as possible. A true triumph for me was he had to give me an A – he hated that, but of course I had to really work to get an A. At graduation he said 'Where are you going?' I said I'm going to be an engineer. He said [I wouldn't make it.]. He was the guiding reason for me to get through some tough times at UIC. The idea of shoving my diploma in his face.

> Men in the organization would complain if I were put on assignment with them. I put up with a lot of grief that I probably shouldn't have. I worked hard to be as good or better than anyone else . . . I had particular skills . . . and a sub-group really wanted me and got an OK, if they could get me at a low salary! I was so naïve that I accepted it, but I think they would have been happier if I didn't accept it. I later got a huge inequity raise.

> I put down a piece of me to be one of the guys. I did things I didn't particularly want to do. I joined the softball team.

The good old boy network poses the greatest impediment to future success for the US women according to the interviewees.

> Sometimes. I do believe there is an old boys' network. It's there. I feel I have to work my way either through it or around it. It happens and pops up. I feel I have to be more aggressive.

> I didn't perceive any barriers starting out . . . Feeling this more now than when I started. Abstract. I'm not taken as seriously.

> It is a man's world – there's more and more women lawyers, but I think the men still have more control. I dealt with and tried to make myself gender-neutral. When I first started I wore cuter clothes.

> There is a big difference between now and 24 years ago. The obstacles are not as blatant . . . I asked what needed to be done to get the promotion. I had to go through many more hoops than my male colleagues. One day after I got

promoted, my male colleague got promoted. 'We couldn't really promote you without promoting him.' I think the obstacles today are a bit harder. As you rise in the organization, it's harder to say . . . [it's due to gender, because there are fewer positions at that level]. It feels like you have to fight twice as hard to get what you want. Today it's harder to get past barriers than then. Then, [barriers were more] blatant – pornography on walls, off-colour jokes. But [today] when people say 'We're all for diversity', but don't deal with the fact that our organizations are not very diverse, we don't have women rising in management.

Biggest obstacle women face today: the men they are dealing with do not see themselves as discriminating, but they behave in ways that discriminate against women and minorities. They don't get it.

SUMMARY AND CONCLUSIONS

Overall, a robust profile of the successful professional woman of the USA emerged from our study: a woman in the midst of a career with which she is absolutely delighted! The women were divided in the extent to which they attributed their success to internal sources (for example, hard work, persistence, personality, people skills, management/leadership styles, aggressive career management, and ability to recognize and seize opportunities) and external sources (for example, family support, mentoring, education, affirmative action and leadership development programmes). The women were articulate in describing the many gender barriers they had faced in their careers, but many believed their gender had worked to their advantage.

A few surprising findings contradicted the assumptions and assertions of prior research literature. Our successful women were reluctant to attribute their success to the help and support of formal or informal mentors. Many described their own management and leadership styles with language such as decisive, autocratic and task oriented – characteristics generally associated with 'masculine' models of leadership. Although the USA has a highly individualistic reputation, almost all the women we interviewed emphasized the centrality of family in their personal and professional development, and, in fact, the individualism/collectivism scores on the survey differed little from those of the women in other countries.

The women were very conscious of living in a period of transition in the way they, and others, viewed their roles as women and as leaders. Their strength shines through in the words of a woman who has succeeded in rising to the top of an archetypical male profession:

I can't emphasize enough the importance of having a very thick skin – I work in a primarily male-dominated profession . . . firefighters . . . men in general . . . have a tendency to manage with a shock factor, to intimidate – Some women, the tears well up . . . But you have to be able to stand up when they test your fortitude. By now, I rarely have problems. I've earned myself a reputation, which will not be suppressed by others. I have a no-nonsense reputation.

With this woman in charge, we may move confidently into the future.

9. Successful professional women in Mexico

Miguel R. Olivas-Luján and
Leticia Ramos Garza

Malinche, Sor Juana Inés de la Cruz, Josefa Ortiz de Domínguez, Frida Kahlo, Martha Sahagún de Fox: these are the names of a few of the most revered and simultaneously criticized Mexican women (see Table 9.1). From pre-colonial times to the twenty-first century, working women in Mexico have played a central, if mostly veiled role in all facets of society. Within this *machista* society – borrowing a characterization from Mexican Nobel Prize winner Octavio Paz (Gutmann, 2001), Mexican women have seen their participation in the workforce improve rapidly in the past 20 to 30 years but, as in many other countries, they still are a long way from reaching parity in most areas.

This chapter is structured as follows: the next section describes how Mexico's long tradition of endorsing international initiatives has gradually increased governmental support for women's issues, although they have not been readily translated into more equitable business practices. Following that, we present an assortment of statistics that describe women's role in the Mexican workforce and factors that have been found to affect it more strongly from a macroeconomic standpoint, including education, fertility rates, civil – including maternity – status and economic need. The section after that presents the results of our empirical study, with details from both quantitative and qualitative components. Finally, we conclude the chapter with some thoughts on how important it is that more attention be given to ensuring an even playing field for women to develop fully their potential at work and increase their contribution to Mexico's goals of development and achieving a better standard of living for all its citizens.

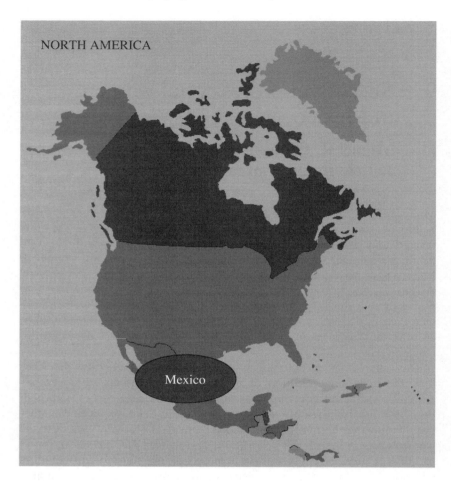

Figure 9.1   Location of Mexico

GAINS AND CHALLENGES FOR MEXICAN
WORKING WOMEN

As a country that has embraced globalization, Mexico has endorsed all the most prominent international conventions and initiatives to achieve gender equity. Starting with the more general Universal Declaration of Human Rights in 1948, Mexico also signed the Vienna Declaration and Programme of Action of the World Conference on Human Rights in 1993, which included a Special Rapporteur on Violence against Women. In 1975,

Table 9.1   Some famous women in Mexican history

	Biographical highlights	Historical legacy
Malinche (*c.*1505–*c.*1529)	Born in a noble Aztec family, she spent her teenage years as a slave in Mayan lands; her multilingual abilities enabled her to be Hernán Cortés' adviser and concubine	Her translation services were instrumental for the Spanish conquerors in getting indigenous allies to subjugate the Aztec empire; her name has become synonymous with 'traitor'
Sor Juana Inés de la Cruz (1646/51–95)	A lady-in-waiting for the Mexican viceroy court as a teenager, later a poet nun, she wrote over 20 theatre plays, several dozen poetry pieces, carols and sonnets. Her challenge to a sermon by then renowned Portuguese Jesuit priest Antonio Vieira earned her an admonishment to which she replied in her *Respuesta a Sor Filotea*	One of the greatest poets on the continent in the seventeenth century, she defended women's rights to an education (from biblical and theological perspectives) in her *Respuesta a Sor Filotea*
Josefa Ortiz de Domínguez (1768–1829)	Daughter of an army captain, she lost her parents at an early age. She married Miguel Domínguez, Querétaro's *corregidor* and became along with him, one of Mexico's most influential Independence war leaders	Her role as organizer and communications co-ordinator was crucial in the development of Mexico's Independence revolution
Frida Kahlo (1907–54)	A renowned painter and active communist supporter, she married famous muralist Diego Rivera; their marriage was full of friction	Kahlo has become a symbol of Mexican feminism for the last half of the twentieth century; her life recently inspired a major motion picture production
Martha Sahagún (1953–)	A strong collaborator of current President Fox from the time he vied for the governorship of Guanajuato state. She married him in 2001, after one year of work as the presidential spokesperson	A potential first female presidential candidate from a major party, her legacy is still be to be defined

Mexico hosted the World Conference of the International Women's Year, an important antecedent for the Convention on the Elimination of All Forms of Discrimination against Women (CEDAW), which was adopted by the UN General Assembly in 1979. The Convention's main objective is to create equal opportunities in political and public life, as well as education, health and employment, and Mexico is one of the few members in full compliance with respect to progress reports and responsiveness (UN, 2005). Mexico has also been an active participant in other influential women's forums such as the Fourth World Conference in Beijing, China in 1995. Of course, this support at the international level embodies significant challenges for actions at the national, state and local levels, and can be little more than 'window dressing' without these.

At the national level, Mexico has accumulated a couple of decades with government efforts whose main purpose is to improve women's situation in the social, health and (more importantly for this chapter) employment arenas. The Comisión Nacional de la Mujer (CONMUJER, National Women's Commission) was founded in 1985. Eleven years later, the Programa Nacional de la Mujer (PRONAM, National Women's Programme) mandated all Federal government agencies to follow its gender equity policies; and more recently, the Instituto Nacional de las Mujeres (InMujeres, National Women's Institute) has co-ordinated the country's gender equity efforts since 2001. Other national efforts that are helping improve women's situation include the Ministry of Statistics (INEGI or Instituto Nacional de Estadística, Geografía e Informática) programmes to measure and follow-up women's progress. Additionally, governments in most Mexican states have their own Women's Institutes with the purpose of advancing gender equity within their borders.

In spite of the government's apparent efforts, support for women's work in the private sector is limited. Zabludovsky (2001), a pioneer of research on gender and work in Mexico, has documented the efforts that IBM and Motorola have exerted to blaze the trail and establish formal programmes that would support their female employees. Other USA-based companies, such as Avon, Mary Kay and Creative Memories, have developed their distribution networks by creating flexible opportunities for women interested in generating their own income; most of these firms' products are usually bought by women.

In general, however, Mexican companies so far do not seem to show a strong interest in promoting gender equity, even for the simple purpose of generating favourable public relations. Within the private sector, it seems that companies which show interest in gender equity do so mainly to promote their products (for example, BANORTE Bank's 'Mujer Banorte' product line that offers checking books and cards with 'feminine' designs).

DEMOSTRADORA URGENTE

Solicito mujer de 182–5 años, estudios mínimos de preparatoria, soltera, *buena presentación*, experiencia en ventas no necesaria de productos alimenticios para trabajar en tienda departamental ubicada en la Colonia Roma, con ganas de trabajar . . .

Hiring advertisements in Mexican newspapers are openly discriminatory, perpetuating the existing gender segregation that sets women apart in lower-paying, subordinate positions like administrative assistant or waitress. The above notice even specifies that less than good-looking women need not apply (emphasis added)! Entry into the higher-paying, prestigious jobs, such as airplane pilot or executive officer, remains a privilege for men (cf. Hesse-Biber and Carter, 2000).

These practices persist in spite of Mexico's very progressive legislation: as far back as 1917, Mexico's Constitution (Article 123, Section A, Paragraph VII) prohibited salary discrimination by sex or nationality, and the Federal Labor Law (Article 3, Paragraph 2) – approved in 1931 – also explicitly forbade any 'differentiation' among workers because of their race, sex, age, religion, political doctrine or social status. Most dramatically, Article 133 from the Federal Labor Law (first paragraph) explicitly proscribes 'employers from denying employment because of applicants' age or sex'. In contradiction, one only needs to open a classified section in any newspaper – or visit the employment section of many a website – to find job advertisements that specify would-be applicants' age range and sex, often adding that *buena presentación* ('good looks') are expected. Clearly, Mexico's problem is not one of lack of appropriate legislation, but of adequate enforcement.

There is also the issue of the *maquiladora* industry (a programme by the Mexican and US governments to create assembly factories that would open employment opportunities in Mexico after the temporary migration programme Bracero was cancelled in 1964). The *maquiladora* programme has been heavily criticized for the intensive use of female unskilled labor (Moure-Eraso et al., 1997; Nauman and Hutchison, 1997; Sánchez, 1989). The strongest criticism from a gender standpoint – that women employees are preferred due to the greater ability to exploit them – has been addressed by Sargent and Matthews (1999), whose ethnographic work shows that, for many *maquiladora* workers, employment in these plants is a better option than other jobs. Additionally, Figure 9.2 shows that the proportion of women workers in the *maquiladoras* has decreased from almost 80 per cent

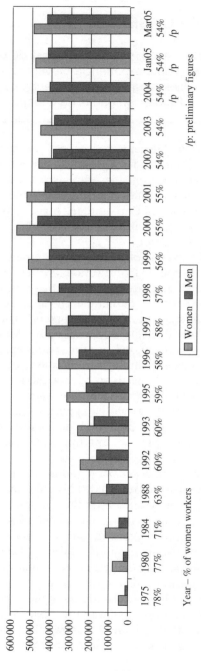

Source: INEGI (2005a).

Figure 9.2 Maquiladora *line workers by sex*

166

in the 1970s (of 57 850 total *maquiladora* line workers) to about 54 per cent in 2005 (of 915 908 total *maquiladora* line workers).

These companies might not be without fault; there is some indication that women workers are paid less than their male counterparts – as women in many other fields and countries are – but it seems that the exploitation theory is receiving less support lately. In fact the *maquiladoras* employ fewer than 3 per cent of the Mexican workforce – in 2004, of the 43 176 958 Mexicans between the ages of 14 and 65, only about 1 124 586 worked for *maquiladoras*, including technical workers and management (INEGI, 2005a). The reason for this intense scrutiny may not be so much women's rights as other less explicit motivations.

In the next section we review the statistics at the national level to assess the most important dimensions of the Mexican female workforce.

SELECTED STATISTICS ON THE MEXICAN FEMALE WORKFORCE

In 2005, INEGI (2005b) reported that there were approximately 105 million Mexicans, of whom 51 per cent were women. Almost 43 per cent of the national population is considered to be part of the economically active population. The traditional female roles of wife-homemaker and mother – along with lack of work opportunities – interact so that only 35.3 per cent (almost 15 million) of Mexican women, compared with 74.6 per cent (over 27 million) of men of working age are part of the workforce (INEGI, 2004d).

Motherhood is perhaps the most important factor that currently affects female work. In 1976, Mexico recorded a 5.7 fecundity rate (number of births per thousand women); this rate went down to 3.8 in 1987, and to 2.2 in 2003 (INEGI, 2004d). From a cultural standpoint, it seems that, in the mid-twentieth century, marriage used to be the life event that would determine women's exit from the workforce. Forty years later, their participation in the workforce is unquestioned, at least until children arrive. In addition, the latest cohorts of women have increased their educational achievements. In 1970, 63.3 per cent of females aged between 6 and 14 attended school; in 2000, the percentage increased to 91.0 per cent; (INEGI, 2003); post-secondary education rates for 2000/01 in Mexico were reported at 21 per cent for men and 20 per cent for women (INEGI, 2004b).

Economic hardship seems to require participating in the workforce even after children are born. Of the approximately 15 million women that work, almost two-thirds (9.9 million) had at least one child, according to projections based on the national employment survey of 2003 (fourth quarter). The same survey estimated that 32.1 per cent of women below the age of

30 that have children (1.79 million of 5.58 million) participate in the work-force (INEGI, 2004c). The percentage grows to 46.5 per cent for mothers between the ages of 30 and 49 (5.81 million of 12.50 million), those who are more likely to have older children. Nonetheless, mothers above 50 have a 27.1 per cent economic participation rate (2.26 million of 8.33 million), as they and their husbands presumably were raised with more traditional attitudes about female work, or perhaps their work is less critical to com-plement the family income, and their offspring have probably 'left the nest'.

On the other hand, mothers with more education show greater commit-ment to participation in the workforce. More than 50 per cent of mothers who had at least some post-high school education were economically active (3.29 million of 6.04 million, or 54.5 per cent), followed by 37.6 per cent of mothers with completed high-school (1.59 million of 4.22 million), then 33.2 per cent for mothers that had finished elementary school and had some high school (2.36 million of 7.09 million) 30.6 per cent of mothers that had not finished elementary school (1.62 million of 5.31 million) and 26.6 per cent of mothers with less education (1.00 million of 3.76 million).

The third crucial factor that influences mother's work in Mexico is civil status. Just over 68 per cent of single mothers in Mexico participate in the workforce (1.15 million of 1.68 million), followed by 44.6 per cent of mothers who reported being widowed, divorced, or separated (2.12 million of 4.76 million), then 33 per cent of mothers married or living with a partner (6.58 million of 19.98 million). Across these categories, working women show higher academic achievement than their non-working coun-terparts, a fact that supports the notion that the more educated women are more committed to work: working single mothers had 8.8 years of school-ing, compared with 6.7 years for non-working single mothers; working mothers married or living with a partner had 8.1 years of schooling, com-pared with 6.3 for non-working counterparts; and for working mothers that were widowed, divorced, or separated, 6.7 years, compared with 3.8 years for their non-working counterparts (INEGI, 2004c).

These national-level figures suggest that education and economic need, in addition to lower fertility rates, are the main factors driving the large increases in female participation in the workforce in Mexico. Still, it is rele-vant to note that there are significant regional differences across the country. First, women tend to have more opportunities in Mexico's metro-politan areas, than in places considered to be rural. Second, women located in the northern regions of Mexico, owing perhaps to its proximity to the USA, also seem to have better opportunities than women in the southern part of Mexico, which exhibit more traditional gender roles. Indeed, when we observe female participation rates at the state level, we find that, in enti-ties like the Distrito Federal (Mexico City), Sinaloa, Jalisco or Hidalgo, the rates exceed 40 per cent (the national rate was 36.6 per cent for the first quarter of 2004), while in other states with less developed metropolitan areas such as Zacatecas, Chiapas, Michoacán, Durango or Guerrero, only about 30 per cent or less of women of working age participate in the workforce (INEGI, 2004b). Related statistics, such as the sum of domestic plus out-of-home work or schooling levels also follow a similar pattern (INEGI, 2004d), The differences in the latter are smaller at the elementary than at the middle or higher education levels.

As has been reported for other countries (Hesse-Biber and Carter, 2000), gender socialization has a strong effect on vocational choices in Mexico as well. Statistics by Mexico's National Association of Universities and Institutes of Higher Education (ANUIES, Asociación Nacional de Universidades e Institutos de Enseñanza Superior) show that women have preferred 'nurturing' specialties such as education, humanities or health-related majors, while males tend to choose 'harder' occupations like agricultural, natural sciences, and engineering and technology-related majors (INEGI, 2004d). The former tend to be less well paid than the latter (Hesse-Biber and Carter, 2000; INEGI, 2003; 2004d); the most recent report by INEGI (2004d) finds that only for the category 'Technicians and specialized personnel' is there parity on median salaries; all other categories in the study (for example, office workers, teachers, sales clerks, industrial supervisors, professionals, and so on) show women's median salaries between 63.6 per cent and 96 per cent of men's. Furthermore, when schooling, number of hours worked and qualifications are statistically controlled for, on average, women make 14.2 per cent less than men.

To sum up, while Mexican women's work situation has improved in the recent past, there is still a long way to go before we can consider that their contribution to the nation's competitiveness is equitably structured and recognized.

THE SUCCESSFUL WOMEN WORLDWIDE PROJECT IN MEXICO

It is in this national context that we set out to work on this Successful Women Worldwide project. The methodology has been described elsewhere in this volume, but for the reader who is focused on this chapter, we used a two-pronged research design, composed of a quantitative (survey) and a qualitative (interview) component. Part of the data was collected during the World Congress of Women Business Owners that took place in Mexico City, and the rest as a part of an optional research seminar for MBAs at the Tecnológico de Monterrey's Graduate School of Business and Leadership

(EGADE). While the data collection was not designed to be statistically representative of successful professional women in Mexico, as there was no scientific selection of respondents, it does represent a wide variety of professional, demographic and regionally different women who have achieved professional success in accordance with the definitions for this study.

Survey Study – Results from the Quantitative Component

The quantitative survey was answered in Mexico by a total of 287 women, but 54 surveys were deleted from the analyses for various reasons (for example, respondent was born or working outside Mexico, her business had been established for less than three years, she was not a manager of managers with subordinates, or other conditions for inclusion in the study were not met – conditions for participation in this study included: owning a business for three or more years; reaching the highest academic levels, such as full professor or a high administrative ranking; being paid heads of organizations with not-for-profit status; having a high-level government job (such as being in charge of a governmental commission or having a law-making post); or supervising managers who also have at least one layer of subordinates) for a total 232 usable surveys. The average respondent to our study was 43 years old (standard deviation = 10.25). A sign of these women's work success is that, on average, they reported average yearly earnings of US$42 114.80, in a country where the per capita gross national income was US$6 230.00 (World Bank, 2004). In other words, on average, these women made 6.76 times the Mexican per capita gross national income for 2003. The most recent national income statistics report an average of approximately US$41 237.86 per year for homes in the top 10 per cent (INEGI, 2003), which suggests our average respondent belongs to this very select group.

Money, of course, is not the only indicator of success; this group of women present several other important indicators; for example, the companies these women own or are part of top management of, had combined sales of over US$306 million in the year before they submitted their responses. The organizations run the gamut from highly feminized industries like education, hospitality and grooming services, to other industries like financial services, metal mechanics, automotive, and medical instruments. Several of our respondents have also held high-level government positions at the national, state and local levels, for example, senators, congresswomen and ministers.

As can be seen in Table 9.2, respondents came from all geographic regions of Mexico, although a 'northern bias' might affect the sample owing to the high proportion of respondents with operations based in the

Table 9.2   Cities and states of origin of participants

Respondents' cities of origin	Cancún, Cd. del Carmen, Cd. Frontera, Coatzacoalcos, Colima, Cuernavaca, Culiacán, Hermosillo, Tijuana, Durango, Ensenada, Guadalajara, Guanajuato, Hermosillo, Irapuato, León, Cd. Madero, Matamoros, Mérida, Mexicali, México City, Monclova, Monterrey, Morelia, Morelos, Nuevo Laredo, Orizaba, Salamanca, Saltillo, San Pedro Garza García, Tampico, Tijuana, Tlaxcala, Toluca, Torreón, Tuxtla Gutiérrez, Villahermosa, Xalapa
Respondents' states (21 of 32 Mexican states)	Baja California, Campeche, Chiapas, Coahuila, Colima, Distrito Federal, Durango, Estado de México, Guanajuato, Jalisco, Michoacán, Morelos, Nuevo León, Quintana Roo, Sinaloa, Sonora, Tabasco, Tamaulipas, Tlaxcala, Veracruz, Yucatán

more economically developed northern states. In short, the lessons that we can draw from this study stem from high earners, highly influential women (in their companies or organization, including government) from most Mexican states (21 of 32). From a demographic standpoint, the large majority of our respondents were company executives (40.95 per cent) or entrepreneurs/business owners (39.22 per cent), followed by independent professionals such as doctors, lawyers, or accountants with their own practice (9.48 per cent), and by public servants (3.45 per cent). Over two-thirds of the sample was employed full time (68.78 per cent), almost another third was self-employed (29.87 per cent) and only a few were working part time (1.36 per cent). The majority of our respondents had a Bachelor's degree as their highest academic attainment (54.83 per cent), almost one in five had already finished a master's degree (19.30 per cent), a small minority had finished PhDs (2.63 per cent), about one-sixth of the sample had only some college studies (16.23 per cent), and only 16 of our respondents report holding only a high school diploma or less (7.02 per cent).

In the personal arena, almost two-thirds of the sample was married (63.88 per cent), followed in frequency by those who were single (19.38 per cent), divorced (13.22 per cent), separated (2.64 per cent) or other (0.88 per cent). In agreement with national statistics, most of these women had two or fewer children (19.05 per cent had none, 13.81 per cent had one and 31.90 per cent had two, for a combined total of 64.76 per cent), but almost one in four had three (24.29 per cent) and slightly more than one of every ten respondents (10.96 per cent) reported four or more children (7.62 per cent had four, 1.43 per cent had five and the same percentage had six; only one respondent reported having seven children, with 0.48 per cent). We should add that the older the survey respondent, the more likely that she had higher studies, and fewer children.

In comparison with the samples from other nations in this study, only the Brazilian and Chilean women had a significantly higher average number of offspring, Argentineans showed no statistically significant difference, and West Indian, Canadian and US respondents had on average a statistically significantly smaller number of children.

Birth order does not seem to play a large role in predicting these women's success, but parental education might. Almost half of our respondents were middle children in their families (48.10 per cent); almost one in three were the eldest child (31.43 per cent), almost one in five were the youngest (18.10 per cent), and only a handful (2.38 per cent) were their parents' only child. Most of the respondents reported growing up with both brothers and sisters (67.13 per cent), and close to one in six grew up among only brothers or only sisters (15.74 per cent and 14.81 per cent respectively).

Father's education seems to be at the higher end of the distribution; our respondents' average age is 43, which suggests that most of their parents must have obtained their education in the 1950s or early 1960s. Most respondents report that their father had a bachelor's degree as their highest academic achievement (38.8 per cent, in addition to 11.2 per cent having obtained 'some college' education, and 1.4 per cent reaching master's level); only 20.6 per cent had high school as their top achievement and 15.4 per cent had only elementary studies. On the mother's side, education also seems to be on the higher end, as respondents report that high school (22.7 per cent) followed by elementary (18.6 per cent), and then some college (14.3 per cent) or bachelor's degrees (14.3 per cent) were their mothers' highest academic achievement. It appears as though most of the professional women in our sample were raised in educated homes, where the father had a higher education level than the mother, and the daughters in turn reached higher educational levels – although almost one in ten of our respondents did not reach college level and still achieved her level of success.

The following sub-sections show the results of both intra- and cross-country comparisons. Intra-country comparisons were designed to compare our responses with other individuals that have not yet achieved professional success, but they have already reached adult age and therefore may be expected to provide a contrast against which we can compare our sample. In the case of the Mexican sample, we collected 42 surveys of adult, undergraduate business students who averaged 20 years old and had little or no work experience (sections on mentoring were excluded from the questionnaire for that reason). Cross-country comparisons below make reference to data collected from successful women in the other countries for this study.

Cultural scales
As described in Chapter 3, we measured three of Hofstede's (2001) dimensions of culture, using Dorfman and Howell's (1988) power distance, individualism/collectivism and uncertainty avoidance scales, in order to verify whether our samples would show similar profiles to those that have appeared in the international management literature. As expected, due to the extraction of respondents from the same culture, the student sample did not score differently from the successful women sample on any of the cultural dimensions. However, the professional Mexican women expressed a significantly higher level of societal acceptance of hierarchical differences in the workplace than the women in the other countries, with an average power distance score of 2.29. The Mexican sample also showed an unexpectedly high level of individualism (3.34), closer to Canada's score than to Argentina's, Chile's or Brazil's. This last result might show support for studies that suggest that wealth and individualism are closely related. Finally, the uncertainty avoidance dimension value was calculated as 3.90 (second highest among the country samples), which is consistent with Hofstede's study; this suggests that the Mexican respondents do not feel comfortable with ambiguous or indeterminate situations.

Personality variables
Details on the personality variables can be found in Chapter 3 in this volume. Mexican respondents, as we expected theoretically, exhibited strong scores for self-efficacy (4.26 on average), which are strongly, statistically different from the student sample (see Appendix D).

The average Mexican score for locus of control (1.95) – also predictably – was strongly internal; in fact, Mexican scores (not distinguishably different from West Indian and Chilean scores) were significantly more internal than the scores obtained from the Canadian, US, Argentinean and Brazilian samples. The student sample exhibited scores that are statistically similar to the professional sample, which might be owing to the fact that the school from which the sample was collected is extremely selective. The strong internal score obtained from the professional sample might suggest that, in order to succeed in a conservative environment like Mexico's, women need to develop and exert a very internal locus of control.

A similar speculation can be inferred by comparing Mexican respondents' need for achievement scores: 13.22 (only the West Indies was higher than Mexico's, but not statistically significantly so). Perhaps successful women in Mexico develop these personality variables more strongly to compensate for the prevalent *machismo* attitudes that might be detrimental to women's careers. The student average (11.83) was (as originally expected) significantly lower than the professional women's.

Mentoring factors

A working hypothesis for this study was that successful women do not become so in isolation. The extant literature suggests that some level of support is necessary, and in organizations this usually takes the form of a mentoring relationship (see Chapter 6 for a more detailed discussion of mentoring). In our survey, the Mexican women reported the highest level of participation in formal mentoring programmes (60.6 per cent), and these relationships (formal or not) take place more often within the organization (63.6 per cent, similar to Chile or the USA). Mentors are more likely to be female for these respondents (63.1 per cent), which represents a departure from the results from other countries, where mentors are more often males. Mentors in the Mexican sample tend to be older: 76.7 per cent, which is similar to most other samples (the USA had the lowest percentage). Consistent with all our country samples, the majority of Mexican respondents reported having had two mentors during their career, followed by three mentors (29.7 per cent), then by one (18.9 per cent).

Most participants in the Mexican sample also report being mentors (84.3 per cent), of younger individuals (72.7 per cent), and most of their mentoring took place within the same organization (62.8 per cent). These results are at odds with prior USA-based reports (Labrich, 1995, cited in Hesse-Biber and Carter, 2000), which suggest that women are less willing to serve as mentors. This would be a fruitful area for further research.

In the next section, we describe the lessons learned from the interview component of our study.

Interview Study – Results from the Qualitative Component

Twenty-nine women participated in personal interviews; most of these women also answered the survey. This section is organized around the following themes: interviewees' demographics, general descriptions of success, attributions for success, internal attributions, external attributions, important others, gender influences, cultural or ethnic influences, management/leadership style, religion, success in general life, great leaders or role models.

The following findings should be interpreted keeping in mind that the limited number of interviews rules out generalizability, the notion that these lessons will apply at the population level. Interviews are a very expensive way to obtain information, but a major advantage is that they also offer a very rich and detailed way to gain a better understanding of the phenomena under study.

Interviewees' demographics

Most of our interviewees were born in the 1950s and 1960s, their average and median age being 46. Our oldest interviewee was 81 years old and the youngest was 31. Most of them (13) had been middle children in their families, and the rest had been born as the eldest (eight) or the youngest (five) sister.[1] They had an average of 5.5 brothers or sisters, with two as the smallest number of siblings and 13 as the largest; five out of six interviewees reported having between three and seven siblings. Three out of four respondents were married, one in six divorced or separated, and one in ten reported being single or widowed. Three of these women reported having four or more children, ten of them had three, eight had two, three had only one and four had none. Eleven of these women reported all their offspring as adults aged 18 or more; four reported at least one teenage child (ages 12 through 17) and nine had younger children. The INEGI latest national survey on the use of time (2002) empirically shows that the type of activities (for example, personal care of children, work out of home) and time spent on them is radically different when a woman's youngest child is below the age of 12. In short, most of our interviewees were at least partially 'done' raising their children, but a few (almost one-third) had offspring at ages that demand much more personal attention and, consequently, the interviewees are less able to dedicate as much time to their work.

In terms of their schooling, 14 respondents had a bachelor's degree, seven reported master's degrees, three had PhDs, two were only high school graduates, one reported a technical degree, and another just elementary school. We should add that the younger the interviewee, the more likely that she had higher studies (Pearson correlation = 0.36, significant at the 0.06 p-level), and – not surprisingly – fewer children (correlation = -0.49, $p < 0.05$)

General descriptions of success

When asked whether they felt successful, three-quarters of the interviewees answered enthusiastically 'Yes', sometimes even followed by 'of course' or 'successful and happy!' The remaining seven interviewees qualified their response by adding 'as a woman', focusing the reply 'on professional life', or comparing themselves to significant referents like friends or mother. Only one of our interviewees answered 'Not yet; I don't feel success has reached me', in spite of being the top financial officer for her city. It is evident that most of our interviewees did feel successful at their current career achievement level.

Attributions for success

The next question in our interview was about the factors to which they attributed their current success level. For our analysis, we decided to call 'major themes' those that appeared in at least 50 per cent of cases, and 'minor themes' those showing up in at least 30 per cent. No 'major themes' appeared for this question, but one 'minor theme' did: almost one-third of the women told us that her 'internal motivation' or 'drive' was a major contributor for her success. Other themes that appeared frequently included 'education' (mentioned by almost 30 per cent of respondents) and 'perseverance, stubbornness, commitment' (about 25 per cent). These themes can be exemplified by the following quote:

> Well, a lot has to do with the way I am, I think; mainly, I feel I am a very tenacious, stubborn, constant person; I don't take my finger away from the line; once I set up an objective I go for it hard and ahead. It also has to do with my upbringing, my family, my education; I think it is a set of all things I have lived, but a lot is what I know, I am very stubborn. (Materials and factor analysis manager, 31 years old)

Of course, some respondents also attributed their success to themes that could be classified as 'external' such as 'family support/values', 'work team', 'parental example', 'mentors' or 'hardship/tragedy', but they were mentioned less frequently. This pattern suggests an internal locus of control, which supports qualitatively the results found in the survey component of this research.

Internal attributions

The next question specifically requested respondents to reflect on the factors 'internal' to their person that have contributed to their success. Again, no major themes appeared, but two minor themes (almost four out of ten respondents) that emerged were 'personal motivation' and 'tenacity/ dedication/perseverance'. The next most frequently reported themes (20 per cent of the interviewees) were 'purposeful choices, setting up goals' and 'discipline/responsibility/reliability'. Other themes appearing less frequently included 'desire to help others [in distress sometimes added]', 'finding the right people', 'self-improvement drive', 'respect for others' and 'ability to respond.' A sample quote for internal attributions now follows:

> You see, first, I think that my current success has to do with design . . . I mean, I feel that I have been called and designed to be a successful woman, as have been . . . by design, all men or women . . . I believe in this part. On the other hand, I think that success is also founded in . . . personal work, a definition of a lifestyle . . . obviously I have worked for a leadership style, focused on people and on results, and it has to do with a professional build-up I have been

developing. (Director of a state organization in support of women, retired physician, 51 years old)

External attributions

Next, we asked interviewees to tell us about the external factors that might have contributed to their success. Three minor themes emerged (no major themes): 'education' (almost 40 per cent), 'parental confidence/support', 'mentors/sponsors/role models' (almost one-third). Other frequently mentioned themes included 'husband's belief in interviewee/support' (20 per cent), 'family upbringing' and 'luck' (16 per cent). A sample quote that illustrates these external attributions is:

> Definitely my family upbringing, my parents, next my education, and currently my family support, my husband and the incentive of [having a] son. (Manufacturing and Technology Manager in an automotive-related company, 32 years old)

Important others

The following question explicitly asked about 'the most important people that have contributed to [interviewees'] success'. Major response themes emerged and consisted of 'father' (almost two-thirds of respondents), 'mother' (almost 60 per cent), followed as minor themes by 'a network of support' (an inferred theme as over 40 per cent of the respondents described in their response several different people, clearly suggesting that there was not one person but a network of them to be recognized) and 'husband' (mentioned by one-third). Also worth mentioning are 'educators (former teachers at the university or other level)' and 'current or former bosses', which were put forward by 20 per cent respondents. Sample quotes follow:

> The thing with me is that I wanted to be as good a professional as my father who was an MD because I identified with his ideals but, at the same time, this was a very ambitious standard, am I clear? I had very educated parents; I could not expect to do less than they did. (Director of a state organization in support of women, retired physician [father, an MD, mother with CPA and Engineering degrees who taught at graduate level], 51 years old)

> Many people have contributed [to my success]; initially, my parents that always supported us, my sisters with whom I competed, my classmates in college, my husband who was my classmate and is a very tough competitor, and my teachers. (High-level university administrator, 47 years old)

> at age 18, I was a data clerk in an important company here in [town] . . . I was quite satisfied . . . In order to get this position, I had to stop studying high school and entered a technical school . . . The day I got married, my husband told me: 'I see too much potential in you . . . as to waste it as a data clerk . . . you

should get a college degree . . .' and well, he bought my new books himself . . . so I could finish high school . . . I finished the final three years in nine months and, definitely, if my husband doesn't insist . . . had he not helped, chances are I would have never thought of it, truly. (Manager of a Telco with regional responsibility [over 210 employees], 47 years old)

Gender influences

The following question was whether respondents felt that their gender had any positive or negative effect in their success. A huge 70 per cent of respondents replied that being a woman had a positive effect. At the same time, four out of ten respondents also acknowledged a negative influence of being a woman at work, and about one of seven said that being a woman was no longer an issue in reference to professional success. Illustrative quotes include:

Being a woman actually helped me . . . you see [my friend who opened doors for my business] would take me to the TV station . . . [her husband] would come to pick me up because I did not even have a car and [he] would take me with his wife . . . [she] was a very nice person with me . . . (Retired entrepreneur whose company once had over 200 salespersons, 86 years old)

I never think of that, of course I might get some doors shut in some places, but I never think that it happened because I am a woman; simply that the doors closed, and I move on to a different place, to see where they open up. (Organizational consultant with international expertise, 48 years old)

Well, I think that [being a woman] puts limits to exert a direct participation in every aspect of society, a patriarchal society in which I have had to surpass some forms of discrimination . . . my gender condition has generated greater difficulties, but we have been able to move forward. (Congresswoman, with overseeing responsibilities in an Equity and Gender Commission, 51 years old)

Sometimes people prefer a woman or a man; at the end of the day, if you add or subtract, you end up the same; it's no more or less for being a woman. (Congresswoman, State legislature, 40 years old)

It is evident that some of these responses show some degree of ambivalence. Still, the fact that a large proportion of these successful women who see their gender as a positive or having no influence makes one wonder if there is some trait in them that shields them from the detrimental effects of gender discrimination (luck?) or a 'self-fulfilling prophecy' at play.

Cultural or ethnic influences

When our respondents were asked if the Mexican culture or their personal ethnic background has been a factor for achieving success, the only minor theme (with three out of every nine responses) was that there was *no* effect. On the other hand, almost three out of ten respondents replied that the national expectations (some even widened the scope to 'global') about the roles for women have had a hampering effect in their careers. Other interviewees commented that the Mexican culture with respect to women is changing rapidly for the better, that Mexican women are obtaining increasing respect in international arenas, and that being born into the middle class or having apparent European ascent or roots (for example, white skin or a non-Hispanic last name) is an advantage in today's Mexican society.

> Personally, I don't think so. I think that, in general, if you do things right, if one works as one should, correctly and showing results, I don't think gender affects here; in my personal case, I don't think I have been affected . . . (Fiscal Planning Director in a medium-sized manufacturer, 34 years old)

> *Machismo* was always present; I think that has let us, women, advance very little, and precisely whatever small achievements we have made are because we have snatched it away, or, insisted upon, with more maturity. (Public Manager, 47 years old)

> in Mexico, there is a class structure that has favored me; I belong to the middle class, and any individual in the middle class . . . man or woman, has more possibilities, I believe, of growing and reaching professional success . . . (University full professor of international fame, 54 years old)

> It's a double-edged sword . . . at school I used to be the only fair-skinned girl and then I saw a number of things that have nothing to do with professional success but somehow make a mark . . . you can see how they see you [differently] sometimes . . . (Congresswoman at the national level, 40 years old)

Management/leadership style
When asked about their management and leadership style, the most frequent response (70 per cent) was 'participative/democratic/inclusive of others', the next was 'task focused' (one of seven respondents), but a few respondents unabashedly described themselves as 'authoritarian/paternalist' or 'situational' leaders. Illustrative responses include:

> Democratic . . . listening to the directors' opinions, establishing goals and joint planning, preparing budgets, etc. (State director of a national organization for women's support, past national Senator, 60 years old)

> Authoritarian! [laughter] I am an authoritarian leader, but . . . of course we have meetings . . . about every two weeks, you see. This is to see how the employees are feeling; we have participation because we definitely depend upon them, don't we? And we also want that they are comfortable working with us . . . I am the one in command [laughter] whether they like it or not [laughter], and many times

men, particularly waiters, don't like a woman giving them orders, right? But that is my position and it is my work and my obligation. (Founder and owner of a prestigious restaurant in northern Mexico, 64 years old)

I work in a team, nobody is better than anyone else, I am here by chance, but we are all equal. (Market research director in a large multinational food company, 44 years old)

Religion

Even though this question was not in the original protocol (and for that reason it was not asked systematically of all of our interviewees), the research team realized that a theme that was emerging from our first interviews (particularly in the West Indies) had religious overtones. We then asked a few of our last interviewees to what extent they considered themselves religious people, in addition to paying closer attention to the interviewees' comments about God or their religion. At least 25 per cent of respondents made comments that would at least partially credit God for their success or the opportunities they had to become successful. The few women we asked about their degree of religiosity did not rate themselves very high on this dimension (with one exception).

Still, a symptom of their attention – even potential affinity – to religion was that Jesus Christ and Mother Teresa of Calcutta were frequently mentioned as 'great leaders', a topic that is explained below. One of our respondents even mentioned that splitting her religious and public life was a way for her to cope with any tensions that might show up in this arena. A few women spoke very fondly about their denomination (mostly Catholic but we had one Evangelical), but this seems to be more the exception than the rule.

I have my own judgements or analyses with respect to why religion is important, basic, or fundamental, or my beliefs on the spiritual. (Director of a state organization in support of women, 51 years old)

Yes, of course [I feel successful]; God has given me much more than what I would have thought I could deserve indeed. (Founder and owner of a prestigious restaurant in northern Mexico, 64 years old)

Success in general life

One of the last questions we asked attempted to assess our interviewees' perception of their life success in general. Six of every seven respondents reported feeling successful with their life in general, but the remainder answered to the effect that they are 'not done yet'. No major or minor themes emerged, but most of the responses included family-related concerns (for example, 'having a stable family', 'raising a family', and so on), offering some support to the idea that, for many Mexican women, success in general life is strongly linked to their family roles as mothers and wives. Some other replies had to do with work achievements, teamwork and even with being a 'good daughter' but they were less frequent.

> Yes, I feel successful because I have managed my family life, my personal life and my professional life. It's like a balance and one has to lean towards one [of these aspects] depending on the circumstances. (Top finance officer in a university, 43 years old)

> No, I believe there are many things I still have to achieve. I am thankful for the life I have had, but I feel I still lack many things. (Top auditor in a public organization, 47 years old)

Great leaders or role models

The last question in our protocol asked our respondents to identify one great leader, and then state the characteristics that made this person a great leader (care was taken to make sure the question was enunciated referring to a man or a woman). The most frequently mentioned individuals were Jesus Christ and Mahatma Gandhi (almost one in every five interviewees for each), followed by individuals in their local leadership positions (about one in seven), Mother Theresa of Calcutta (one in ten), the interviewee's mother or father, Nelson Mandela and Beatriz Paredes (former president of the Revolutionary Party). Now, on a second pass with an eye to finding commonalities among the names mentioned, it turns out that the vast majority of these 'great leaders' made (or are in the process of making) a contribution to society in the *political* realm; for example, Margaret Thatcher, John F. Kennedy, Nelson Mandela, Franklin D. Roosevelt, Winston Churchill, Charles de Gaulle, Richard Nixon, Hilary Clinton, Mexican president Vicente Fox (23 respondents came up with one or more of them). Next, the category that captured more attention was *spiritual* and included Jesus Christ, Mahatma Gandhi, and Mother Teresa, as described above. A few others are known for their *intellectual or artistic* legacy: Virginia Wolf, Sor Juana Inés de la Cruz and Diego Rivera. Answers to this question included 23 males and 25 females.

The most frequent reasons given for these choices of great leaders included 'congruency between public and private life' (one in six), 'commitment with their cause', 'principle- or idea-based actions', and 'self-effacing or sacrificing actions' (one in seven). These categories give us an idea of what is important for our interviewees in terms of what a leader should be like or do. Only in two cases did a respondent cite gender-related characteristics: one woman explained that the leader she named had 'broken gender expectations' and another respondent talked about her leader's 'feminine vision of the world'. From these responses, it does not seem that gender would be a strong factor in defining our respondents' work identity.

CONCLUSION

In this chapter, we have shown a variety of statistical evidence suggesting that the institutional environment – legal, governmental, even cultural – for women's work has been steadily improving in Mexico, in spite of the lack of legal enforcement of its laws. We have also reported the results of our Successful Women research project, which indicate that, while there may be many routes to achieving professional success, some useful generalizations and comparisons with other countries can be drawn. This should help both practitioners and academics to design developmental programmes to enable future generations of working women to achieve even higher levels of success than the women of this project.

It is our hope that, within the framework of the Successful Women Worldwide project, this chapter makes a significant contribution to the endeavours to make Mexico a more competitive and a fairer nation for these and future generations.

NOTE

1. We had 29 interviewees, but not all answered all questions; consequently, for some answers, adding up all frequencies results in numbers lower than 29.

10. Successful women: a vision of Brazil

Neusa Maria Bastos F. Santos

Brazil is an integral part of the South American continent. The population of almost 170 million is 50.7 per cent female (IBGE, 2002; Publifolha, 2002). Over 70 per cent of the women work in the formal market. Many of them are successful in their personal and/or professional lives. Here is a quote from one successful Brazilian woman that captures the Brazilian spirit of success:

> A successful person should be before everything else a happy person. Accomplishment leads to human growth, even if it means recognizing human limits. I share the achievements that I have had because the positive results were not achieved alone. This assumes my own mistakes are a learning opportunity that transforms me to be even better. Above all, 'everything is grace'; this is how I want to be a successful person.

POLITICAL, SOCIAL, ECONOMIC AND CULTURAL PANORAMA

Brazil is the largest country in South America, occupying 47 per cent of the South American territorial area, which is divided into five areas – North, North-east, South-east, South and Centre-west. See the map in Figure 10.1. The Brazilian population is composed of several ethnic groups: in the South and South-east German, Italian and Japanese prevail and in the North the African and Dutch prevail. In spite of this great heterogeneity, Brazil does not have any dominant ethnic group. Portuguese is the official language of Brazil, but English is widely spoken in tourist areas. It is a largely Catholic country (88 per cent). Life expectancy is 70 years for women and 63 years for men.

Culturally, Brazil is diverse and heterogeneous, and one can expect to find cultural difference across such a vast country. Nevertheless, according to Hofstede (1980), the Brazilian culture is classified as collectivist, high

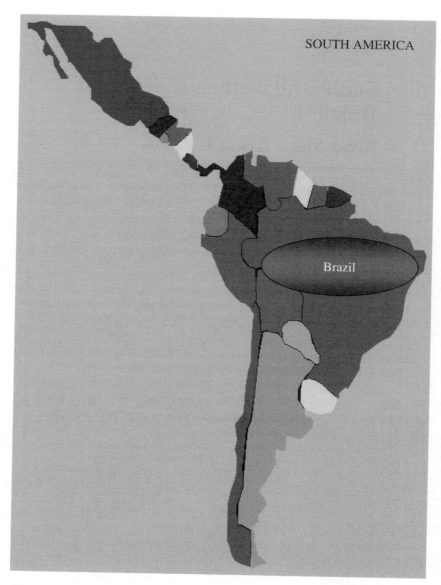

Figure 10.1   Location of Brazil

power distance and having a strong aversion to uncertainty (high on uncertainty avoidance).

WOMEN'S PARTICIPATION IN THE BRAZILIAN JOB MARKET

Between 1985 and 2002, Brazilian women's participation in the labour force grew from 32 per cent to 40 per cent (Bruschini and Lombardi, 2004); in 2002, of the total of 28.7 million formal jobs, 11.4 million represented the female population. Over 70 per cent of the women worked in the formal market. This tendency is also consistent with jobs in the public service; in 1985, 16.3 per cent of the female jobs were contracted in the public sector and by 2002 this percentage had increased to 31.8 per cent. In 1992, 83.6 per cent of the positions of female work were governed by CLT (Consolidation of Labour Laws). In the past 17 years, labour market trends found in the public sector were duplicated in the areas of the education and health.

According to Ministry of Education and Culture (MEC), women are not studying in the areas of science, mathematics, computing, agriculture, veterinary, engineering, production and construction. The great contingent of women is still concentrated in the areas of education, services, health, humanities and arts, social sciences and business, in this respective order.

SUCCESSFUL WOMEN: A VISION OF BRAZIL

According to Godinho et al. (2005), Brazilian women have travelled a long road in their search for educational opportunities. Today, women are at all levels of education, and at the university level their achievements are superior to those of men – according to the MEC (2005), of 100 graduates, 37 men and 63 women complete higher education. Although women's educational achievements are impressive, and the proportion of women in higher education is growing every year, this has not translated into increased salaries. Women have, nevertheless progressed substantially in Brazil in recent years as we see in the following discussion of various groups.

Academic Women

In 1996, women's participation as teachers at the higher education level was 38.7 per cent and by 2003 this had risen to 43.4 per cent. Women's participation in teaching also inspired an increase in women with master's and doctorate degrees. In 1996, there were 20 622 women (44 per cent of the total) with master's degrees versus 24 860 men (56 per cent) men. By 2003, the number of women reached 45 263, while the number of men increased to 51 247 – women's share had increased by 3 per cent to 47 per cent of the total. In 1996, there were 10 504 women (34 per cent of the total) with doctorates versus 20 569 men (66 per cent). In 2003, the number of women reached 21 431, while for the men it increased to 34 807 – women's participation had increasd by 4 per cent to 38 per cent.

Women Entrepreneurs

Women's participation in Brazil's job market is growing every year (GEM, 2003). In 2000, women's participation was only 29 per cent compared with 71 per cent for men. By 2003, women's participation has risen dramatically to 46 per cent. Sixty-four per cent of Brazilian women entrepreneurs are aged between 25 and 44 years, 61 per cent are married and 32 per cent single.

Executive Women

According to Bruschini and Puppin (2004), of the 42 276 management positions in Brazil, 23.6 per cent were occupied by women. In management positions women are usually in community and social services (50.2 per cent), cultural services (47.3 per cent), social services (42.2 per cent) and clinical services and hospitals (30.5 per cent). Several researchers (Bruschini and Lombardi, 2004; Bruschini and Puppin, 2004; Junqueira, 2001; Pecht, 1999; Puppin, 1994; Santos, 1999; 2000; Soares, 2001) have found that women have more opportunities to reach higher positions in public administration than in the private sector. Women hold 21 per cent of the management positions in the private sector compared with 44.8 per cent in the public sector.

The earlier discussion illustrated the progress that Brazilian women have made in the world of work in recent years. This discussion also highlighted the challenges that women still face. In spite of the challenges, women in Brazil, as elsewhere, have often achieved substantial success. The objective of the remainder of this chapter is to illustrate and discuss the characteristics and success of the Brazilian women included in the research project. We begin by presenting the information relating to the survey and then turn to the results of the interviews.

SURVEY DATA COLLECTION AND RESULTS

The survey consisted of 505 questionnaires, distributed to successful female academics, entrepreneurs and executives. The response rate was

41.6 per cent – a total of 210 respondents, comprising 53 (25.23 per cent) academics, 52 (24.77 per cent) entrepreneurs and 105 (50 per cent) executives. Job titles included managers, directors, lawyers, professors and vice-presidents. The following is a summary of the main findings.

Demographics

One hundred seventy-eight (84.76 per cent) of the women worked full time and 23 (10.95 per cent) were employed part time. Their average age was 42.81 years (ranging from 21 to 75). Ninety-eight (46.67 per cent) were married, 60 (28.57 per cent) single and 15 (18.57 per cent) divorced. The average number of children was 1.08, but some had up to five children.

In terms of birth order of the women themselves, 86 (40.95 per cent) are eldest children, 47 (22.38 per cent) youngest children, 45 (21.43 per cent) middle children and 22 (10.48 per cent) only children. Regarding education level, 35 (16.67 per cent) of the successful Brazilian women have a university education, 42 (20 per cent) have master's degrees and 32 (15.23 per cent) doctorates.

Mentoring

Mentors had a moderate influence in the psychological aspects (mean = 3.65). The entrepreneurs' mentoring score is significantly higher than that for executives and academics. The mean for career mentoring was 3.54, indicating the mentors also had a moderate influence with regard to women's careers. (See Appendix D.)

Personality Characteristics

The results of the measures of personality characteristics – self-efficacy, locus of control and need for achievement – were:

- *Self-efficacy*: the mean was 4.07, indicating a high level of self-efficacy.
- *Locus of control*: the mean was 2.46 indicating an internal locus of control.
- *Need for achievement*: the mean was 12.42, indicating a high need for achievement.

Cultural Characteristics

The results of the measures of culture – individualism/collectivism, power distance and uncertainty avoidance – were:

- *Individualism/collectivism*: the mean was 3.55, indicating a slight tendency towards collectivism. In contrast, Hofstede's earlier results had suggested that Brazilians were more strongly collective.
- *Power distance*: the mean was 2.02, indicating low power distance (note that the internal consistency for this scale is somewhat low, 0.57; therefore, these results should be considered with some caution). In contrast, Hofstede's earlier results had suggested that Brazilians were high on power distance.
- *Uncertainty avoidance*: the mean was 3.73, indicating a somewhat high aversion to uncertainty. Hofstede's earlier work had also indicated that Brazilians were high on uncertainty avoidance.

Satisfaction

Satisfaction includes the degree to which the successful women were satisfied with their professional and personal life. The mean was 6.13 (on a scale of 1 to 7), indicating a high degree of satisfaction among the successful women in relation to their work and personal lives.

INTERVIEW DATA COLLECTION AND RESULTS

Seventeen interviews were conducted with 12 executives, three academics and two entrepreneurs who live and work in the city of São Paulo. The executives were in accounting, banking, consulting, cosmetics, human resources management (a public company), law and real estate. The entrepreneurs were in accounting and jewellery. The following summarizes the results of the interviews

Demographic Profile of Successful Women

Nine (52.94 per cent) women were born in São Paulo; 88.24 per cent (15) were descendants of Europeans. In their own families, 76 per cent (14) of the women were oldest daughters, and they had a maximum of two siblings. Twelve (70.59 per cent) of the successful Brazilian women interviewed were married, four (23.53 per cent) were single and one (5.88 per cent) woman was widowed. Ten of the women (58.82 per cent) did not have any children, four (23.53 per cent) had two children, and three (17.65 per cent) had only one child. Eleven of the women (64.71 per cent) possessed university degrees; the medium age was 46 years, (with a range of 30 to 66 years). Nine (52.94 per cent) have domestic help (maids) that aids them in the administration of the home. They have almost no help from the husband or other family members in domestic responsibilities.

The Impact of Religion

In terms of religion, there was a predominance of Catholicism – nine of the successful women interviewed were Catholic. For these successful women, religion did not affect their careers; they are not practising, but they believe in God, whom they seek more as spiritual support and faith.

> I am Catholic . . . religion didn't affect my career. I am not a person that frequents Mass regularly. I prefer to speak with God when I have the need. The companies that I worked for are not interested in my religion. (Technology manager of a Brazilian bank)

> I'm Catholic. In spite of not frequenting the church, I believe in God. My religion had little affect on my career. But believing in God always gave me more strength to struggle, for believing that he would be at my side protecting me. (Project manager of a consultancy)

A second group comprised eight women who were non-Catholic or non-religious; they were Christian, Kardecists, Buddhists, Espiristas, and Cabbalist. For all of these women, their beliefs helped to establish patterns of values, ethics and norms of conduct that were transported to the world of the work and for their own lives.

> Kardecist and apprentice . . . it helped me to establish relationship criteria and norm of conduct. (Process manager of a large Brazilian bank)

> I don't have religion, I am a student of Logosófia, that is a science . . . Logosófica affected my career in the sense of ethics, morals, and in having better relationship with my fellow persons. (Teacher and partner-director of an accounting office)

The Impact of Education

Of the 17 interviewees, five stated that education was important for their professional success, particularly because it is necessary to stay current in one's profession.

> Constant investment in education, to be up to date in my profession. (Technology manager of a Brazilian bank)

> Without a doubt, education. It is understood as an accomplishment and updating through courses, participation in conferences. I try to read and I learn a lot

in contact with the people. (Graduate Programme working for Co-ordinator a public university)

The Impact of Gender

The Brazilian women were divided on the subject of gender. Ten women felt that 'being a woman' had no negative effect on their professional path, but also that it did not help them – they did not receive any privileges because they were women. Gender was a neutral factor in their success.

> I never suffered any discrimination, but I also had never had any privilege for being a woman. (Project manager)

Three women explained that 'being a woman' did not affect their careers because they work in companies where there is a larger contingent of women in management positions. Two women also stated that, until a certain point in their careers, being female did not affect their professional paths, however, if they wanted to move to higher levels, they will face barriers because of their organizations' culture.

> In my work, I never suffered discrimination for being woman. Maybe because, in my area, the majority are women. (Accounting manager of a Brazilian bank)

> In my profession . . . if I try for higher positions, depending on the company, I can find barriers in obtaining such positions because of 'machismo' or organizational culture. (Technology manager of a Brazilian bank)

Seven successful women interviewed stated that because of organizational culture they were skipped over for promotions at the highest levels in the organization; they work with men with 'macho' personalities that hinder and delay their career development. The 'macho' aspect of Brazilian society and its impact on women's professional success was a major issue, as the following quotes emphasize.

> The Brazilian culture is very macho, this impedes us, a lot of times, and we are passed over for higher positions in the organization. (Technology manager of a Brazilian bank)

> No matter how much it is spoken in the women's emancipation and in society, the Brazilian culture is macho, which sometimes interrupts women's professional growth. (Back-office manager of a Brazilian bank)

> The Brazilian machismo disrupts the women's ascension into the leadership positions. (Project manager of consultancy of computer science)

While the 'macho' culture in Brazil was mentioned by many of the women, some also felt that Brazil was changing in this regard.

> Brazil is a country where machismo still exists . . . it is a cultural problem, but in some segments it is already starting to dissipate. In spite of having an Italian background and being the only girl with three brothers, the women in my family (my grandmothers and my mother) were always part of a matriarchy. (Process manager a great Brazilian bank)

> On the international scene, in other words, when I have participated in international seminars and courses, a lot of people were surprised to find a Brazilian that spoke English and who is interested in International Rights. Culturally, our country has inherent barriers from a past that no longer of exists, but many people outside of Brazil are still not convinced of that. (Lawyer)

Internal Factors

Among the 17 women interviewed, nine affirmed that motivation, persistence and willpower were fundamental to reach the objectives for their professional and personal lives. Some executives said:

> Perseverance and persistence . . . (Process manager of a large Brazilian bank)

> Motivation to reach results, a lot of internal force during the accomplishment of plans . . . persistence. (Co-ordinator of postgraduate course in a public university)

> Willpower and perseverance. I wanted to be an executive woman and I struggled to reach my objective. (Accountant)

External Factors

While internal factors were clearly very important to the successful Brazilian women, external factors were also mentioned. Opportunity and recognition of their work were mentioned frequently. Seven women thought that their success also came from taking advantage of the opportunities that they were offered, and were the fruits of recognition of their work.

> I look to take advantage of the opportunities that appear. I make an effort to 'win' with events that are sad, negative, or frustrating in my life (for not losing more than is already lost – I don't like to win 100 per cent). These opportunities are very important . . . (Graduate Programme Co-ordinator working for in a public university)

> The company in which I work provides me opportunities for professional growth, because they believed in my work. (Accounting manager of a Brazilian bank)

I would say that opportunity is a fundamental factor in the conquest of success, as well as alliances with influential people in prominent positions . . . Education is also important. (Technology manager of a Brazilian bank)

Leadership Style

Sixteen of the interviewees described their leadership style as participative and collective, and said that work is valued by the team. Their leadership styles are shared, and are not authoritarian.

I am a direct person, participative, [I] delegate functions and responsibilities, this way allowing, people to grow . . . I delegate responsibilities. (Technology manager of a Brazilian bank).

To work in team; vision participation; balance between reason and sensibility; to know to delegate tasks; to divide knowledge and to inspire trust. (Teacher and accountant)

Participative, advisory, collective. I am a person that delegates responsibilities . . . I have under my command more than 50 people. (Back-office manager of a Brazilian bank)

Support and Mentoring and Success

Five (married women) of the 17 Brazilian women interviewed stated that family support and the support of their husband were important to help them in the growth of their careers, as they tell the interviewees:

My family was the main factor that contributed to my success, because my parents were enterprising people and they have had their own business more than 30 years . . . they motivated me to have my own business. (Entrepreneur, jewellery)

Temperament for the work and a lot of co-operation of my husband has motivated my career. (Graduate Programme Commission President working for an outstanding private university)

The women's answers with respect to mentoring specifically were quite varied. The successful women look for mentoring as psychological support from a very early stage in their careers. This support is seen as showing the women the appropriate values, norms and behaviours in business, and giving advice on how to act in the business world. Family members were especially important in the Brazilian sample. Seven women mentioned their mother as mentors, six their father, four their husband, four teachers, and only one mentioned her boss as a mentor.

My parents always taught me that difficulties don't exist, there is willpower and determination. They were the people in which I mirrored myself in several aspects. I remember that I had a manager, about 20 years ago, who motivated me, forcing me to overcome barriers. (Process manager of a large Brazilian bank)

My mother did not distinguish between the boys and girls in the sense of education, domestic tasks, freedom to go out at night. My father is also a mentor, guiding me in the steps to reach in a profession. My husband always motivates me and, in my absences, having the pleasure to be with our daughter . . . (Teacher and partner-director of an accounting office)

My husband. With certainty, his support was fundamental for my growth, because, we shared all our activities in relation to administration of the home and our children's education; this allowed me, in a certain way, to be devoted to my career. (Back-office manager of a Brazilian bank)

My sister – she always struggled and she got what she wanted, and for me she was always a great example, and she gave me great advice. (Project manager)

Satisfaction with Personal and Professional Life

Nine of the 17 women said they were happy and satisfied with their personal and professional lives, but the answers were quite varied as the quotes below illustrate:

In a certain way, yes. I never had children and I don't know to what extent my life would be different if I had them. I cannot deny that, as with other woman, I was born with the natural maternal instinct. Maybe not having children is why I am so devoted to my professional career. No matter how superficial it may seem, success is measured in relation to having material goods, but we cannot forget that success is also personal accomplishment. To have pleasure in what we do is also to reach success. (Process manager of a major Brazilian bank)

Yes, I am satisfied, but I would like to conquer some areas of my life. I have a family that I love, an affectionate husband, and a work that I adore to do. (Back-office manager of a Brazilian bank)

In contrast, eight women were unsatisfied for several reasons. One of the reasons is attributed to the conquest of material goods. Some feel that they could have done even better in their professional activities, others had difficulties reconciling their careers with their personal lives. One woman attributed her dissatisfaction to her own personality style – always looking for new challenges and constant growth.

In development . . . I am recognized as a serious professional, but I look for much more. I would like to know more . . . to be more competent, happier personally and professionally . . . I need more time to be home with my husband and daughters . . . (Co-ordinator of postgraduate course in a public university)

[I am] somebody that is always unsatisfied with what I did, thinking I could have done more and better. I would like to write more, to publish more . . . (President of the postgraduate courses in a private university)

CONCLUSION

Based on the research conducted in Brazil, we can conclude that Brazilian women are moving into higher-level positions of the organization, in spite of the relatively small number today. Brazilian women want to expand their participation in public society. In spite of this, prejudices still impede women's participation in several segments of society – in positions of power in both politics and organizations. These prejudices promote professional segregation into feminine and masculine work categories, contributing to the salary divergence between men and women. Brazilian society needs to find new ways of living with gender differences, respecting these differences and creating new policies for men and women to work together. For Brazilian women to obtain a competitive advantage they must invest substantially in education, look for new work opportunities and, at the same time, reconcile their professional and personal lives

Brazilian women were similar to the successful women from other countries in the study. Brazilian women possess high levels of self-efficacy, a high need for achievement and an internal locus of control. As with the women in other countries, the quantitative and qualitative data together provide a picture of successful women who are highly motived and hard-working. The Brazilian women are generally satisfied – the surveys indicated a high level of satisfaction, but interviewees raised some issues to be considered in terms of satisfaction. Uniformly, the successful Brazilian women described their leadership as paricipative and focusing on teamwork.

The cultural values expressed by the Brazilian women were somewhat different from those described in the Hofstede (1980) study. The women were moderate on individualism/collectivism, although somewhat more collective, whereas Hofstede had described Brazil as quite collective. They were low on power distance, whereas Hofstede had described Brazil as high on power distance. The women's relatively high score on uncertainty avoidance was essentially consistent with Hofstede's findings.

11. Argentina: returning to its glorious past

Silvia Inés Monserrat, Griselda Lassaga and Claudia D'Annunzio

To the rest of the world, Argentina means 'tango', 'pampas' and 'soccer'. In the past few years Argentina could also mean 'crisis and default'. In fact, Argentina is all of that – and much, much more. Among the 200 countries in the world, Argentina is the eighth largest nation in terms of territory, after Russia, Canada, China, the USA, Brazil, Australia and India (Microsoft® Encarta® Online Encyclopedia, 2005). In 2005, Argentina had a population of 39 537 943, giving the country an overall population density of 14 persons per square kilometre (37 per square mile), one of the lowest in the world. More than one-third of the population lives in or around Buenos Aires; 90 per cent of the people live in urban areas.

Located in South America (Figure 11.1), Argentina has an area of almost 2.3 million square miles. It is 2300 miles long, from north to south. Argentina's main geographic characteristic is the enormous contrast between the immense eastern plains and the impressive Andes mountain range to the west. Owing to its vast land mass, the country displays a great variety of climates, from the hot and dry north-western provinces, to the cold and rainy forests of the Patagonian Andes.

Argentina's cultural roots are mainly European, and this is clearly reflected in its architecture, music, literature and lifestyle. The people of Argentina share a feeling of being somewhat European. However, because Argentina is located so far to the south in the southern hemisphere, it suffers the consequences of being isolated from the most important economic and cultural centres of the northern hemisphere. Geographically and psychologically, Argentina is viewed as a distant country – far away for trading and far away for travelling. Argentina is too far away to be well known by the rest of the world.

Nowadays, because of technology and mass media, this vast 'distance' has begun to be overcome. Argentina's place in the world will no longer depend as much on its geographic situation, as on its technological development.

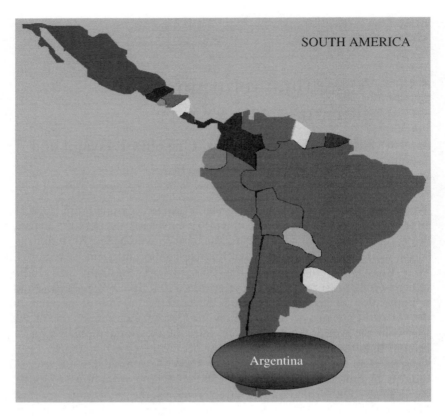

Figure 11.1   Location of Argentina

HISTORICAL AND CULTURAL BRUSHSTROKES

Argentina is by far the 'most European' country in Latin America, with 97 per cent of the population of Spanish, Italian, British and German ethnic origin. Large-scale European immigration in the decades after 1880 reaffirmed the European ties, spurring modernization and development (Sennholz, 1982). Argentineans feel European, and have grown up looking towards Europe. On the questionnaires, when asked about their race or ethnic background, more than 50 per cent answered 'European'. One woman stated:

> We all feel ourselves as Europeans. (Sociologist, ex-politician, feminist activist, married, four children, born in 1949)

By the 1930s, Argentina had the seventh largest economy in the world. During this period, it was considered the 'barn of the world' because a large portion of the world depended on Argentina's agricultural exports. But in 1930 General Uriburu began a revolution against Hipólito Yrigoyen's constitutional government. With Uriburu's revolution, the black history of military dictatorship began. From 1930 until the end of the twentieth century, 24 different presidents governed Argentina, of whom only 12 were constitutionally elected (Monserrat-Lluna, 2000). This was arguably one of the causes of what happened to Argentina's economy. In 2002 in terms of GDP, Argentina had fallen to twenty-fourth place, but in terms of GDP per capita Argentina had fallen to the seventieth place.

In 1983 Argentina returned to democracy after seven years of military government. That period, because of intense fighting between 'guerrilleros' and the state, was called the time of the 'dirty war'. Since 1983 three presidents have governed the country: two from the 'Peronista party', the other from the 'Unión Cívica Radical' party. These are the two parties that most influenced Argentina's contemporary history.

In recent decades, Argentina has experienced both inflation and recession. Privatization and other economic reforms begun by President Menem in the early 1990s produced unprecedented economic growth, but significant economic problems remained, including high unemployment and a massive national debt. The economy was hurt by Brazil's recession and currency devaluation in the late 1990s, but the pegging of the peso to the dollar and other reforms requested by the International Monetary Fund, combined with Argentina's own economic problems, resulted in economic collapse in 2001. The economy did not begin to grow strongly again until 2003. In 2004, Argentina's economy was growing at a brisk 11 per cent, exports were surging and poverty was declining. Dr Robert Lavagna, Minister of Economy, has been very successful in negotiating foreign debt.

As discussed in Chapters 1 and 3, the SWW research examines three of Hofstede's variables (Hofstede, 1984). Argentina appears to be moderately low on power distance, similar to the USA and Canada. Implications for the workplace include:

- subordinates expect to be consulted
- boss should be resourceful democrat
- inequalities between people should be minimized
- organizational hierarchy is viewed as exploitative.

In the current study, women interviewed demonstrated a low power distance with the following quotes:

> There are not hierarchies. I have a friendly relationship with my employees. (Entrepreneur, single, no children, born in 1968, small business owner, high school education)

> I accept suggestions; I like my employees to participate in the business. (Small business owner, general manager, widow, no children. She did not want to say her date of birth but she is over 65)

Argentina is also high on uncertainty avoidance, similar to Chile, Brazil and Mexico. A high level of this characteristic indicates low tolerance for uncertainty and ambiguity. This creates a rules-oriented society that institutes laws, regulations and controls in order to reduce the amount of uncertainty. Argentina is moderately collectivist on individualism/ collectivism, more so than the USA and Canada, but less so than Chile. Argentineans are friendly people, who enjoy being together, studying together and working together in teams. This cultural preference may explain why Argentina's athletic championships have always been in team sports (soccer, volleyball, basketball). However, that preference does not prevent individuals from making decisions that need to be made, regardless of what their teammates may think.

> I had very good teams; I believe a lot in teamwork, colleagues that have worked with me and have contributed to success in my long diplomatic career . . . No one does anything alone. (Lawyer, career diplomat, postgraduate, single without children, born in 1940)

> I like working on teams. I am consultative. But if I am sure about something, the decision is always mine . . . (I) do not care what they say to me. (Organizational consultant, entrepreneur, divorced, two children, born in 1954)

> The final decision on my enterprise is mine. (Accountant, MBA, entrepreneur, married, one son, born in 1959)

WOMEN IN ARGENTINA

Education Rate

Women attend school at a greater rate than men. In the major urban areas, women's (from 15 to 17 years old) education rate is 84.6 per cent while it is 78.6 per cent for men. For, students between 18 and 24 years, the rate are 48.6 per cent for women and 41.5 per cent for men (SIEMPRO, 1999).

Labour Force Participation

In the past decade, Argentina's female labour force increased (1990 = 27.4 per cent, 2001 = 33.2 per cent, 2004 = 48.5 per cent) (INDEC, 2005). Despite legal prohibitions, perhaps because the country remains a patriarchal society, there is still discrimination against women, making it more difficult for women to be considered equal to men. On average, women are paid 75 per cent of men's pay for equivalent work (Correia, 1998). But this gap is the lowest in Latin America, and compares favourably to many industrialized countries. The gender gap narrows for women with more education and, for women aged 14 to 49, the less education and the older the women, the wider the gap.

POLITICIANS: FROM EVA PERÓN TO CRISTINA KIRCHNER

The struggle for women's emancipation was long and had its very beginning in the early years of the twentieth century. During the decades of the 1920s and 1930s, Alicia Moreau de Justo and Carolina Muzzili, socialist activists, demanded women's suffrage. In 1934 the first Argentinean woman, Dr Ema Costa, was elected in a provincial election. But it was not until 1947, during Domingo Peron's presidency, that women were given rights to run for national election. Today 48 per cent of Argentina's voting population are women.

Eva Duarte de Perón, as First Lady of Argentina, was supportive of women's suffrage. The first national election with the participation of women was held on 11 November 1951. Eva Perón went beyond securing the formal right to vote; she brought the need to increase women's participation in the political process to the very centre of the Peronista Party. Owing to her influence, a quota law created the 'Women's branch' of the Peronista Party. In 1951 women got 15.5 per cent of the total seats in the lower house and by 1955, the number had increased to 22 per cent. But this did not remain stable in subsequent periods of political turbulence. From the return to democracy in 1983 until 1991, an average of only 4 per cent of the legislators elected to the Chamber of Deputies were women. In 1991, legislation was passed (the Quota Law) which contained two important requirements (Jones, 1995):

1. That a minimum of 30 per cent of all candidates on the party lists in all 24 electoral districts be women (Argentina elects its national deputies via a closed list arrangement).

2.   That these women be placed in elected positions on the lists and not only in decorative positions providing little chance of election.

In the 1993 Chamber election, following the implementation of the law, 21.3 per cent of the deputies elected were women, compared with only 4.6 per cent in the election of 1991. But victory is still very far away. (Htun, 2000). As of 2000, there were only three women state secretaries, and five vice-secretaries Furthermore, of the 25 provinces, there was not a single woman governor, and only four vice-governors.

What is true is that women's leadership in Latin America has changed (Htun, 2000). Argentina is not an exception. In the past, women who attained power were wives (more commonly, widows), daughters or sisters of prominent men. Isabel Peron, the only woman president Argentina has had, was Peron's wife, and arrived at the presidency because of Peron's death. In contrast, today Cristina Fernandez de Kirchner (President Kirchner's wife) has won her own political position, and she is Senator because of her attitude and skills, not because of her marital situation. Today, Cristina Fernandez de Kirchner is considered by many to be a leading figure in Argentine politics.

METHOD

Argentina's surveys were collected by three researchers from Universidad Nacional del Centro, a public university located in the centre of Buenos Aires Province. A fourth researcher from Universidad de Belgrano provided expertise on issues related to professional women.

PARTICIPANTS

The first barrier for the survey was that in Argentina there was no place from which to obtain a list of professional women. A database needed to be built by searching the Internet and contacting women who had reached high-level positions or were well known because of their work, their professions or their enterprises.

Argentina's population distribution is quite skewed. Of a total female population of 18 601 058, almost 46 per cent live in Buenos Aires City and Buenos Aires Province, about 8 per cent live in Cordoba province and fewer than 4 per cent live in the remaining 22 provinces of the country. To reflect this population distribution, the researchers' decision was to sample women living in Buenos Aires, Greater Buenos Aires (representing 32 per cent of the total population of women in the country) and Tandil. Questionnaires to women living in Buenos Aires and Greater Buenos Aires were sent by e-mail; surveys to women living in Tandil were distributed in person. An association for women entrepreneurs, with online services, distributed the questionnaires to their associates who had owned an enterprise for at least three years. The average time in business for Argentinean's women entrepreneurs surveyed was 15 years.

The first attempt to reach women was during the last quarter of 2002. By then Argentina was going through a great economical, political and social crisis. Perhaps because of heightened feelings and concerns at that time, few responses were obtained. During the second half of 2003, and at the beginning of 2004, data collection resumed, and 105 surveys were returned. In addition, 97 undergraduate students (men and women) from both universities were used as a comparison group.

The final sample comprised executives (14.3 per cent), entrepreneurs (45.7 per cent), academics (7.6 per cent), professionals (26.7 per cent) and public officials (5.7 per cent). Of the respondents, 59.4 per cent were employed full time, 32.7 per cent were self-employed and only 7.9 per cent were employed part time. Also, 53.5 per cent were married, 26.7 per cent were divorced, and 18.8 per cent were single. In terms of birth order and gender of siblings, 44.1 per cent were the eldest, and 44.8 per cent had brothers and sisters. The educational level of the respondents was quite high: 96 per cent had superior studies, 18.4 per cent some college, 47.6 per cent were college graduates, and almost 30 per cent were postgraduates.

THE VOICES OF SUCCESSFUL ARGENTINEAN WOMEN

A second part of the study consisted of in-depth interviews to further probe issues related to the success of women in Argentina. Ten successful women were interviewed.

Success Defined in Their Own Words

Success is counted sweetest. (Emily Dickinson)

When asked if they considered themselves successful, the women we interviewed were split into two camps: those who rejected the very notion of 'success' and those who embraced it. The first group felt 'success' was somehow a frivolous notion, impossible to apply to a scientific or academic career. For these women the word – not the significance we give in this successful women project – was in some way embarrassing.

> I don't know what the definition of successful really is.

> Yes, [I feel successful] but with a very low profile. I feel embarrassed even though I recognize some characteristics (of successful women).

> It is difficult to describe myself as a successful person, but I think I have achieved all the goals I've set for myself.

> In general I don't use that word to describe myself. I think I've been a lucky person, especially in my professional career . . .

This is one woman who said success was both material and non-material, as discussed in Chapter 2:

> Yes, but not only a material success, an economic success. Yes, I do feel myself to be successful.

The other women, most of them entrepreneurs with risk-taking personalities, were happy to speak about 'success' and to consider themselves successful.

> Yes, I think in life there are always successes and failures. I'm happy with what I have achieved in this business.

> Yes I consider myself successful.

> I feel successful; I got to the top positions at foreign office.

> I think so. I am not a humble person.

> Yes, I think so. The business has grown from 1995 to now. And I can say I have grown from having nothing to having four successful businesses.

Being a Woman in Argentina

In the past few decades Argentina's families have changed. The recent tendency is to have smaller families. The fertility rate decreased (from 3.0 children per woman in 1980 to 2.47 in 2000 and 2.24 in 2004); at the same time the divorce rate has increased. Almost 30 per cent of families are headed by women (INDEC, 2005). In our study, Argentinean women have the highest rate of divorce: almost four times that of Canada and more than double that of the women from the USA.

The working Argentinean woman does not forget that domestic labour is her duty. Employing domestic help is part of the national way of life and almost all interviewees indicated they employed some domestic help. Some husbands and children contribute to domestic work, but never equally to women. In fact, it does not matter how successful an Argentinean woman is, her family will be waiting for home-made food upon returning home. When the children need to stay at home, because of illness or vacation time, or just because the nurse did not come to work, mothers are expected to stay home with them. Despite all of this, professional women in Argentina do not give up on having a family (Heller, 1996; in press). In fact 76 per cent of our sample have children and of these women, 33.7 per cent have at least two and 25 per cent have more than two children. The concerns of Argentinean women are how to balance family and work, rather than whether or not to have children. This explains why marital status was viewed by our interviewees as central to their feelings of personal success. Success was very closely related to achieving family goals and, perhaps because of our Judeo-Christian socialization when growing up, divorce is very much seen as a frustration that whittles away at our sense of having achieved personal success. This is evident in the words of three divorced respondents:

> No, because I had to make a great effort to develop my professional goals at the same time as I developed my personal ones. Only recently have I become more balanced.

> No, I had only one family and because the family broke down (she divorced), I could not consider that a success.

> No, I would never have wanted to be an entrepreneur, a corporation woman. I would have wanted to be a mother with many children. This was not in my plans.

Meanwhile the married women answered:

> Yes, I do feel myself as successful.

> Yes, I have been. Especially successful because of the family I have.

Gender

As with most Latino cultures, Argentina is pretty 'machista'. During the period of 1870 through to 1929, women were considered incapable (Novick, 2001). Even today, despite legal prohibitions and international agreements, Argentina's mainly patriarchal society still encourages discrimination against women, from unequal pay to gender-specific recruitment advertising.

Eva Perón, surely the best-known Argentinean woman, said:

> The world suffers a great absence: women.
> Everything, absolutely everything in this contemporary world had been
>   built following men's measures.
> We are absent in governments
> We are absent in Parliaments
> On International organism
> We are not in the Vatican or the Kremlin
> . . . We are not on the Atomic Energy Commission
> Or in big consortiums
> We are not on secret societies
> We are not in any of the great centres that constitutes power in the world
> Despite that we have been always in agony times and in all bitter
>   humanity's hours . . . (Eva Perón, 1997)

Do the perceptions of our Argentinean interviewees bear out the reality
that in this country gender remains a barrier to women's professional
success? Let us hear their voices.

> I feel that things are more difficult for women. At this university, especially,
> where most of the students and the graduates are males.

> In general, in this society where we live . . . women view successful women with
> envy . . .

> Well I also thought that gender was indifferent to me, but now I have a male
> partner, and I understand that males are able to open doors that are usually
> locked for women. My work context is a female world, but now my partner is
> opening doors to the corporate world for me. And the corporate world is a male
> world.

> You might think that since my business is related to the beauty and cosmetic
> industry, the fact of being a woman is a positive aspect. However, in real life it
> is not like that. Most businesses are run by men, and although they use women
> as their visible face, the leadership belongs to them.

But not all of them perceive gender discrimination:

> I never feel my gender was a barrier.

> I have never believed in gender differences. Although my business in particular
> is a man's world everybody respects me.

The rest of the successful Argentinean women interviewed suggest there is
a balance between positive and negative aspects of being a women:

Has contributed a lot. There are like two different questions. In some aspects it has contributed [positively] and in others I have had to fight. There have been many more years in which we women have been discriminated against. It is always easier if you are male.

I don't think of any aspects as positive or negative, but of course mostly there are men everywhere I go: congress, suppliers, negotiations . . . It is weird because making marmalade is a woman's job, but in industry men are in the majority, women's participation is very low.

Attribution of Success: Internal and External Factors

I can see a balance between internal and external factors.

The Argentinean women's voices confirm this tendency. A common theme was their determination for success is a sum of all things, a balance between internal and external factors. And not very surprisingly, women who had lived in Argentina during its worst 50 years of history, expressed the belief that internal factors are not enough when you have to survive and try to achieve your goals in an unstable environment. A woman who had experienced that period of Argentina's history explained:

I can see a balance between internal and external factors. One matter has to do with the other. It goes from what is external to what we create. Motivation? I was driven by my hunger for having my own business.

Internal factors
In Chapter 3, locus of control was introduced as a key characteristic related to professional success.

In analysing the results of the surveys it was determined that the successful women had a significantly greater self-efficacy (women = 4.06, students control group mean = 3.61); internal locus of control (women = 2.45, students 2.49), need for achievement (women = 12.80, students = 10.46) and were more satisfied (women = 6.13, students = 5.64) than the undergraduates. (See Appendix D.) Appendix D shows that in our survey, the successful women of Argentina were less internal (2.45), along with Brazil, than the successful women of the USA, Mexico, Canada, Jamaica/Barbados and Chile.

Elaborating on the internal causes of their own success, the women mentioned several key themes, including dedication, tenacity, determination, natural skills, disciplined work and strong personality in general. When asked to what to they attribute their success, they said:

It's a sum of all things, not only one of those items [motivation, internal factors, external factors] all are interesting . . .

Because I worked hard.

I am a good 'storm pilot' . . . a strong personal actor . . .

It required hours and hours of hard work. Determination, I had to fight to get what I have now, it was not easy.

My natural skills.

To an internal work discipline . . . to be open-minded . . .

I am very determined in what I do.

To my personality. How I am, especially internal factors.

'To tenacity and to work.'

External factors

When asked about external factors related to their success, Argentineans' choices were: luck, family upbringing, education and work teams.

I had a little bit of luck . . . My family education, my formal education in Argentina . . . I had very good teams; I believe a lot in teamwork.

I think I've been lucky . . . I grew up, with [role] models . . .

My education, my formal education, the university.

How we grow up in our family. What we receive from our families.

Education is vital.

But also luck.

Relationships with peers and family orientation.

Mentors   The results for mentoring in Argentina were very unpredictable. Previous international research connects success to mentoring (See Chapters 2 and 6). In Argentina we did not find any literature on this particular theme. Often, mentoring in Argentina appears to be an informal relationship between a mentor and a mentee, perhaps based on their proximity (work, family, studies, and so on, but not because of a formal programme). This was confirmed by the results from our survey, in which psychosocial and career mentoring (mean = 3.51 and 3.47 respectively) were not as high as might be expected from the literature on mentoring. Furthermore, when asked if they were mentors, over 84 per cent reported that they were not. Because of the absence of 'mentoring roles' and 'mentoring programmes' from Argentinean work culture, these results are not surprising. In addition, 52 per cent of the respondents of the survey who themselves had been mentored, indicated that the topic of workplace mentoring needs to be studied in future research.

It is noteworthy that when the interviewees stated that they had mentors, the majority did not mention mentors at work, but rather members of their own families: parents, father, mother, husband, grandfather, husbands and mothers-in-law.

My husband; my mother . . . she taught me about life, values, work culture.

My mother was the person that led us through education. The one who taught us to be constant. The family context: My father moved me.

My second husband also helped me a lot

My parents who supported me.

My parents, there is the origin of my personality, and my grandparents.

Management style and leadership style   When speaking of their management and leadership styles, the successful women were divided into two groups: one that recognized tough, driven management, and one that was more participative, consultative and very fond of delegating. Even the more participative or consultative women admitted, however, that they always continued to be in control and that the final decision is their sole propriety. Here is what they said about their management styles:

I am obsessive, very careful person, and a little too directive.

Order and austerity. I'm an incredibly fussy person.

I do understand I have a tough management style. It is because of my personality, when I want to get something I am tough.

I am participative and consultative.

I accept suggestions. I like to give my employees participation in the business.

Participative, collective, I am not dictatorial at all.

I am very participative . . . But in management style in general I think women are more so . . .

Leadership

Almost all the successful women believe that they lead because of their natural skills, and that they act as role models for others.

> I believe in delegation without losing control.

> But I have a career that could be an example for others. I like working on teams. I am consultative. But if I am sure about something, the decision is always mine; I don't care what they say to me. I ask, check . . . but . . . In my organization I feel that others identify me as the person who 'supports' others.

> I think I am a natural leader.

> Yes, I always have a leadership role, but a very democratic one.

> I think I am a natural leader, it's how I am . . . this is also true in my personal life.

What does not kill you makes you stronger

For Argentinean women, stability, economic growth, a stable environment, democracy and predictability have not been everyday words. With a median of 47 years old, successful Argentinean women have grown up and lived in the worst 50 years of Argentinean history. But for Argentineans, what did not kill them made them much stronger:

> In this country we learn to research, because we have goals and need to search for the roads to arrive at the goals . . . The Argentinean context, the crisis, is a real challenge to me. The crisis is not going to defeat me.

> Because of our country's context, we need to be very attentive, and that gives us an unbelievable flexibility, and a high-speed reaction that I think few other countries have. It is an advantage. And we also have a high level of stress adaptation. Others die for things that for us are possible to get through.

In the past few years Argentina's women have written many pages of our history. Whether it has been defending their children or fighting for accounts of their 'disappeared' grandsons like 'Madres y Abuelas de Plaza de Mayo'; or beating the 'cacerolas' against Dr De la Rua's government, and demanding their savings from the bank. From the successful corporate woman leading the two principal banks in Argentina, to the women thrown into the workforce because of male unemployment, every successful woman is prepared to fight for her dreams. She is an empirical demonstration that however unfavourable the environment, her goals can be achieved. More than anything else, it depends on how strong are her desires and goals, and how hard she can work to achieve them.

Eva Perón, beloved or hated, was a woman who rose from her illegitimate birth to become, undeniably, a world-famous leader – a woman who had nothing contributing to her success except her own personal characteristics, her hunger for the struggle and her vision for Argentina.

CONCLUSION

It is not chance that has brought me to this position, to this life I lead.
In the lives of peoples, as in the lives of men, everything is not done by destiny.
It is necessary for peoples, like men, to help their destiny. (Perón, 1997)

Argentina is trying to recover its glorious past. The road is long and hard, and all human resources, especially the best ones, will be needed on the journey. Argentinean women today make up more than 50 per cent of the total population. They have a higher life expectancy, and are getting more advanced degrees with better grades than men. Argentinean successful women who have achieved their goals have proven that success can be reached without sacrificing one's family life. This can serve as a powerful role model for women in other countries of the world as well. We hope that this research will encourage others to follow the same road. Despite the unfavourable economic environment in Argentina, women have shown that their personal characteristics can lead them to success.

12. The successful women of Chile

Mahia S. Saracostti, Silvia Inés Monserrat and ComunidadMujer[1]

CHILE: LAND OF POETS

Chile is located in south-west South America (Figure 12.1), stretching far south to Antarctica, a country of startling contrasts and extreme beauty, with attractions ranging from the towering volcanic peaks of the Andes to the ancient forests of the Lake District. As home of Literature Nobel Prize winners, Pablo Neruda and Gabriela Mistral, Chile is, indeed, the Land of Poets.

Gabriela Mistral was the first Latin American woman to win the Nobel Prize for Literature in 1945. In her acceptance speech she said: 'At this moment, by an undeserved stroke of fortune, I am the direct voice of the poets of my race and the indirect voice for the noble Spanish and Portuguese tongues.' With both a European and native American heritage, she personifies the Chilean culture: a blending of Hispanic and European elements brought by the soldiers, missionaries and women who colonized the Chilean territory from 1535, combined through intermarriage with the indigenous civilizations that were already established in that territory: Aymaras, Diaguitas, Changes, Quechuas, Mapuches, Picunches, Pehuenches, Onas and Yamana among others.

Most of these original indigenous peoples no longer exist, except for the Aymara (close to 90 000) and Atacameños (around 10 000) in the north; Mapuche, or people of the earth, (around a million) in the south-central zone; Rapanui (3500); and some Kawaskhar and Yagans on the islands of the extreme south. Their customs and cultural heritage are protected by the Indigenous Law, which recognizes the unique character of these people and their right to live according to their own customs and cultural patterns.

The overwhelming majority of the people live in the middle of Chile. Nearly two-thirds of Chile's population lives in the fertile region surrounding Santiago, its capital. Roman Catholicism is the dominant religion, Because of the Catholic Church's strong opposition to divorce,

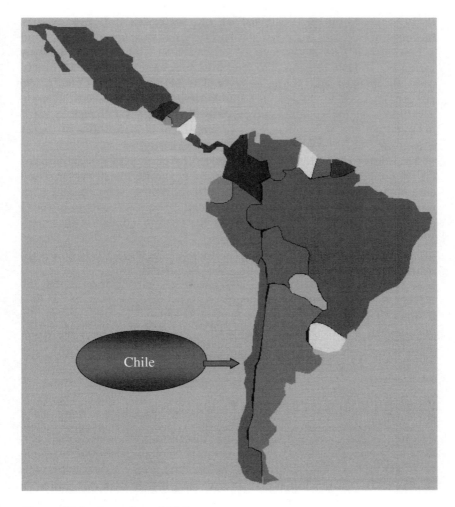

Figure 12.1   Location of Chile

Chile had been, until 2004, one of only three countries in the world where divorce was banned.

Chile is one of the leading industrialized nations of Latin America. It has a strong economy based on mining, especially copper mining, and agricultural goods, largely for export. Chile is the world's largest producer and exporter of copper. It also exports fruits and vegetables, and its wines have become popular in many countries. Since the return to civilian government in 1990, spending on social welfare has increased, although exports, business investments and consumer spending have also grown.

During that period, the level of education in Chile has continuously increased. Today Chile can guarantee a 12-year basic education for practically all children and young persons. The national literacy rate of 96 per cent is one of the highest in Latin America. Total annual enrolment in institutions of higher education in 2000–2001 was 452 177 and, in 2002, men and women had similar levels of enrolment in institutions of higher education, 52.5 per cent and 47.5 per cent respectively.

According to the study by Selamé (2004), 81.4 per cent of women employees are concentrated in the tertiary sector – including social, personal and community services, financial services, transportation, retailing and communication. Total average income of women is about 65 per cent of men's average income. This gap decreases as the level of education decreases. Women without a university degree receive 83 per cent of the income earned by men without a university degree, but women with university degrees earn less than 44 per cent than men with university degrees earn.

In the past 12 years (1990 to 2002) women's participation in the job market increased from 31.3 per cent to 35.6 per cent, as given in the 2002 National Census. Also, in 2003, men represented 52.1 per cent of the unemployed, while women represented 47.5 per cent. However, it should be recognized that men and women represent, respectively, 62 per cent and 38 per cent of the workforce (CASEN, 2003).

CHILE IN HOFSTEDE'S STUDY

Chapter 3 describes Hofstede's cultural dimensions of individualism/collectivism, power distance, and uncertainty avoidance. In his research, Hofstede (2001) found Chile to be moderately high on power distance, similar to Brazil, but lower than Mexico and higher than Argentina. In countries with high power distance, obedience to authority (parent, boss, officials) is expected; language is filled with power or hierarchy indicators; and managers/teachers tend to be autocratic, while subordinates expect direct supervision (Tidwell, 1999). A study comparing Chilean, Mexican and Canadian public officials determined that Chilean officials have a stronger sense of authority than their counterparts in Mexico and Canada. They give more importance to hierarchy and formal roles, and believe in the necessity of defining employees' roles when tasks become more complex (Proulx, 2003).

The Chilean women in Hofstede's study scored high on uncertainty avoidance, similar to Argentina, Brazil and Mexico. Chilean society is characterized by inequalities of power and wealth as well as low tolerance for uncertainty and ambiguity. In an effort to minimize or reduce this level of uncertainty, strict rules, laws, policies and regulations are adopted and implemented. People do not accept change easily and are risk adverse, but their collectivistic culture is manifest in a close long-term commitment to their 'member group' (family, extended family or extended relationships). They had the lowest score on the individualism/collectivism cultural index. Argentina, Brazil and Mexico appear to be moderately individualistic, while Chile is the most collectivistic country in the Latin American sample. Loyalty in a collectivist culture is paramount, and this appears to be reflected in the voices of the Chilean women we interviewed:

> I like to delegate when I trust, build good work teams, I care very much on building good teams.

> There is a time that your team's performance is because you built a truthful environment.

> I am very horizontal, but I trust on teamwork. I am very good delegating, and trust completely in my team's work.

BEING A WOMAN IN CHILE

'The world belongs to women', 'Women rule', 'Politics is conjugated in feminine form', 'Women are the mega tendency of today', 'Female winds are blowing', 'Being female is in style' and 'The workforce has a female face', are all popular phrases that are used in today's Chilean slang as well as in Chile's mass media.

Recently, much emphasis has been placed on the possibility that for the first time in Chilean history a woman could win the presidency. There is little doubt that Soledad Alvear, a Christian Democrat, and Michelle Bachelet, a Socialist, both have strong possibilities of occupying the presidential seat in March 2006. Yet it is difficult to believe that gender will critically boost their chances of winning the presidency. It is also difficult to believe that these popular slogans glorifying women in leadership truly reflect profound advances in Chilean women's access to decision-making power at various levels of national politics.

During the first half of the twentieth century, a group of Chilean women obtained the right to vote. It was an arduous struggle but only the tip of the iceberg as regards the rights of the Chilean woman. Today in Chile, women have the right to vote, to work and to study, yet they continue to suffer discrimination in many fields, especially in terms of acquiring leadership positions in the political, academic and private business arenas.

The creation of the National Service for Women (SERNAM) in 1990 led to a strong interest in studying the problems that Chilean women were facing. Today SERNAM is the driving force behind the Equal Opportunity Plan between men and women, which strives to secure the most egalitarian and democratic manner in which both genders can coexist.

Today Chilean women live longer than men; they marry less frequently and are more likely to seek marital annulments and divorces.[2] Furthermore their fertility has diminished. These realities reveal a number of questions, doubts and decisions facing Chilean women in today's society.

Female participation in the labor force is at 36 per cent (CASEN, 2003). Although it remains predominantly in the areas of services and commerce, this figure demonstrates that Chilean women are slowly but surely entering the public sphere. Yet in spite of increased labour participation, women's wages are approximately 30 per cent lower than men's wages for the same work (Selamé, 2004), and this gap worsens as female educational levels increase.

Chilean women have also failed to enter into the critical political spheres where decisions are made about the country's public policies. Owing to the low number of female senators and representatives, women lack influence in the political sphere, leaving the discussion of laws that affect women and families largely in the hands of Chilean men.

THE SUCCESSFUL WOMEN OF CHILE STUDY

The survey used in the present study had been pre-tested in a Chilean context by administering it to 24 undergraduate students at Universidad del Desarrollo, Santiago, Chile. The survey was then completed by 84 successful women: executives and professionals, university professors (tenured associates or higher), entrepreneurs/small business owners and government officials.

At the same time, 11 very successful women from Santiago, Chile, were interviewed. They were asked how they defined success and what made them successful. The interview consisted of open-ended questions designed to provide more in-depth information than could be interpreted from the questionnaire items and to uncover other perceived important characteristics of success.

Women included in the study were identified through ComunidadMujer (2005), a non-profit corporation whose objective is to bring women's perspective to the public arena. Their aim is to foster harmony between family and work, and to gain greater consideration of women's issues.

Results

Most of the successful women had professional careers (42.9 per cent) or were in executive positions (28.6 per cent). The majority of the women had at least a bachelor degree (over 90 per cent), were married (58.3 per cent), had three children (32.9 per cent) and work full time (75.9 per cent).

Taking into consideration both survey and interview results, the following sections summarize the main characteristics of successful Chilean women.

Internal factors related to success

The results of the survey indicated that successful Chilean women share certain personality and experiential characteristics. Compared with the undergraduate comparison group, the successful women had a significantly greater self-efficacy (4.25 versus 3.83). Their need for achievement (12.33 versus 11.30) was also slightly higher, but not significantly so. Mentoring (psychosocial: 3.72 and career-related: 3.61) was relatively important to the successful women. (See Appendix D.)

These findings were reinforced by the interviews with the successful women. The major themes that emerged related to personality and internal motivation of success: goal driven, full of aspiration, ambitious and hard-working. On the other hand, the successful women said that their management or leadership style was consultative. They used terms such as 'forming teams', 'motivating people' and 'building good work teams'. They also stated that they were 'participative', 'collaborative', 'horizontal leadership' and 'team-oriented'.

External factors related to success

In terms of the external factors that influence their success, the women mentioned the *social support* of their families or upbringing, especially their fathers and their mothers. One successful woman stated, 'Success has to be with birth factors. To be born in a family that has a good economical situation gives you the guidelines, this will mark you strongly'.

Most of the successful Chilean women said that their *education* helped them succeed. One woman said: 'professional study gives you a tool for life'. Other woman stated: 'I received an excellent education, in private schools and abroad.' On the other hand, in terms of *role models or mentors*, the most frequently cited were fathers and colleagues.

Two important themes emerged from the interviews: successful Chilean women find themselves in the paradox between advancement and retreat; and successful Chilean women are shaping their own female leadership style.

Between advancement and retreat: how far have Chilean women really come?
Even though we perceive advances of Chilean women in positions of authority in the business, political and academic spheres, true power and leadership opportunities continue to evade most Chilean women.

Women are entering higher education in massive numbers; half of the youth that matriculate year after year in higher education are women (Correa and Monckeberg, 2001). However, although women are more educated, they have not yet had the opportunity to capitalize on their educational achievements by accessing leadership positions in the social, cultural, economic and political spheres of Chilean society. It is here that we find what is called the paradox of the Chilean woman.

Many of the Chilean women with whom we spoke emphasized the importance of education as a major factor in their success; others stressed personal experiences and attitudes.

> Luckily I received an excellent education, in private schools and abroad. A home where everyone talks very much, discusses about the country, the culture.

> I think that professional study gives you a tool for life, but is not necessary for success. Professional education helps you a lot, as a 'presentation letter', but what we do after, about our career development, about the corporation, where you work . . . I think that success is much more an attitude in life, that is far and away the most important.

> Success has to do with birth factors. To be born into a family that has a good economical situation gives you the foundation; this will mark you strongly. Educational options, to be able to finish your studies, to travel, and to learn from interesting people and on the jobs I tackle . . . things had gone OK, even though I have been changing, but things have worked out. I was a lucky person and I feel myself successful.

In spite of the supportive factors mentioned above, Chilean women have a difficult time becoming leaders because the culture erects important barriers to women seeking leadership positions in Chilean society.

> It is not easy to achieve the recognition you deserve . . . we always need to make more effort than men in order to go to the top positions.

> I think, in general, it is harder for women. There is a discourse that women have the same skills, but culturally there are more barriers for women. I get the impression that today we still have less weight and what women says have less value.

In this sense, Chilean women are thwarted in their efforts to become leaders by the strong *machista* face of Chilean society.

I think that [Chilean] society is pretty 'machista'. I think that in their developmental stages women don't feel enough freedom, and enough incentive
to promote those characteristics that should turn us into leaders. I think we are
too concerned about adapting ourselves, because everything requires us to
adapt. Family, love, the necessity to be beautiful or successful in social terms,
characteristics that distract you from the serious necessity to be on a competitive level.

We are in a very 'machista' society. Women, who are able to move up, are able to
do so because they have particular characteristics, not because the environment
allows or stimulates them. It is because of their personal conditions, because
they have resources that allow them, because they live in a special time, but not
because the environment favors them.

It is interesting to highlight a second aspect of this paradox, the incongru-
ence between beliefs about women's opportunities for advancement and the
concrete achievements of Chilean women. A study conducted by the
Future Foundation (Fundación Futuro, 2003) surveyed Chilean men and
women about women's opportunities in Chile. Of those surveyed, most
respondents believed a woman could become Supreme Court President
(93.8 per cent), president of a large company (99 per cent), Chilean president (86.5 per cent), or commander-in-chief of the army (74.2 per cent).
However, the actual achievements and advancements in leadership positions do not match those beliefs. When the question is whether women
really attain positions of political power or if they occupy strategic positions in companies, the answer is categorically 'No'.

For every 9 parliamentarians only 1 parliamentary is female; for every 7
mayors only 1 female mayor; for every 4 town councilors only 1 is female; for
every 20 judges on the supreme court 1 is female; for every 3 men in the directive
of the Workers Union (CUT) 1 female; for every 5 men in the directive positions in political parties only 1 woman. (Servicio nacional de la Mujer
(SERNAM), 2006)

The paradox of the Chilean woman leads to a number of questions: why
do Chilean women remain at the lower levels of their organizations when
it is time to transform themselves into leaders or speakers? Why do some
Chilean women leaders act with a male style or have the tension between a
male style and a female style? Why have Chilean women reached such a
high level of participation in higher education but have not yet been able to
use their knowledge in leadership positions? Finally, why does such incon-
gruence exist between what women and men perceive and believe about
women's potential for success and what women have actually achieved in
decision-making positions?

To the rescue of female leadership in Chile

Women play essential roles in every aspect of human history, in human reproduction and in human survival. Yet they have often not been heard or seen because of their consistent exclusion from traditional spheres of power.

For years, women who have reached higher positions, and have assumed leadership functions in organizations, have experienced the stigma of 'masculinization' – many men and women alike have believed that women must act as men in order to achieve or maintain power. Today, we continue to encounter this viewpoint, but at the same time we discover a female style of leadership in the research of Chilean experts, and in the words of the successful women in our study.

A few Chilean investigators, such as Nureya Abarca (2004), allude to the fact that the new organization of today requires the abilities of female leaders; specifically a leadership style oriented to forming teams, to motivating people, and a more personal treatment that is neither too hierarchical nor formal. This is reflected in the voices of our interviewees:

> I like to delegate when I trust, build good work teams, I care very much about building good teams. I am very demanding. I want people to achieve their goals. I want people to be very rigorous, but I also want them to be OK, to have a family and personal life . . .

> I am very horizontal, and I believe in teamwork. I am very good at delegating, and trust completely in my team's work.

> I believe in horizontal leadership, where a person feels that opportunities exist. The best motivation in my kind of leadership comes from understanding people's skills and contributing to their development. I believe that is very important, so I see myself as a leader of opportunities rather than restrictions.

> I am a leader that pushes the carriages . . .

Women are more oriented towards strengthening links, and their strengths lie in the management of interpersonal relationships. A world in which I demand and you obey, in which obedience is rewarded and disobedience punished, is slowly coming to an end. There is a new current in which emphasis is placed on taking care of people, treating them well, inspiring them and assuring their satisfaction. Women have an advantage because they are capable of forming a type of home atmosphere in the workplace. In today's world, people feel the pressure of brutal competition and seek a pleasant working environment, one that a woman is capable of generating. Women can lead the way towards new forms of organization at work.

Female leadership is characterized by a participatory style, which summons and invites teamwork. Women in general are more open and prepared to share information; collaborators are permitted to interrupt at any moment, and periodic meetings are held to support team members under women's leadership. Women like involving their teams in making decisions.

Chilean investigator Karina Doña (2004) suggests that when female leadership is discussed, people feel that the way women lead emerges from their inherent femininity. The notion that the female leader's greatest strength is being a woman was also reflected in the comments of several of the successful women we interviewed:

I believe that we can derive major benefits using the intelligence, intuition, and wisdom of our female natures.

People are attracted to the mix of fragility and strength.

CONCLUSIONS

The successful women in this survey scored internally on locus of control, and high on need for achievement and self-efficacy. This is an important finding for policy-makers and educators, academics and practitioners interested in harnessing the benefits of women professionals and women's entrepreneurship to stimulate economic growth and employment. These attributes can be taught and/or enhanced. From an early age, both girls and boys should be encouraged to set high goals, strive to accomplish them and take personal responsibility for work outcomes.

NOTES

1. ComunidadMujer is a private, non-profit corporation whose objective is to bring women's perception to the public arena – in order to make society more humane – aiming at harmonization between family and work and at a greater consideration of women's issues.
2. Chile is one of the last countries in the world that has not legalized divorce. A law permits marital separation under certain conditions, but it does not terminate the conjugal bond.

13. The big picture from polar winds to tropical breezes

Betty Jane Punnett, John Miller and Donald Wood

Women are achieving in all kinds of positions, and succeeding at all levels, around the world. During the week of 3 August 2005, the BBC (British Broadcasting Corporation) World Service's *Today* programme ran a series of interviews with women in jobs traditionally associated with men. The women included Marin Alsop, the first woman to head a major US orchestra, Sandra Edokpayl, Nigeria's first female mechanic, Holly Bennett, one of Europe's only female explosive engineers, and Tahany Al-Gebaly, Egypt's first woman Supreme Court judge. These success stories illustrate what women can achieve. At the same time, the very fact that these women are unusual indicates the challenges that women face in traditionally male preserves.

The BBC's interest in successful women highlights the rationale for this book. We, the authors, began by saying something like 'there are amazing examples of successful women, no matter where we look, yet we know women face major challenges in succeeding – let's find out about these women'. Our initial interest was simply to describe successful women from different countries and identify how they were similar to or different from one another. Much like the BBC's interviews, we wanted to hear what successful women said about their success.

We were fascinated by the stories from the women we surveyed and interviewed, and we believe our readers will find their stories equally interesting. The comments of the women we interviewed are remarkably similar to those reported by the BBC. For example, in the BBC interview, Marin Alsopp said:

> I always tried to improve myself . . . I think that was a big key to my success.

> It's not what people are used to and they're not comfortable, so some get a little upset and agitated.

> I'm soldiering on and persevering, and being passionate, and not giving up.

I think the best thing I have been able to do is never interpret these obstacles or rejections as gender-based, and try to make myself better.

These quotes from Marin Alsopp are reminiscent of the things said by the successful women who are the basis for this book. The successful women we interviewed across the Americas are hard-working people who believe in their ability to succeed. These women know that they face challenges, but they face these challenges and succeed in spite of them, or sometimes because of them.

Women are clearly a major resource for companies, and increasingly companies are recognizing their potential. We argued early on in this book that using the leadership and management potential of women would give companies a competitive advantage. The results of our study support this contention.

Yet, consider the following excerpt from *The Times* newspaper (Judge, 2003): 'so much for smashing the glass ceiling and using their unique skills to enhance the performance of Britain's biggest companies. The triumphant march of women into the country's boardrooms has instead wreaked havoc on companies' performance and share prices'.

The article was based on an analysis of companies' performance and share prices when women were hired for top positions. So, perhaps we were wrong. Perhaps women may seem to be successful, but are really not very good in the business world. Perhaps we should agree to discard the results of the past several years.

Fortunately, the reality seems not to be as described in *The Times*. A study from Exeter University (Ryan and Haslam, 2005) shows clearly that what we are seeing in this data is not women who are less competent, but an example of what they term the 'glass cliff'. According to their study, women's leadership appointments are more likely to be made in problematic organizational circumstances and are thus more precarious, as the following quote from their study indicates:

[I was] promoted to manager at a time when failure of the company was inevitable. In my estimation I needed six months to put new practices in place and put the company on an even keel – I was made redundant after three and a half months.

Further, in these high-risk and difficult situations, the women's performance is carefully monitored, internally and externally, and bad performance is closely scrutinized, with explanations focusing on their individual abilities.

Paul Rincon of the BBC noted that Ryan and Haslam's study of the phenomenon showed that women are often only hired for top positions when a company is doing badly, and that companies were more likely to choose a female candidate, rather than a male one, when a company was doing badly. Further, the glass cliff is not confined to business; there is also evidence that women in the legal profession are often given more difficult cases than men.

So, the challenges continue for women to succeed, but women continue to rise to the challenges, and succeed in spite of them. Another quote from the Exeter study illustrates this:

> I am a geologist and I have always had great difficulty getting jobs in mining. I have found that picking and accepting glass cliff situations has helped me get jobs . . . I have proved that I can and as a consequence I now charge accordingly.

We can conclude based on our own research and the women we met and interviewed, as well as the other research we have cited in this book, that women can and will succeed professionally. At the same time, women can expect to face challenges in the world of work for the foreseeable future. Their personality strengths in terms of a high level of self-efficacy, an internal locus of control, as well as a high need for achievement, will continue to be important in their quest for success. So will the support they receive from their families, and mentors, continue to be important, as this support helps women deal effectively with the challenges they face. One of the authors of this book noted:

> My husband and family are very supportive, particularly because they ensure that we celebrate my successes. When I succeed, my husband takes great pride in it – often, more than I do myself.

Drawing together what we have learned from this project is a difficult task, because we agree that we have learned many things, and we agree on many of the things we have learned, but each of us also has learned different things. This chapter attempts to capture as many of these themes as possible. We begin with some comments from those intimately involved in the project.

BETTY JANE PUNNETT

I was in many ways the originator of this project, as explained in Chapter 4. This led to colleagues who participated in the project designating me 'mother'. Mothers, by definition, have children, and this involves giving birth. Giving birth involves a substantial gestation period, and the birth event itself is both painful and rewarding. This describes the process of this research project, and its output – including this book – rather well. Those of us involved in the project from the beginning are amazed at how long we have worked together, we wonder at the challenges we have overcome, and we rejoice at the completion of a major milestone. The research project, and particularly the book, has required close co-operation among researchers from a variety of countries; we have each brought our particular views to the process, and it has not always been easy to reconcile these, but we have succeeded. As 'mother' I have encouraged, cajoled, reconciled, threatened . . . all the things that mothers do, and it has been both challenging and rewarding. I have been particularly fascinated by the 'voices' of the women who participated in the research. These voices give one a great sense of accomplishment and positive potential.

TERRI R. LITUCHY

The most interesting result for me was that the successful women – regardless of country or occupation – had similar personalities, and were significantly different from the students. In Canada, we compared the successful women to MBA students as well as undergraduates, and while there were more similarities than with the general undergraduates, they were still significantly different on most personality variables. This is what we hypothesized, but I was nevertheless really struck by the similarities.

SILVIA INÉS MONSERRAT

The most important outcomes of the project were how much these women have in common. From their stories, without knowing their nationalities, you could not tell where they came from. The project also provided insights regarding the possibility that women can be empowered. The final results showed that internal factors, for the majority of the women surveyed, had heavily contributed to their success. In future, women can succeed, no matter what the environment, no matter how many barriers they face, no matter what the local economy is like, the political issues or the lack of opportunities. Success has much more to be with what women want to achieve and how hard they work towards their goals, than with how developed is the country where she lives. Women coming from Latin American countries, where fecundity rates are high, also show that family and professional success are not opposite alternatives. Women can be professionally successful without losing the opportunity of being wife and mother, and success will depend mostly on how she is able to balance both aspects of her life, and how her family environment accompanies her on the road to success.

JO ANN DUFFY

The most important outcomes of the project were learning how similar successful women tend to be in terms of their self-reliance and resiliency. Probably coming to understand how important it is to scan your environment and grab hold of opportunities is the most important learning outcome for me, and one I will communicate to my students. The project provided insights regarding the importance of patience and not overreacting to situations. So many times I just wanted to say 'I'm finished; count me out' but I knew we needed to 'hang together' because our quest to understand more about the characteristics of successful women was an important one. I have come to admire and respect BJ and Suzy for their ability to find a common ground on which we could all stand. I think everyone in the core group brought talents and skills essential to the success of the project; it was amazing how much synergy was created from our diversity. One last thing, I now fully appreciate the value of face-to-face interactions; this would never have worked had we not come together a few times.

SUZY FOX

It was amazing how similar professional women across the Americas really are, and how similar are the challenges we continue to face. We have different views of the roles and importance of religion, family, community, and so on, but we also share a certain strength. We just need to learn how to harvest that strength of character, of commitment, of concern, in order to achieve even greater levels of leadership in business and society. Personally, working in an international, virtual team brought both riches and frustrations beyond my expectations. It is amusing and a source of insight to realize how much all that we teach and study about cross-cultural teamwork, communication, negotiation, motivation, decision-making and leadership applies to ourselves, as scholars and as friends. We tend to look at ourselves as 'exceptions', but we are really not.

ANN GREGORY

The project provided insights indicating that women everywhere have similar problems and characteristics but that there are differences, some owing to different stages of women's development and others owing to cultural aspects. Joan Dewling, my co-researcher, and I were struck by the impact of culture upon the successful women in Newfoundland we interviewed, most of whom were Newfoundlanders. For most, their primary identification was as Newfoundlanders, not Canadians. Many, too, discussed the impact of their ethnicity (both pro and con), including the negative influence of the colonial mind-set. What I learned personally was the importance of occasional face-to-face communication and interactions among group members in a project where most of the time we needed to rely on communication via e-mails and occasionally 'talking' via MSN Messenger. These face-to-face meetings were infrequent but very enjoyable.

The previous comments serve to highlight a number of interesting aspects of this project:

- Clearly, all of us involved in doing the research were struck by the similarity of responses from such a wide array of countries. While we had hypothesized that successful professional women would share certain characteristics, we had all expected more variation. When we first brought together the results from several of the countries, at a symposium in Montreal, the overwhelming feeling was 'it's incredible how similar the results are'. Interestingly this was true both for the survey results and the interview results. Although the interviews brought out the differences in women from various countries, their collective 'voice' was much the same, as we illustrated in the quotes that begin this book.

- One of the really interesting aspects of this project, and one which has formed a substantial part of this book, is the voices of the women themselves. Each of us from time to time comments on something special from 'our' interviews (those we were personally involved in) that made our respondents in some way unique. The project gave us a profound sense of respect for successful women. We felt we liked them, even when their voices were second-hand, because they were competent, hard-working and caring. Some of our own experiences are also mirrored in those of our respondents. For example, our successful women, to a large extent, felt that fathers, husbands and sons had been particularly helpful and supportive in their success, and some of the researchers had had the same experience.

- We have all also experienced the challenges of the project. It has not been easy to complete, and we have both loved and hated our colleagues, and the project, from time to time. We have learned a substantial amount about the realities of a virtual project. We have also experienced the joys of the project. We have developed into a cohesive group, and enjoyed many fulfilling encounters.

Because the core group of researchers all came from an academic background, an important aspect for us was the rigour of the research. We set out to design a research project that would be credible in academic circles. The early chapters of this book described the research in some detail, and each of the country chapters reported on the results relative to the factors being investigated. The rest of this chapter examines the assumptions and hypotheses underlying the project, and discusses what our overall results suggest about these hypotheses.

CHALLENGES FACED BY WOMEN

We took an in-depth look at the literature on women in management. This literature clearly outlined the challenges that women face in a variety of situations. Without question, we can conclude that women do face challenges in succeeding in areas that have generally been considered 'male'. In the BBC interviews described at the beginning of this chapter, the women interviewed were 'the first' in their field. The women in our sample were all in positions where there are relatively few women. The women we interviewed, overall, acknowledged the barriers that women face, and they agreed that women have to work especially hard, and have to prove themselves in a 'man's world', if they are to succeed. Several US women talked of a 'glass cliff' rather than walls or ceilings, to illustrate the difficulties faced by women. It seems that the underlying assumption of the project is substantiated – women continue to face challenges professionally, and women continue to succeed in the face of these challenges.

We also explored the expected relationships between culture, personality and success. Our hypotheses were that culture/national origin might significantly impact on how women became successful. Our results do not support major cultural/national differences among successful professional women. We identified some differences based on culture or national identity, but we were more surprised by the similarity we found among the women we surveyed and interviewed. In effect, we found a very similar profile for the women in our study, even though they came from very different cultural and national backgrounds. This suggests that women everywhere share an ability to be successful, even though they face a variety of challenges in the world of work. The differences which we found across nations were subtle, and emerged from the interviews rather than the surveys.

SOME CONCLUSIONS

Across the board, surveys and interviews in all the countries, showed that women had some things in common – people skills, a caring management style, self-efficacy and confidence, a seize-the-opportunity attitude, a high need for achievement, internal attributions of success, and so on. The literature considers most of these attributes to be trainable and this has important implications about developing programmes for training women in these attitudes and attributes.

This has been an exciting project for all of us involved. We believe that the outcomes will be valuable to women everywhere, and we look forward to moving on with this project in ways that can benefit women around the world.

Appendix A: SWW e-mail survey for the USA

SUCCESSFUL WOMEN WORLDWIDE
A GLOBAL RESEARCH PROJECT

E-MAIL SURVEY FOR THE USA

Coordinated by:
JO ANN DUFFY, PH.D.
Gibson D. Lewis Center for Business and Economic Development
Sam Houston State University
and
SUZY FOX, PH.D.
Institute of Human Resources and Industrial Relations
Loyola University Chicago

Welcome to an exciting, new project. This project looks at the characteristics of successful women in the Americas, and around the world. This is being done as part of a collaborative global research network. The project includes a mail survey, as well as interviews. You have been identified, based on our criteria, as one of the successful women in the USA to receive the mail survey. Thank you for participating in this exciting project!

The survey is intended to describe some characteristics of successful women, so that we can compare successful women from different countries and regions. There are no 'right' or 'wrong' answers to the survey questions. In addition to questions dealing with personal and social characteristics, there are questions dealing with information about the respondent – these will be helpful to us in analyzing the data, and we hope you will answer these questions as well. The survey should take about 25 minutes to complete.

Responses to the survey are anonymous and all survey material is strictly confidential. Results will be reported in a summary form only. Of course, your participation is completely voluntary. By continuing with this questionnaire, we understand that you are giving your informed consent to participate in this study.

Thank you for taking time out of your busy schedule to complete the survey. If you have any questions at all, please feel free to contact us at:

Suzy Fox   *Jo Ann Duffy*
(312) 915–7518   *(936) 294–1256*
Sfox1@luc.edu   *mgt_jxd@shsu.edu*

This project has been reviewed by Sam Houston State University's committee for the Protection of Human Subjects (936) 294–3621.
This project has been reviewed by Loyola University Chicago's Institutional Review Board for the Protection of Human Subjects (773) 508–2479.

On the following pages are 'sets' of questions from standardized tests. Each question 'set' has directions for completing the test.

Please read the directions for each set of questions before responding. Your first response is the best response, so please do not spend a lot of time trying to interpret the questions . . . there is no 'right' answer.

To what extent does each statement describe you? Indicate your level of agreement by typing in the appropriate number

1=Strongly Agree   2=Agree   3=Neutral   4=Disagree
5=Strongly Disagree

---	A1	When I make plans, I am certain I can make them work.	1 2 3 4 5
---	A2	One of my problems is that I cannot get down to work when I should.	1 2 3 4 5
---	A3	If I can't do a job the first time, I keep trying until I can.	1 2 3 4 5
---	A4	When I set important goals for myself, I rarely them.	1 2 3 4 5
---	A5	I give up on things before completing them.	1 2 3 4 5
---	A6	I avoid facing difficulties.	1 2 3 4 5
---	A7	If something looks too complicated, I will not even bother to try it.	1 2 3 4 5
---	A8	When I have something unpleasant to do, I stick to it until I finish it.	1 2 3 4 5
---	A9	When I decide to do something, I go right to work on it.	1 2 3 4 5
---	A10	When trying to learn something new, I soon give up if I am not initially successful.	1 2 3 4 5
---	A11	When unexpected problems occur, I don't handle them well.	1 2 3 4 5
---	A12	I avoid trying to learn new things when they look too difficult for me.	1 2 3 4 5
---	A13	Failure just makes me try harder.	1 2 3 4 5
---	A14	I feel insecure about my ability to do things.	1 2 3 4 5
---	A15	I am a self-reliant person.	1 2 3 4 5
---	A16	I give up easily.	1 2 3 4 5
---	A17	I do not seem capable of dealing with most problems that come up in my life.	1 2 3 4 5

Please note that in the last set of questions agree was on the left and disagree on the right. On this page, disagree is on the left, and agree is on the right.

Please type in the number indicating how much you agree with the following statements:

**1=Disagree very much   2=Disagree moderately   3=Disagree slightly
4=Agree slightly   5=Agree moderately   6=Agree very much**

---	B1	A job is what you make of it.	1 2 3 4 5 6
---	B2	On most jobs, people can pretty much accomplish what they set out to accomplish.	1 2 3 4 5 6
---	B3	If you know what you want out of a job, you can find a job that gives it to you.	1 2 3 4 5 6
---	B4	If employees are unhappy with a decision made by their boss, they should do something about it.	1 2 3 4 5 6
---	B5	Getting the job you want is mostly a matter of luck.	1 2 3 4 5 6
---	B6	Making money is primarily a matter of good fortune.	1 2 3 4 5 6
---	B7	Most people are capable of doing their jobs well if they make the effort.	1 2 3 4 5 6
---	B8	In order to get a really good job you need to have family members or friends in high places.	1 2 3 4 5 6
---	B9	Promotions are usually a matter of good fortune.	1 2 3 4 5 6
---	B10	When it comes to landing a really good job, who you know is more important than what you know.	1 2 3 4 5 6
---	B11	Promotions are given to employees who perform well on the job.	1 2 3 4 5 6
---	B12	To make a lot of money you have to know the right people.	1 2 3 4 5 6
---	B13	It takes a lot of luck to be an outstanding employee on most jobs.	1 2 3 4 5 6

---	B14 People who perform their jobs well generally get rewarded for it.	1 2 3 4 5 6
---	B15 Most employees have more influence on their supervisors than they think they do.	1 2 3 4 5 6
---	B16 The main difference between people who make a lot of money and people who make a little money is luck.	1 2 3 4 5 6

Now think of a person (or persons) who has influenced your career development (in other words, someone you consider your mentor, sponsor or role model). Please type in the number that best represents your agreement with the following items, in accordance to the following scale:

1=Not at all   2=To a slight extent   3=To some extent
4=To a large extent   5=To a very large extent

The person (or persons) that have more strongly influenced your career has:

---	C1	encouraged you to try new ways of behaving on the job	1 2 3 4 5
---	C2	assigned responsibilities to you that have increased your contact with people who will judge your potential for future advancement	1 2 3 4 5
---	C3	discussed your questions or concerns regarding feelings of competence, commitment to advancement, relationships with peers and supervisors or work/family conflicts	1 2 3 4 5
---	C4	reduced unnecessary risks that could have threatened your opportunities for promotion	1 2 3 4 5
---	C5	served as a role model	1 2 3 4 5
---	C6	helped you meet new colleagues	1 2 3 4 5
---	C7	demonstrated good listening skills in your conversations	1 2 3 4 5
---	C8	given you assignments or tasks that have prepared you for positions	1 2 3 4 5
---	C9	conveyed feelings of respect for you as an individual	1 2 3 4 5
---	C10	helped you finish assignments or tasks or meet deadlines that otherwise would have been difficult to complete	1 2 3 4 5
---	C11	encouraged you to talk openly about anxieties and fears that detract from your work	1 2 3 4 5
---	C12	encouraged you to prepare for advancement	1 2 3 4 5

---	C13 shared personal experiences as an alternative perspective to your problems	1 2 3 4 5
---	C14 given you assignments that present opportunities to learn new skills	1 2 3 4 5
---	C15 displayed attitudes and values similar to your own	1 2 3 4 5
---	C16 given you assignments that have increased your contact with higher level managers	1 2 3 4 5

Please give us some information about the one person that has been most influential in your career.

Was (or is) this person:

C17 Part of a formal program in your organization?   Yes   No

C18 in the same organization as you?   Yes   No

C19 Male   Female

C20 Older   About the same age   Younger

C21 If you have had mentors, approximately how many have you had during your career? _____

C22 Do you feel that you currently play the role of mentor for other people?

Yes   No

C23 If yes, do they work in the same organization?   Yes   No

C24 Are those you mentor   Older   About the Same Age   Younger

Please use the following scale for the statements below:

**1=strongly disagree   2=disagree   3=neutral   4=agree
5=strongly agree**

---	D1	Managers should not delegate important tasks to employees	1 2 3 4 5
---	D2	Group success is more important than individual success	1 2 3 4 5
---	D3	Employees should only pursue their goals after considering the welfare of the group	1 2 3 4 5
---	D4	Individuals may be expected to give up their goals in order to benefit group success	1 2 3 4 5
---	D5	It is important to have job requirements and instructions spelled out in detail so that employees always know what they are expected to do	1 2 3 4 5
---	D6	Standard operating procedures are helpful to employees on the job	1 2 3 4 5
---	D7	Being accepted by the members of your group is very important	1 2 3 4 5
---	D8	It is frequently necessary for a manager to use authority and power when dealing with subordinates	1 2 3 4 5
---	D9	Managers should avoid off the job social contacts with employees	1 2 3 4 5
---	D10	Managers should encourage group loyalty even if individual goals suffer	1 2 3 4 5
---	D11	Employees should not disagree with management decisions	1 2 3 4 5
---	D12	Managers expect employees to closely follow instructions and procedures	1 2 3 4 5
---	D13	Group welfare is more important than individual rewards	1 2 3 4 5
---	D14	Rules and regulations are important because they inform employees what the organization expects of them	1 2 3 4 5

---	D15 Instructions for operations are important for employees on the job	1 2 3 4 5
---	D16 Managers should make most decisions without consulting subordinates	1 2 3 4 5
---	D17 Managers should seldom ask for the opinions of employees	1 2 3 4 5

Please read the statements below and think about whether you **agree (A)** or **disagree (D)** with it. Check the appropriate response.

agree   disagree

E1	People should be more involved with their work	___A ___D
E2	I enjoy difficult work	___A ___D
E3	I have rarely done extra studying in connection with my work	___A ___D
E4	I try to work just hard enough to get by	___A ___D
E5	I will not be satisfied until I am the best in my field of work	___A ___D
E6	I do not let my work get in the way of what I really want to do	___A ___D
E7	In my work I seldom do more than is necessary	___A ___D
E8	My goal is to do at least a little bit more than anyone else has done	___A ___D
E9	I often set goals that are difficult to reach	___A ___D
E10	People seldom think of me as a hard worker	___A ___D
E11	It doesn't really matter to me whether or not I become one of the best in my field	___A ___D
E12	I seldom set standards which are difficult to reach	___A ___D
E13	As a child I worked a long time for some of the things I earned	___A ___D
E14	I don't mind working while other people are having fun	___A ___D
E15	I am not really very certain what I want to do or how to go about doing it	___A ___D
E16	I would work just as hard whether or not I had to earn a living	___A ___D

The following group of questions asks how you view your present job, and for the last question, your life as a whole. For each statement indicate the extent to which you agree with it by typing the number of the appropriate response, using the following choices.

**1 = Disagree very much   2 = Disagree moderately   3 = Disagree slightly
4 = Neutral   5 = Agree slightly   6 = Agree moderately
7 = Agree very much**

---	F1 In general, I don't like my job.	1 2 3 4 5 6 7
---	F2 All in all, I am satisfied with my job.	1 2 3 4 5 6 7
---	F3 In general, I like working here.	1 2 3 4 5 6 7
---	F4 I am satisfied with my life as a whole.	1 2 3 4 5 6 7

Demographic Information

Please provide the following information to assist us in our analysis:

G1   Profession _____

G2   Title _____

G3   Employment Status (for example unemployed, self-employed, part-time, full-time) _____

G4   If you own your own business, how long has it been in operation? _____

G5   Number of Employees in Your Organization _____

G6   Year of Birth _____

G7   Marital Status _____

G8   Number and Age of Children _____ _____

G9   Your Birth Order (for example only child, oldest, middle, youngest) _____

G10 Gender of your siblings _____ _____

G11 Education level you have achieved (for example Bachelor's, Master's) _____

G12 Parents' Education and Profession _____ _____

G13 Place of Birth _____

G14 Nationality _____

G15 Ethnicity (for example African, European, Chinese, Indian, Lebanese) _____

G16 Your Salary Range (specify currency) _____

G17 Do you have managerial responsibility over people who manage other workers/people?

Yes   No

G18 Which of the following categories most characterizes your work? Please check one.

Academic: tenured full professor or above

Owned own business for at least 2 years

Manager of managers

Other _____

_____

_____

☺ **Thank you very much for your help!**

If you'd like to receive a report of our findings (it may be several months away!) please e-mail me (Suzy) to put you on the feedback list.

If you have any further comments or questions about this project, please feel free to contact us at:

Suzy Fox
sfox1@luc.edu

or

JoAnn Duffy
mgt_jxd@shsu.edu

Appendix B: Form A: interview questions – Successful Women Project

Demographic Information

Name _____ Profession _____

Title _____ Employment Status _____

Owners of business – length of operation _____

Employees in your Organization _____

Year of Birth _____ Marital Status _____

Number and Age of Children _____

Respondent's Birth Order (for example only child, oldest, middle,

youngest) _____

Gender of siblings _____

Current Help in Housekeeping Activities (for example role of spouse,

children, household help, mother/father, extended family)

_____

Education Level Achieved (for example A levels, Bachelor's, Master's)

_____

Parents' Education and Profession _____

Place of Birth _____

Nationality _____

Ethnicity _____

Form A – Personality, External Factors, Management and Leadership

Overall, to what do you attribute your success?

What is it about you as a person that you believe has contributed to your success?

What factors external to you have contributed to your success?

Have there been others in your life who have contributed substantially to your success? Who are the most important people and how have they contributed?

How do you feel that your gender has contributed, either positively or negatively, to your success?

Are there aspects of your ethnic or national culture that you feel have helped or hindered you, as a woman, in achieving professional success?

How would you describe your own management style?

Do you see yourself in a leadership role? How do you approach this role?

In life generally, do you feel that you have succeeded in doing what you hoped to do?

If you had to choose one person to describe as a 'A great leader', who would it be?

Why do you feel this person was a 'A great leader'?

Would you describe yourself, as we do, as a successful person?

Would you like to receive a copy of the results of the study in our region?

Appendix C: Milestones of the project: presentations of the SWW Core Team

- The Successful Women Worldwide (SWW) Symposium, Huntsville, Texas, February 2005.
- The Successful Women Worldwide (SWW) Symposium, Montreal, June 2004.
- Academy of Management Conference, Seattle, August 2003.
- International Western Academy of Management, Lima, Peru, July 2002.
- Academy of Management, Professional Development Workshop, Toronto, August 2000.
- Academy of Management, Professional Development Workshop, Chicago, August 1999.

Other National and International Conferences

- Decision Science Institute Conference, San Francisco, November 2005.
- Academy of Business Disciplines, Fort Myers, Florida, November 2005.
- Academy of International Business UK, Bath, April 2005.
- International Business Information Management (IBIMA) Conference, Cozumel, Mexico, December 2004.
- Decision Science Institute Conference, Boston MA, November 2004.
- European Institute for the Advanced Studies in Management, Female Managers, Entrepreneurs and the Social Capital of the Firm, Brussels, November 2004.
- XVIII Jornadas Nacionales de Administración, Villa Gesell, Argentina, November 2003.
- Global Business and Technology Association Conference, Budapest, July 2003.
- European Applied Business Research Conference, Venice, Italy, June 2003.

- IHRM Conference, Limerick, Ireland, June 2003.
- University of the West Indies Interdisciplinary Conference, SVG, May 2003.
- First International Conference of the Academia de Ciencias Administrativas (ACACIA), Mexico, 2002.

Appendix D: Statistical results: successful women and comparison groups

	N	Personality Self Efficacy	Locus of Control	Need for Achieve	Mentoring Psycho-social	Career-related	Collect Ind	Culture Power Distance	Uncert Avoid	Satisfact
ARGENTINA Women	105									
Mean/Sum**		4.06	2.45	12.80	3.51	3.47	3.68	2.29	3.60	6.13
Alpha		0.76	0.77	0.39	0.87	0.89	0.78	0.61	0.67	0.68
Comparison Group	97									
Mean/Sum**		3.61	2.49	10.46	NA	NA	3.54	2.45	3.63	NA
Alpha		0.82	0.73	0.68	NA	NA	0.53	0.48	0.55	NA
t-statistic		6.44***	−0.34	6.30***	NA	NA	1.39	−1.78	0.93	NA
BRAZIL Women	210									
Mean/Sum**		4.07	2.46	12.42	3.65	3.54	3.55	2.02	3.73	6.13
Alpha		0.89	0.73	0.52	0.86	0.85	0.71	0.57	0.73	0.68
Comparison Group	30									
Mean/Sum**		3.95	3.00	10.73	NA	NA	3.30	2.06	3.70	NA
Alpha		0.79	0.87	0.47	NA	NA	0.67	0.78	0.54	NA
t-statistic		1.12	−3.45	4.00	NA	NA	1.97	−0.39	0.24	NA
(p-value)		(0.265)	**	***	NA	NA	**	(0.695)	(0.892)	NA
CANADA Women	199									
Mean/Sum**		4.23	2.04	12.75	3.57	3.37	3.29	1.94	3.64	6.23
Alpha		0.79	0.82	0.66	0.84	0.85	0.73	0.44	0.71	0.76
Comparison Group	93									
Mean/Sum**		3.81	2.63	10.50	NA	NA	3.32	2.26	3.78	NA

	A	B	C	D	E	F	G	H	I
Alpha	0.88	0.78	0.68	NA	NA	0.59	0.60	0.61	NA
t-statistic	6.91	−8.38	6.06	NA	NA	−0.33	−4.98	−2.20	NA
(p-value)	***	***	**	NA	NA	(0.744)	***	*	NA
CHILE Women 84 Mean/Sum**	4.25	2.11	12.33	3.72	3.61	3.57	2.06	3.59	6.10
Alpha	0.68	0.77	0.73	0.73	0.86	0.75	0.19	0.71	0.80
Comparison Group 24 Mean/Sum**	3.83	2.27	11.30	NA	NA	3.56	2.19	3.64	NA
Alpha	0.73	0.79	0.73	NA	NA	0.75	0.65	0.75	NA
t-statistic	4.61	−1.16	1.60	NA	NA	0.09	−1.18	−0.30	NA
(p-value)	***	(0.248)	(0.114)	NA	NA	(0.925)	(0.241)	(0.765)	NA
MEXICO Women 232 Mean/Sum**	4.26	1.95	13.22	3.86	3.77	3.34	2.29	3.90	6.32
Alpha	0.76	0.75	0.65	0.80	0.83	0.71	0.55	0.67	0.73
Comparison Group 43 Mean/Sum**	3.95	2.09	11.83	NA	NA	3.53	2.16	3.69	NA
Alpha	0.84	0.85	0.74	NA	NA	0.74	0.58	0.67	NA
t-statistic	4.06	−1.38	2.92	NA	NA	−1.47	0.30	1.92	NA
(p-value)	***	(0.170)	**	NA	NA	(0.143)	(0.193)	*	NA
USA Women 126 Mean/Sum**	4.22	2.32	12.57	3.51	3.43	3.19	2.14	3.54	6.16
Alpha	0.82	0.86	0.70	0.85	0.87	0.67	0.54	0.84	0.88
Comparison Group 128 Mean/Sum**	3.82	2.40	11.23	NA	NA	3.18	2.41	3.88	NA
Alpha	0.87	0.81	0.67	NA	NA	0.64	0.45	0.82	NA
t-statistic	6.42	−0.98	4.00	NA	NA	0.17	−4.08	−4.32	NA
(p-value)	***	(0.330)	***	NA	NA	(0.864)	***	***	NA

247

Appendix E: Women in the workforce worldwide: trends

Ann Gregory

A striking trend in recent decades is the increasing proportion of women entering the labour force, reaching a world average of 63 per cent (ILO, 2004a). North Africa and the Middle East are exceptions, with only two out of every ten women of working age employed (ILO, 2004a) – see Figure E.1.

Women also have higher unemployment rates, significant pay differentials (see ILO, 2004a); and persistent occupational segregation continues (World Bank Policy Research Report, 2001). Women are overrepresented in service occupations, technical jobs, and clerical and sales jobs, and men are overrepresented in production and higher-paying administrative and managerial positions. This contributes to pay inequity. 'Recent empirical studies from 71 countries indicate that, on average in developed countries women earn 77 per cent as much as men, and in developing countries, 73 per cent as much' (World Bank Policy Research Report, 2001).

The International Labor Organization (1997) has characterized the rate of progress for women in managerial positions as slow and uneven, but, in most countries studied (several in each continent), progress was being made.

The share of women's professional jobs in 2000–2002 was highest in Eastern Europe and the Confederation of Independent States (CIS); the highest proportion was in Lithuania, which was 70.2 per cent. Other than the above countries, the data show that countries in the Americas have a higher share of women in managerial jobs than most other countries in the world. Although the proportion of women in top management has increased over time within industrialized countries, this proportion is still typically reported as less than 5 per cent. In Japan, women are less represented on all levels of management. In 1989 the percentage of middle-level managers was 2.5 per cent; by 2002 it was 8.7 per cent and the percentage of those who were department heads (upper ranks of middle management) rose from 1.2 per cent to 3.2 per cent (International Labour Organization, 2004a). In developing countries the trend is for increasing numbers of women to enter lower and middle levels of management, but very few have penetrated upper levels.

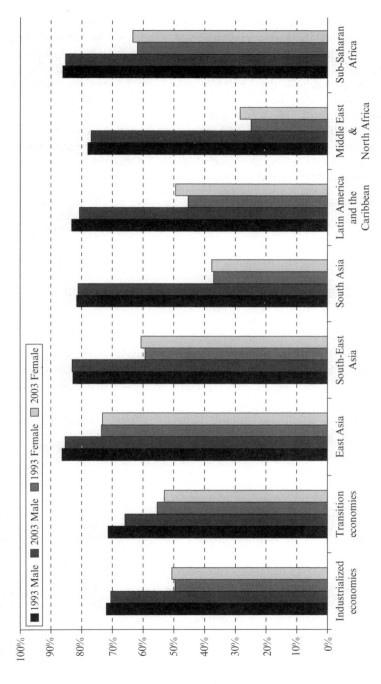

Source: ILO (2003; 2004a).

Figure E.1 Labour force participation rates, by sex and region, 1993 and 2003

Research in North America, Europe, Asia, Latin America, Africa and Australia report on the higher proportion of women in the public sector, but found that gender segregation in functional areas is quite prevalent, as is the crowding of women into lower-level and middle-level positions (Antal and Krebsbach-Gnath, 1994; Black et al., 1992; Hanninen-Salmelin and Petajaniemi, 1994; Izraeli, 1994; Malveaux, 1982; Mansor, 1994; Serdjenian, 1994; Still, 1997). In general, at the beginning of their career, women tend to be placed in positions that have a lower value in terms of skill requirement and remuneration than their qualifications warrant, and they tend to be placed in 'non-strategic' areas, such as human resources and public relations (International Labour Organization, 2004a).

References

Abarca, N. (2004), *Inteligencia Emocional en el Liderazgo*, Santiago, Chile: El Mercurio Aguilar.

Allen, T.D. and Eby, L. (2004), 'Factors related to mentor reports of mentoring functions provided: gender and relational characteristics', *Sex Roles*, **50**, 129–39.

Altus, W.D. (1966), 'Birth order and its sequalae', *Science*, **151**, 44–9.

American Association of University Women (2005), www.aauw.org/index.cfm, 12 July 2005.

American Bar Association Commission on Women in the Profession (1994), *Options and Obstacles: A Survey of the Studies of the Careers of Women Lawyers* (eds M. Tucker and G.A. Niedzielko), Washington, DC: ABA.

Anderson, C.R. (1977), 'Locus of control, coping behaviors, and performance in a stress setting: a longitudinal study', *Journal of Applied Psychology*, **62**, 446–51.

Andrew, C., Coderre, C. and Denis, A. (1994), 'Women in management: the Canadian experience', in N.J. Adler and D.N. Izraeli (eds), *Competitive Frontiers: Women Managers in a Global Economy*, Cambridge, MA: Blackwell, pp. 377–87.

Antal, A.B. and Krebsbach-Gnath, C. (1994), 'Women in management in Germany: East, West, and reunited', in N. Adler and D.N. Izraeli (eds), *Competitive Frontiers: Women Managers in a Global Economy*, Cambridge, MA: Blackwell, pp. 206–23.

Asia Pacific Foundation (2003), 'Population by ethnic origin', www.asiapacific.ca/data/people/demographics_dataset1_byprovPrint.cfm, 30 June 2005.

Auster, E.R. (2001), 'Professional women's midcareer satisfaction: toward an explanatory framework', *Sex Roles*, **44** (11–12), 719–50.

Axtell, R.E. (1993), *Do's and Taboos Around the World*, New York: Wiley.

Axtell, R.E., Briggs, T., Corcoran, M. and Lamb, M.B. (1997), *Do's and Taboos Around the World for Women in Business*, New York: Wiley.

Babcock, B.A. (2001), 'A real revolution', *University of Kansas Law Review*, **49** (4), 719–31.

Bailyn, L. (2003), 'Academic careers and gender equity: lessons learned from MIT', *Gender, Work and Organization*, **10** (2), 137–58.

Bandura, A. (1986), *Social Foundations of Thought and Action: A Social Cognitive Theory*, Englewood Cliffs, NJ: Prentice-Hall.

Bandura, A. (1997), *Self-efficacy: The Exercise of Control*, New York: W.H. Freeman

Barling, J. and Sorensen, D. (1997), 'Work and family: in search of a relevant research agenda', in C.O.L. Cooper and S.E. Jackson (eds), *Creating Tomorrow's Organization*, New York: Wiley, pp. 157–69.

Barnes, J.A. (1954), 'Class and committees in a Norwegian island parish', *Human Relations*, **7**, 39–58.

Bartol, K. (1974), 'Male versus female leaders: the effect of leader need for dominance on follower satisfaction', *Academy of Management Journal*, **17**, 225–33.

Bartol, K. (1978), 'The sex structuring of organizations: a search for possible causes', *Academy of Management Review*, **3**, 805–15.

Bartol, K. and Butterfield, D.A. (1976), 'Sex effects in evaluating leaders', *Journal of Applied Psychology*, **61**, 446–54.

Baruch, Y., O'Creevy, M.F., Hind, P. and Vigoda-Gadot, E. (2004), 'Prosocial behavior and job performance: does the need for control and the need for achievement make a difference?', *Social Behavior & Personality*, **32** (4), 399–411.

Bass, B.M. (1981), 'Women and leadership', in *Ralph Stogdill's Handbook of Leadership: A Survey of Theory and Research*, 2nd edition, New York: Free Press.

Bass, B.M. (1985), *Leadership and Performance Beyond Expectations*, New York: Free Press.

Bass, B.M. (1990), *Bass & Stogdill's Handbook of Leadership: Theory, Research, and Managerial Applications*, 3rd edition, New York: Free Press.

Bass. B.M. (1999), 'Two decades of research and development in transformational leadership', *European Journal of Work and Organizational Psychology*, **8**, 9–32.

Belcourt, M. (1987), 'Nothing to lose: entrepreneurial behavior of female entrepreneurs', *Canadian Journal of Administrative Sciences*, **4** (2), June, 199–210.

Berger, J., Fisek, M.H., Norman, R.Z. and Zelditch, M. Jr (1977), *Status Characteristics and Social Interactions: An Expectation States-approach*, New York: Elsevier Science.

Bernard, J. (1966), *Academic Women*, Cleveland and New York: World Publishing.

Berry, J. (1999), 'Intercultural relations in plural societies', *Canadian Psychology*, **40** (1), 12–21.

Bhagat, R.S., Kedia, B.L., Perez, L.M. and Moustafa, K.S. (2004), 'The role of subjective culture in organizations: progress and pitfalls twenty years later', in B.J. Punnett and O. Shenkar (eds), *Handbook for International Management Research*, Ann Arbor, MI: Michigan University Press, pp. 189–208.

Bird, G.W., Bird, A. and Scruggs, M. (1984), 'Determinants of family task sharing: a study of husbands and wives', *Journal of Marriage and the Family*, **46**, 345–55.

Black, J.S., Stephens, G.K. and Rosener, J.B. (1992), 'Women in management around the world: some glimpses', in U. Sekaran and F.T. Leong (eds), *Womanpower: Managing in Times of Demographic Turbulence*, Newbury Park, CA: Sage, pp. 223–51.

Blair-Loy, M. and Wharton, A.S. (2002), 'Employees' use of work–family policies and the workplace social context', *Social Forces*, **80** (3), 813–45.

Blaisdell, S., Bogue, B., Cyr, M. and Schade, C. (2002), 'Getting off the plateau: increasing the representation of women beyond 20%', paper presented at the WEPAN Conference, San Juan, Puerto Rico.

Bowen, D.D. and Hisrich, R.D. (1986), 'The female entrepreneur: a career development perspective', *Academy of Management Review*, **11**, 393–407.

Bowman, M. (2000), 'The diversity of diversity: Canadian–American differences and their implications for clinical training and APA accreditation', *Canadian Psychology*, **41** (4), 230–43.

Boyacigiller, N., Kleinberg, J., Phillips, M. and Sackman, S. (2004), 'Conceptualizing culture', in B.J. Punnett and O. Shenkar (eds), *Handbook for International Management Research*, Ann Arbor, MI: Michigan University Press, pp. 99–167.

Boyd, M., Goyder, J., Jones, F.E., McRoberts, H.A., Pineo, P.C. and Porter, J. (1981), 'Status attainment in Canada: findings of the Canadian mobility study', *Canadian Review of Sociology and Anthropology*, **18** (5), 657–73.

Brazilian Institute of Geography and Statistics (IBGE) (2005), http://www.ibge.gov.br/english/default.php, 19 September 2005.

Brenner, O.C., Tomkiewicz, J. and Schein, V.E. (1989), 'The relationship between sex role stereotypes and requisite management characteristics revisited', *Academy of Management Journal*, **32**, 662–9.

Breton, R. (1998), 'Ethnicity and race in social organization: recent developments in Canadian society', in R. Helmes-Hayes and James Curtis (eds), *The Vertical Mosaic Revisited*, Toronto: University of Toronto Press, pp. 60–115.

Brockman, J. (2001), *Gender in the Legal Profession: Fitting or Breaking the Mould*, Vancouver, BC: University of British Columbia Press.

Brown, S.M. (1979), 'Male versus female leaders: a comparison of empirical studies', *Sex Roles*, **5**, October, 596–611.

Brown, S.P., Ganesan, S. and Challagalla, G. (2001), 'Self-efficacy as a moderator of information-seeking effectiveness', *Journal of Applied Psychology*, **86**, 1045–51.

Bruschini, C. and Lombardi, M.R. (2004), 'Banco de dados sobre o trabalho das mulheres. Fundação Carlos Chagas', www.fcc.org.br/mulher/apres.html, 11 August.

Bruschini, C. and Puppin, A.B. (2004), 'Trabalho de mulheres executivas no Brasil no final do século XX', *Cadernos de Pesquisa*, **34** (121), 105–38.

Bruschini, C. and Puppin, A.B. (2005), 'Gender and women executives in Brazil', in S. Maxfield (ed.), *Gender Dimensions of Corporate Life in Latin America: Women's Roles and Women's View*, Bogota: Universidad de Los Andes.

Brush, C.G. (1992), 'Research on women business owners: past trends, a new perspective and future direction', *Entrepreneurship Theory and Practice*, **16** (4), 5–30.

Burke, R. (2002), 'Organizational values, job experiences and satisfactions among managerial and professional women and men: advantage men?', *Women in Management Review*, **17** (5), 228–36.

Burke, R. and McKeen, C. (1994), 'Effect of employment gaps on satisfactions and career prospects of managerial and professional women', *International Journal of Career Management*, **6**, 52–66.

Burke, R.J., McKeen, C.A. and McKenna, C. (1993), 'Correlates of mentoring in organizations: the mentor's perspective', *Psychological Reports*, **72**, 883–96.

Burke, S. and Collins, K.M. (2001), 'Gender differences in leadership styles and management skills', *Women in Management Review*, **10**, 744–56.

Burns, J.M. (1978), *Leadership*, New York: Harper & Row.

Cammann, C., Fichman, M., Jenkins, D. and Klesh, J. (1979), 'The Michigan organizational assessment questionnaire', unpublished manuscript, University of Michigan, Ann Arbor.

Campbell, J. (1992), 'Beyond the organization: women entrepreneurs', in S. Olsson (ed.), *The Gender Factor*, Palmerston North: Dunmore Press.

Carli, L.L. and Eagly, A.H. (1999), 'Gender effects on social influence and emergent leadership', in G. Powell (ed.), *Handbook of Gender & Work*, Thousand Oaks, CA: Sage Publications, pp. 203–22.

CASEN (2003), *Encuesta de Caracterización Socioeconómica Nacional. Principales resultados de empleo*, Santiago: MIDEPLAN.

Cassell, J. (2000), *The Woman in the Surgeon's Body*, Cambridge, MA: Harvard University Press.

Catalyst (1993), 'Successful initiatives for breaking the glass ceiling to upward mobility for minorities and women', press release, December.

Catalyst (2000), 'Catalyst census finds 50 companies with significant numbers of women corporate officers, a 100% increase since 1995', press release, 13 November, New York: Catalyst.

Catalyst (2001), 'Women in law: making the case', www.catalystwomen. org/ knowledge/titles/title.php?page=lead_wlmkcase_01, 8 July.

Catalyst (2002), 'Catalyst census of women corporate officers and top earners', www.catalystwomen.org/knowledge/titles/title.php?page=cen_ WOTE02, 8 July.

Catalyst (2003a), 'Catalyst census of women board directors', www.cata-lystwomen. org/knowledge/titles/title.php?page=cen_WBD03, 8 July.

Catalyst (2003b), 'Women in US corporate leadership', press release, June, http://www.catalystwomen.org/press_room/press_releases/20030603.htm.

Catalyst (2004), *Women and Men in US Corporate Leadership: Same Workplace, Different Realities?* New York: Catalyst.

Catalyst (2005a), 'Catalyst census of women corporate officers and top earners of Canada', www.catalystwomen.org/knowledge/titles/title. php?page= cen_WOTE_can, 8 July.

Catalyst (2005b), 'About Catalyst: mission and history', www.catalyst-women.org/ about/mission.shtml, 8 July.

Center for American Women and Politics (2005), Eagleton Institute of Politics, Rutgers University, www.cawp.rutgers.edu/Facts.html, 10 May.

CFHSS-FCSH (2002), 'Selected indicators of the status of women in - universities in Canada', www.fedcan.ca/english/policyandadvocacy/win/ indicators-women.cfm, 25 June 2004.

Chaganti, R. and Parasuraman, S. (1996), 'A study of the impacts of gender on business performance and management patterns in small businesses', *Entrepreneurship: Theory and Practice*, **21** (2), 73–5.

Chemers, M.M. and Ayman, R. (1993), *Leadership Theory and Research: Perspectives and Directions*, San Diego: Academic Press.

Chinese Culture Connection (1987), 'Chinese value dimensions and the search for culture-free dimensions of culture', *Journal of Cross Cultural Psychology*, **18** (2), 143–64.

Chiu, C. (1998), 'Do professional women have lower job satisfaction than professional men? Lawyers as a Case Study', *Sex Roles*, **38** (7/8), 521–37.

CIA (2005a), 'The world factbook – Canada', www.cia.gov/cia/publica-tions/ factbook/geos/ca.html, March, various occasions including 17 January 2006.

CIA (2005b), Factbook website, http://www.cia.gov/cia/publication/fact-book, various occasions including 17 January 2006.

Clanton, K. (2001), Glass ceilings and sticky floors: minority women in the legal profession, *University of Kansas Law Review*, **49** (4), 761–74.

Clark, R.D. and Rice, G.A. (1982), 'Family constellations and eminence:

the birth orders of Nobel prize winners', *Journal of Psychology*, **110** (2), 281–8.

ComunidadMujer (2005), www.comunidadmujer.cl/cm/home.asp, 7 July.

Correia, M. and Monckeberg, M. (2001), *Mujeres Chilenas. Estadísticas para el Nuevo Siglo*, Santiago: SERNAM e INE.

Correll, M. (1998), 'Gender portfolio review Argentina, Chile, Uruguay program', The World Bank, Latin American Region, Poverty Reduction and Economic Management, www.acdi-cida.gc.ca/cida_ind.nsf/8949395286e4d3a58525641300568be1/54c32f24d3df2b7185256b66006afeaa?OpenDocument, 3 April 2005.

Cuba, R. Decenzo, D. and Anish, A. (1983), 'Management practices of successful female business owners', *American Journal of Small Business*, **8** (2), 40–45.

De Janasz, S.C., Sullivan, S.E. and Whiting, V. (2003), 'Mentor networks and career success: lessons for turbulent times', *Academy of Management Executive*, **17** (4), 78–91.

Deaux, K. and Emswiller, T. (1974), 'Explanations of successful performance on sex-linked tasks: what is skill for the male is luck for the female', *Journal of Personality and Social Psychology*, **29**, 80–85.

Deaux, K. and Farris, E. (1977), 'Attributing causes for one's own performance: the effects of sex, norms, and outcome', *Journal of Research in Personality*, **11**, 59–72.

Delaney, R., Brownlee, K. and Sellick, M. (2001), 'Surviving globalization: empowering rural and remote communities in Canada's provincial north', *Rural Social Work*, **6** (3), 4–11.

Denis, W. (1999), Language policy in Canada, in P.S. Li (ed.), *Race and Ethnic Relations in Canada*, 2nd edition, Don Mills, Ontario: Oxford University Press pp. 178–216.

Dewling, J. (2003), 'A historical perspective – the women of Newfoundland and Labrador: their position and work', unpublished paper, Faculty of Business Administration, Memorial University of Newfoundland.

Diaz, M. (2001), 'Mexico: free trade agreements anyone? United States–Mexico Chamber of Commerce', www.usmcoc.org/n1.html, 12 July 2005.

Dobbins, G.H. and Trahan, W. (1985), 'Sex bias in performance appraisal: a meta-analysis and critical review', paper presented at the Academy of Management, Chicago.

Dominguez, C.M. (1992), 'Executive forum – the glass ceiling: paradox and promises', *Human Resource Management*, **31** (4), 385–92.

Doña, K. (2004), 'Liderazgo femenino: ¿Mito o realidad?', Agenda Pública, Dept. de Gobierno y Gestión Pública del Inst. de Asuntos

Públicos de la Universidad de Chile. AÑO III – N°5, DICIEMBRE-ENERO 2004, www.agendapublica. uchile.cl/2_dona.html, 10 January 2005

Dorfman, P.W. and Howell, J.P. (1988), 'Dimensions of national culture and effective leadership patterns: Hofstede revisited', *Advances in International Comparative Management*, **3**, 127–50.

Dreher, G.F. and Cox, T.H. (1996), 'Race, gender and opportunity: a study of compensation attainment and the establishment of mentoring relationships', *Journal of Applied Psychology*, **81** (3), 297–308.

Duryea, S., Edwards, A.C. and Ureta, M. (2001), 'Women in the Latin American labor market: the remarkable 1990s', Primer Seminario Técnico de Consulta Regional sobre temas Laborales, Ciudad de Panamá, Panamá, November.

Eagly, A.H. (1987), *Sex Differences in Social Behavior: A Social-role Interpretation*, Hillsdale, NJ: Lawrence Erlbaum.

Eagly, A.H. (1997), 'Sex differences in social behavior: comparing social role theory and evolutionary psychology', *American Psychologist*, **52**, 1380–83.

Eagly, A.H. and Johnson, B.T. (1990), 'Gender and leadership style: a meta-analysis', *Psychological Bulletin*, **168**, 233–56.

Earley P.C. and Singh, H. (2000), *Innovations in International and Cross-Cultural Management*, Thousand Oaks, CA: Sage.

Eby, L.T. (1997), 'Alternative forms of mentoring in changing organizational environments: a conceptual extension of the mentoring literature', *Journal of Vocational Behavior*, **51**, 125–4.

Epstein, C.F. (1970), *Woman's Place: Options and Limits in Professional Careers*, Berkeley, CA: University of California Press.

Epstein, C.F. (1993), *Women in Law*, 2nd edn, Urbana, IL: University of Illinois Press.

Epstein, C.F. (2001), 'Women in the legal profession at the turn of the twenty-first century: assessing glass ceilings and open doors', *University of Kansas Law Review*, **49** (4), 733–60.

Epstein, C.F., Saute, R., Oglensky B. and Gever, M. (1995), 'Glass ceilings and open doors: women's advancement in the legal profession', *Fordham Law Review*, **64**, 291–448.

Erdwins, C.J., Buffardi, L.C., Casper, W.J. and O'Brien, A.S. (2001), 'The relationship of women's role strain to social support, role satisfaction, and self-efficacy', *Family Relations: Interdisciplinary Journal of Applied Family Studies*, **50** (3), 230–38.

Fagenson, E.A. (ed.) (1993), *Women in Management: Trends, Issues and Challenges in Managerial Diversity*, Newbury Park, CA: Sage.

Fagenson, E.A. and Horowitz, S.V. (1985), ' "La Difference" in organizations: a test of three perspectives', paper presented at the American Psychological Association, Los Angeles.

Falbo, T. (1981), 'Relationships between birth category, achievement, and interpersonal orientation', *Journal of Personality and Social Psychology*, **4** (1), 121–31.

Falkenberg, L. and Rychel, C.J. (1985), 'Gender stereotypes in the workplace', Concordia University Faculty of Commerce and Administration Working Paper Series, Montreal, Quebec, pp. 85–123.

Florentine, R. (1988), 'Sex differences in success expectancies and causal attributions: is this why fewer women become physicians?', *Social Psychology Quarterly*, **51** (3), 236–49.

Forestell, N.M. (1995), 'Times were hard: the pattern of women's paid labour in St. John's between the two World Wars', in C. McGrath, B. Neis and M. Porter (eds), *Their Lives and Times: Women in Newfoundland and Labrador: A Collage*, St John's: Killick Press, pp. 76–92.

Foundation of Canadian Entrepreneurs (2002), 'Best practices for women entrepreneurs in Canada', unpublished report, Royal Bank.

Fox, R. and Schuhmann, R. (2001), 'Mentoring experiences of women city managers: are women disadvantaged?', *American Review of Public Administration*, **31** (4), 381–92.

Fox, S. and Spector, P.E. (1999), 'A model of work frustration-aggression', *Journal of Organizational Behavior*, **20**, 915–31.

Fundación Futuro (2003), available at http://www.fundacionfuturo.cl/estudios_pub.php, August 2004.

Galinsky, E., Salmond, K., Bond, J.T., Kropf, M.B., Moore, M. and Harrington, B. (2003), 'Leaders in a global economy: a study of executive women and men', Boston College, The Center for Work and Family.

Giscombe, K. and Mattis, M.C. (2002), 'Levelling the playing field for women of color in corporate management: is the business case enough?', *Journal of Business Ethics*, **37**, 103–19.

Global Entrepreneurship Monitor (GEM) (2003), *Empreendedorismo no Brasil 2003: Relatório Nacional*, Paraná : Instituto Brasileiro de Qualidade e Produtividade.

Godinho, T., Ristoff, D., Fontes, A., Xavier, I.M. and Sampaio, C.E.M. (2005), 'Trajetória da mulher na educação brasileira: 1996–2003', Brasília: Instituto Nacional de Estudos e Pesquisas Educacionais Anísio Teixeira, www.inep.gov.br/download/catalogo_dinamico/titulos_avulsos/2005/trajetoria_ mulher_1.pdf, 9 May.

Goffee, R. and Scase, R. (1985), *Women in Charge: The Experience of Female Entrepreneurs*, London: Allen and Unwin.

Gordon, J.R. and Whelan-Berry, K.S. (2004), 'It takes two to tango: an empirical study of perceived spousal/partner support for working women', *Women in Management Review*, **19** (5), 260–73.

Goulet, L.R. and Singh, P. (2002), 'Career commitment: a reexamination and an extension', *Journal of Vocational Behavior*, 61 (1), 73–91.

Greenhaus, J.H. and Parasuraman, W. (1994), 'Work-family conflict, social support, and well-being', in M.J. Davidson and R.J. Burke (eds), *Women in Management: Current Research Issues*, London: Paul Chapman publishing, pp. 213–29.

Gregory, A. (1990), 'Are women different and why are women thought to be different? Theoretical and methodological perspectives', *Journal of Business Ethics*, **9**, 257–66.

Gutmann, M.C. (2001), 'Mexican Machos and hombres', *ReVista*, an online magazine of Harvard's Faculty of Arts and Sciences, www.fas.harvard.edu/~drclas/publications/revista/mexico/Gutmann.html, Fall, 1 June.

Hackett, G. and Betz, N.E. (1981), 'Applications of self-efficacy theory to the career assessment of women', *Journal of Career Assessment*, **5** (4), 383–402.

Hall, E.T. (1976), *Beyond Culture*, New York: Anchor Books.

Hall, E.T. (1983), *The Dance of Life: The Other Dimension of Time*, Garden City, NY: Anchor Press/Doubleday.

Hall, E.T. and Hall, M.R. (1990), *Understanding Cultural Differences: Germans, French, and Americans*, Yarmouth, ME: Intercultural Press.

Hamlin, N. (1994), 'The impact of corporate restructuring & downsizing on the managerial careers of minorities and women: lessons learned from nine corporations', US Government Reports, Glass Ceiling: Background Papers.

Hanninen-Salmelin, E. and Petajaniemi, T. (1994), 'Women managers, the challenge to management? The case of Finland', in N.J. Adler and D.N. Izraeli (eds), *Competitive Frontiers: Women Managers in a Global Economy*, Cambridge, MA: Blackwell, pp. 175–89.

Harris, H. (1995), 'Organizational influence on women's career opportunities in international management', *Women in Management Review*, **10** (3), 26–31.

Heider, F. (1958), *The Psychology of Interpersonal Relations*, New York: Wiley.

Heilman, M.E. (1980), 'The impact of situational factors on personnel decisions concerning women: varying the sex composition of the applicant pool', *Organizational Behavior and Human Performance*, **26**, 386–95.

Helgesen, S. (1990), *The Female Advantage: Women's Ways of Leadership*, New York: Doubleday.

Heller, L. (1996), *Porque llegan las que llegan?*, Buenos Aires: Feminaria Editoria.

Heller, L. (in press), 'Mujeres Líderes en Argentina: Estudios comparativo en diferentes empresas', in S. Maxfield (ed.), *Gender Dimensions of Corporate Life in Latin America: Women's Roles and Women's View*, Bogotá: Universidad de Los Andes.

Hennig, M. and Jardim, A. (1976), *The Managerial Woman*, Garden City, NY: Anchor Press/Doubleday.

Hesse-Biber, S. and Carter, G.L. (2000), *Working Women in America – Split Dreams*, New York: Oxford University Press.

Hewlett, S.A. (2002), 'Executive women and the myth of having it all', *Harvard Business Review*, **80**, April, 66–74.

Higgins, M.C. and Kram, K.E. (2001), 'Reconceptualizing mentoring at work: a developmental network perspective', *Academy of Management Review*, **26** (2), 264–288.

Hinze, S.W. (2000), 'Inside medical marriages: the effect of gender on income', *Work and Occupations*, **27**, 464–99.

Hisrich, R.D. and Brush, C.G. (1983), 'The woman entrepreneur: implications of family, education and occupational experience', in J.A. Hornaday, J.A. Timmous and K.H. Vesper (eds), *Frontiers of Entrepreneurs Research*, Wellesley, MA: Babson College, pp. 255–71.

Hisrich, R.D. and O'Brien, M. (1981), 'The woman entrepreneur from a business and sociological perspective', in K. Vesper (ed.), *Frontiers of Entrepreneurship Research*, Wellesley, MA: Center for Entrepreneurial Studies, Babson College, pp. 21–9.

Hofstede, G. (1980a), *Culture's Consequences: International Differences in Work-Related Values*, Beverly Hills, CA: Sage Publications.

Hofstede, G. (1980b), 'Motivation, leadership and organization: do American theories apply abroad?', *Organizational Dynamics*, **9** (1), p. 42–63.

Hofstede, G. (1984), *Culture's Consequences: International Differences in Work-Related Values*, Newbury Park, CA: Sage Publications.

Hofstede, G. (1991), *Cultures and Organizations: Software of the Mind*, London: McGraw-Hill.

Hofstede, G. (2001), *Culture's Consequences: Comparing Values, Behaviors, Institutions and Organizations across Nations*, 2nd edition, Thousand Oaks, CA: Sage Publications.

Hollway, W. and Mukurasi, L. (1994), 'Women managers in the Tanzanian civil service', in N.J. Adler and D.N. Izraeli (eds), *Competitive Frontiers: Women Managers in a Global Economy*, Cambridge, MA: Blackwell, pp. 343–57.

Horner, M. (1968), *Sex Differences in Achievement Motivation and*

Performance in Competitive and Non-Competitive Situations, Ann Arbor, MI: University of Michigan.

Htun , M.N. (2000), 'El Liderazgo de las Mujeres en América Latina: Retos y Tendencias', New School University Diálogo Interamericano, www. ndipartidos.org/pdf/LP2003/Htunlead.pdf, August.

Hui, M., Laroche, M. and Joy, A. (1997), 'Psychometric properties of an index measure of ethnicity in a bicultural environment', *Canadian Journal of Administrative Sciences*, **14**, 14–27.

Hull, K.E. and Nelson, R.L. (2000), 'Assimilation, choice or constraint? Testing theories of gender differences in the careers of lawyers', *Social Forces*, **79**, 229–64.

Ibarra, H. (1992), 'Homophily and differential returns: sex differences in network structure and access in an advertising firm', *Administrative Science Quarterly*, **37**, 422.

Ibarra, H. (1997), 'Paving an alternative route: gender differences in managerial network structure and access in an advertising firm', *Social Psychological Quarterly*, **60**, 91–102.

Ibarra, H. and Daly, K.M. (1995), 'Gender differences in managerial behavior: the ongoing debate', Harvard Business School Note, 9-495-038.

IBGE (2002), 'Sinopse Preliminar do Censo Demográfico 2000', Brasília: Instituto Brasileiro de Geografia e Estatística, www.ibge.gov.br/home /estatistica/ populacao/sinopse_preliminar/Censo2000sinopse.pdf, 10 May.

INDEC (National Women's Council) (2005), 'Instituto nacional de estadistica y censo', www.indec.mecon.ar/principal.asp, 7 July.

Inderlied, S.D. and Powell, G. (1979), 'Sex-role identity and leadership style: different labels for the same concept', *Sex Roles*, **5**, 613–25.

INEGI (2002), *Encuesta nacional sobre uso del tiempo*, Aguascalientes, Ags.: Instituto Nacional de Estadística, Geografía e Informática.

INEGI (2003), *Mujeres y hombres en México 2003*, Aguascalientes, Ags.: Instituto Nacional de Estadística, Geografía e Informática.

INEGI (2004a), *Mujeres y hombres en México 2004*, Aguascalientes, Ags.: Instituto Nacional de Estadística, Geografía e Informática.

INEGI (2004b), *Agenda estadística de los Estados Unidos Mexicanos*, Aguascalientes, Ags.: Instituto Nacional de Estadística, Geografía e Informática.

INEGI (2004c), *Estadísticas a propósito del día de la madre – Datos nacionales*. Aguascalientes, Ags.: Instituto Nacional de Estadística, Geografía e Informática

INEGI (2004d), Mujeres y hombres en México 2004, Aguascalientes, Ags.: Instituto Nacional de Estadística, Geografía e Informática.

INEGI (2005a), 'Estadística de la Industria Maquiladora de Exportación', Aguascalientes, Ags.: Instituto Nacional de Estadística, Geografía e Informática.

INEGI (2005b), *Estadísticas a propósito del día de la madre – Datos nacionales*, Aguascalientes, Ags.: Instituto Nacional de Estadística, Geografía e Informática.

International Labour Office (1997), *'Glass Ceiling' Separates Women from Top Jobs*, Geneva: ILO.

International Labour Organization (ILO) (2003), *Global Employment Trends*, Geneva: ILO.

International Labour Organization (ILO) (2004a), *Global Employment Trends for Women 2004*, Geneva: ILO.

International Labour Organization (2004b), *Breaking Through the Glass Ceiling: Women in Management: Update 2004*, Geneva: ILO

Ismail, M. (2003), 'Men and women engineers in a large industrial organization: interpretation of career progression based on subjective-career experience', *Women in Management Review*, **18**, 60–67.

Izraeli, D.N. (1994), 'Outsiders in the promised land: women managers in Israel', in N.J. Adler and D.N. Izraeli, *Competitive Frontiers: Women Managers in a Global Economy*, Cambridge, MA: Blackwell, pp. 301–24.

Izraeli, D.N. and Adler, N. (1994), 'Competitive frontiers: women managers in a global economy', in N.J. Adler and D.N. Izraeli (eds), *Competitive Frontiers: Women Managers in a Global Economy*, Cambridge, MA: Blackwell, pp. 3–21.

Jackson, D.N. (1989), *Personality Research Form Manual*, Port Huron, MI: Sigma Assessment Systems, Research Psychologists Press.

Jago, A.G. and Vroom, V.H. (1982), 'Sex differences in the incidence and evaluation of participative leader behavior', *Journal of Applied Psychology*, **67**, 776–83.

Javidan, M., Bemmels, B., Devine, K.S. and Dastmalchian, D. (1995), 'Superior and subordinate gender and the acceptance of superiors as role models', *Human Relations*, **48**, 1271–84.

Jex, S.M. and Bliese, P.D. (1999), 'Efficacy beliefs as a moderator of the impact of work-related stressors: a multilevel study', *Journal of Applied Psychology*, **84**, 349–61.

Jones, M. (1995), 'Gender quotas and PR in Argentina. Increasing women's representation', www.fairvote.org/reports/1995/chp 7/jones.html, 17 January 2006.

Judge, E. (2003), 'Smashing through the glass ceiling – women on board: help or hindrance?', *The Times*, 11 November, London.

Judge, T.A., Thoresen, C.J., Pucik, V. and Welbourne, T.M. (1999),

'Managerial coping with organizational change: a dispositional perspective', *Journal of Applied Psychology*, **84**, 107–22.

Junqueira, E.B. (2001), 'Mulheres advogadas: espaços ocupados', in C. Bruschini, and C.R. Pinto (eds), *Tempo e lugares de gênero*, São Paulo: FCC: Editora 34.

Kalbach, M. and Kalbach, W. (1999), 'Demographic overview of ethnic origin groups in Canada', in P.S. Li (ed.), *Race and Ethnic Relations in Canada*, 2nd edition, Don Mills, Ontario: Oxford University Press. pp. 21–51.

Kanter, R.M. (1977), *Men and Women of the Corporation*, New York: Basic Books.

Kay, F.M., Dautovich, N. and Marlor, C. (1996), *Barriers and Opportunities within Law: Women in a Changing Legal Profession: A Longitudinal Study of Ontario Lawyers 1990–1996. A Report to the Law Society of Upper Canada*. Toronto: Law Society of Upper Canada.

Kelly, M.R. and Marin, D.A.J. (1998), 'Position power and women's career advancement', *Women in Management Review*, **13**, 53–66.

Kirchmeyer, C. (2002), 'Gender differences in managerial careers: yesterday, today, and tomorrow', *Journal of Business Ethics*, **37**, 5–24.

Kirkman, B.L. and Shapiro, D.L. (2001), 'The impact of cultural values on job satisfaction and organizational commitment in self-managing work teams: the mediating role of employee resistance', *Academy of Management Journal*, **44** (3), 557–69.

Kluckhohn, F. and Strodtbeck, F. (1961), *Variations in Value Orientations*, Westport, CT: Greenwood Press.

Kobasa, S.C. (1979), 'Stressful life events, personality, and health: an inquiry into hardiness', *Journal of Personality & Social Psychology*, **37**, 1–11.

Krakauer, L. and Chen, C.P. (2003), 'Gender barriers in the legal profession: implications for career development of female law students', *Journal of Employment Counseling*, **40**, 65–79.

Kram, K.E. (1983), 'Phases of the mentor relationship', *Academy of Management Journal*, **26**, 608–25.

Kram, K.E. (1985), *Mentoring at Work*, Glenview, IL: Scott, Foresman.

Krefting, L.A. (2003), 'Intertwined discourses of merit and gender: evidence from academic employment in the USA', *Gender, Work and Organization*, **10** (2), 260–78.

Kroeber, A.L. and Kluckhohn, C. (1952), 'Culture: a critical review of concepts and definitions', paper of the Peabody Museum of American Archaeology and Ethnology 47(1), Cambridge, MA: Harvard University.

Labrich, K. (1995), 'Kissing off corporate America', *Fortune*, 20 February, pp. 44–7, 50, 52.

Lane, H. and DiStefano, J.J. (1988), *International Management Behavior*, Toronto: Kent.

Lankau, M.J. and Scandura, T.A. (2002), 'An investigation of personal learning in mentoring relationships: content, antecedents, and consequences', *Academy of Management Journal*, **45** (4), 779.

Lazarsfeld, P. and Merton, R. (1954), 'Friendship as a social process: a substantive and methodological analysis', in A. Berger and C. Page (eds), *Freedom and Control in a Modern Society*, New York: Van Nostrand, pp. 18–66.

Leavitt, N. (2001), 'Keeping feminism in its place: sex segregation and the domestication of female academics', *University of Kansas Law Review*, **49** (4), 775–807.

Lee-Grosselin, H. and Grisè, J.(1990), 'Are women owner-managers challenging our definitions of entrepreneurship? An in-depth survey', *Journal of Business Ethics*, **9**, 423–33.

Lenartowicz, T. and Roth, K. (2004), 'The selection of key informants in IB cross-cultural studies', *Management International Review*, **44** (1), 23–51.

Leuprecht, C. and McCreery, C. (2002), 'Machiavelli's machine: a Canadian rationalization of the endemic nature of electoral fraud', The Canada Page, www.thecanadapage.org/Machiavelli.htm, 14 May.

Lewis, S. (1997), ' "Family friendly" employment policies: a route to changing organizational culture or playing about at the margins', *Gender, Work and Organization*, **4** (1), 13–23.

Li, P.S. (1999), 'Race and ethnicity', in P.S. Li (ed.), *Race and Ethnic Relations in Canada*, 2nd edn, New York: Oxford University Press, pp. 3–20.

Liff, S. and Ward, K. (2001), 'Distorted views through the glass ceiling: the construction of women's understandings of promotion and senior management positions', *Gender, Work and Organization*, **8**, (1), 19–36.

Little, B. (2002), 'It's true: women are gaining ground in every job category', *Globe and Mail*, 4 March, p. B2.

Lituchy T.R. and Reavley, M. (2003), 'Women small business owners in Poland and the Czech Republic', in A. Staszalek (ed.), *Values in an Era of Transformation*, Lodz, Poland: Wydanie Pierwsze Press, pp. 245–73.

Lituchy, T.R., Bryer, P. and Reavley, M.A. (2003), 'Small business in the Czech Republic and Japan: successes and challenges for women entrepreneurs', in H. Etemad, and R. Wright (eds), *Globalization and Entrepreneurship: Policy and Strategy Perspectives*, Chelterlava, UK and Northampton, MA, USA: Edward Elgar, pp. 1–51.

Loden, M. (1985), *Feminine Leadership or How to Succeed in Business Without Being One of the Boys*, New York: Times Books.

Lorber, J. (1993), 'Why women physicians will never be true equals in the American medical profession', in E. Riska and K. Wegbar (eds), *Gender, Work and Medicine: Women and the Medical Division of Labour*, London: Sage, pp. 62–76.

Lueger, R.J., Lueger, S.A. and Heon, S. (1984), 'Reducing sex-role stereotypes in hiring managers', paper presented at the American Psychological Association, Toronto.

Luthans, F., Envick, B.R. and Anderson, R.D. (1995), 'The need for achievement and organizational commitment of entrepreneurs: a gender comparison', in W.D. Bygrave, B.J. Bird, S. Birley, N.C. Churchill, M. Hay, R.H. Keeley and W.E. Wetzel, Jr (eds), *Frontiers of Entrepreneurship Research*, Babson Park, MA: Center for Entrepreneurial Studies, Babson College.

Maier, M. (1999), 'On the gendered substructure of organization: dimensions and dilemmas of corporate masculinity', in G.N. Powell (ed.) *Handbook of Gender and Work*, Thousand Oaks, CA: Sage, pp. 69–93.

Mainiero, L.A. (1994), 'Getting anointed for advancement: the case of executive women', *Academy of Management Executive*, **14** (3), 136–9.

Malveaux, J. (1982), 'Moving forward, standing still: women in white collar jobs', in P.A. Wallace (ed.), *Women in the Workplace*, Boston, MA: Auburn House, pp. 101–29.

Manaster, G. and Corsini, R. (1984), *Individual Psychology Theory and Practice*, Itasca, IL: F.E. Peacock.

Mansor, N. (1994), 'Women managers in Malaysia: their mobility and challenges', in N.J. Adler and D.N. Izraeli (eds), *Competitive Frontiers: Women Managers in a Global Economy*, Cambridge, MA: Blackwell, pp. 101–113.

Marchandani, K. (1999), 'Feminist insight on gendered work: new directions in research on women and entrepreneurship', *Gender, Work and Organization*, **6**, October, 224–35.

Marshall, J. (1984), *Women Managers: Travellers in a Male World*, Chichester: Wiley.

Mattis, M.C. (2004), 'Women entrepreneurs: out from under the glass ceiling', *Women in Management Review*, **19** (3), 154–63.

Mavin, S. (2001), 'Women's career in theory and practice: time for change?', *Women in Management Review*, **16** (4), 183–92.

Maxfield, S. (2005), 'Women in corporate Latin America', in S. Maxfield (ed.), *Gender Dimensions of Corporate Life in Latin America: Women's Roles and Women's View*, Bogotá: Universidad de Los Andes.

Maznevski, M.L., Distefano, J.J., Gomez, C.B., Noorderhaven, N.G. and Wu, P.C. (1997), 'The cultural orientations framework and international management research', AIB Annual Meeting, Monterrey, Mexico.

McBrier, D.B. (2003), 'Gender and career dynamics within a segmented professional labor market: the case of law academia', *Social Forces*, **81** (4), 1201–66.

McCann, P. (1988), 'Class, gender and religion in Newfoundland education, 1836–1901', unpublished paper, Memorial University of Newfoundland Centre for Newfoundland Studies.

McClelland, D.C., Atkinson J.W., Clark, R.A. and Lowell, E.L. (1976), *The Achievement Motive*, New York: Irvington.

McIlwee, J.S. and Robinson, J.G. (1992), *Women in Engineering: Gender, Power, and Workplace Culture*, New York: SUNY Press.

McQuarrie, F.A.E. (1994), 'Are women set up for failure on the road to the executive suite?', *Academy of Management Executive*, **8** (4), 84–5.

Microsoft® Encarta® Online Encyclopedia (2005), http://ca.encarta.msn.com.

Miller, G.E. (2004), 'Frontier masculinity in the oil industry: the experience of women engineers', *Gender, Work and Organization*, **11** (1), 47–73.

Ministério Da Educação E Cultura (MEC) (2005), 'Censo Escolar 2004', São Paulo, www.inep.gov.br/basica/censo/Escolar/resultados.htm, 10 May.

Moore, D.P. (1999), 'Women entrepreneurs: approaching a new millennium', in G.N. Powell (ed.), *Handbook of Gender and Work*, Thousand Oaks, CA: Sage, pp. 371–89.

Moore, D.P., Buttner, E.H. and Rosen, B. (1992), 'Stepping off the corporate track: the entrepreneurial alternative', in U. Sekaran and F. Leong (eds), *Womanpower: Managing in Times of Demographic Turbulence*, Newbury Park, CA: Sage, pp. 85–110.

Morris, D. (2004), *The Naked Woman*, London: Jonathan Cape.

Morrison, A.M. (1992), *Breaking the Glass Ceiling: Can Women Reach the Top of America's Largest Corporations?*, Reading, MA: Addison-Wesley.

Moser, J.W. (1998), 'Physician income trends in the last ten years', in M.L. Gonzalez and P. Zhang (eds), *Socioeconomic Characteristics of Medical Practice 1997/1998*, Washington, DC: AMA, Center for Health Policy Research, pp. 29–37.

Moure-Eraso, R., Wilcox, M., Punett, L., MacDonald, L. and Levenstein, C. (1997), 'Back to the future: sweatshop conditions on the Mexico–US border', *American Journal of Industrial Medicine*, **31**, 587–99.

Muhonen, T. and Torkelson, E. (2004), 'Work locus of control and its relationship to health and job satisfaction from a gender perspective', *Stress & Health: Journal of the International Society for the Investigation of Stress*, **20** (1), 21–8.

Muller, H.J. and Rowell, M. (1997), 'Mexican women managers: an emerging profile', *Human Resource Management*, **36**, 423–35.

Murray, H.C. (1979), *More than Fifty Percent: Woman's Life in a Newfoundland Outport 1900–1950*, St John's: Breakwater Books.

Nauman, A.K. and Hutchison, M. (1997), 'The integration of women into the Mexican labor force since NAFTA', *American Behavioral Scientist*, **40**, 950–56.

Niemeier, D.A. and Gonzalez, C. (2004), 'Breaking into the Guildmasters' Club: what we know about women's science and engineering department chairs at AAU universities', *NWSA Journal*, **16** (1), 157–71.

Noe, R.A. (1988), 'Women and mentoring: a review and research agenda', *Academy of Management Review*, **13**, 65–78.

Nossel, S. and Westfall, E. (1998), *Presumed Equal: What America's Top Women Lawyers Really Think about Their Firms*, 2nd edition, Franklin Lakes, NJ: Career Press.

Novick, S. (2001), 'Argentina's recent population policies and demographic trends', European Population Conference 2001, Helsinski, 7–9 June, www.iussp.org/ Brazil2001/s 30/S35_03_Novick.pdf, 17 January 2006.

O'Neil, D.A., Bilimoria, D. and Saatcioglu, A. (2003), 'Women's ways of instituting careers: a typology of women's career development', Academy of Management Best Conference Paper 2003.

O'Neill, R.M. (2002), 'Gender and race in mentoring relationships: a review of the literature', in D. Clutterbuck and B.R. Ragins (eds), *Mentoring and Diversity: An International Perspective*, Oxford: Butterworth-Heinemann, pp. 1–22.

Ohlott, P.J., Ruderman, M.N. and McCauley, C.D. (1994), 'Gender differences in managers' developmental job experiences', *Academy of Management Journal*, **37** (1), 46–67.

Olivas-Luján, M.R., Harzing, A.W. and McCoy, S. (2004), 'September 11, 2001: two quasi-experiments on the influence of threats on cultural values and cosmopolitanism', *International Journal of Cross Cultural Management*, **4** (2), 211–28.

Oliveira, A.M.H.C. (2001), 'Occupational gender segregation and effects on wages in Brazil', paper presented at the 24th General Population Conference IUSSP.

Olson, J.E., Good, D.C. and Frieze, I.H. (1985), 'Income differentials of male and female MBAs: the effects of job type and industry', paper presented at the Academy of Management, San Diego.

Paddock, J.R. and Schwartz, K.M. (1986), 'Rituals for dual-career couples', *Psychotherapy*, **23**, 453–9.

Paik, Y. and Vance, C.M. (2002), 'Evidence of back-home selection bias against US female expatriates', *Women in Management Review*, **17** (2), 68–79.

Parsons, T. (1951), *The Social System*, New York: Free Press.

Pecht, E.R.L. (1999), 'Mulher empresária e empresária mulher: trajetórias de vida e estilos de gerência', São Paulo, Dissertação (Mestrado em Administração) – Pontifícia Universidade Católica de São Paulo.

Perón, E. (1997), 'La razón de mi vida y otros escritos' Planeta Pub Corp edition', 1 July, www.pjbonaerense.org.ar/peronismo/escritos_eva/razon _de_mi_vida/ gran_ausencia.htm, 17 January 2006.

Porter, J. (1965), *The Vertical Mosaic: An Analysis of Social Class and Power in Canada*, Toronto: University of Toronto Press.

Powell. G.N. (1990), 'One more time: do female and male managers differ?', *Academy of Management Executive*, **4**, 68–75.

Powell, G.N. (1993), *Women and Men in Management*, 2nd edition, Newbury Park, CA: Sage.

Powell, G.N. (1999), 'Reflections on the glass ceiling: recent trends and future prospects', in G.N. Powell (ed.), *Handbook of Gender & Work*, Thousand Oaks, CA: Sage, pp. 325–45.

Preston, A.E. (2004), 'Plugging the leaks in the scientific workforce', *Issues in Science and Technology*, **20** (4), 69–74.

Proulx, D. (2003), 'Los factores axiológicos en la implementación de nuevos modelos de gestión', VIII Congreso Internacional del CLAD sobre la Reforma del Estado y de la Administración Pública, Panamá, http://unpan1. un.org/intradoc/groups/public/documents/CLAD/clad 0047335.pdf, 5 May.

Publifolha (2002), *Enciclopédia do mundo contemporâneo: estatísticas e informações completas de todos os países do planeta*, São Paulo: Editora Abril.

Punnett, B.J. (1998), 'The impact of individual needs on work behavior: China and North America', *Journal of Asia-Pacific Business*, **2** (3), 23–44.

Punnett, B.J. (2004a), 'The developing world: toward a managerial under-standing', in H. Lane, M.L. Maznevski, M.E. Mendenhall and J. McNett (eds), *Handbook of Global Management*, London: Blackwell, pp. 387–405.

Punnett, B.J. (2004b), *International Perspectives on Organizational Behavior and Human Resource Management*, Armonk, NY: M.E. Sharpe.

Punnett, B.J. and Ricks, D. (1997), *International Business*, Cambridge, MA: Blackwell.

Punnett, B.J. and Shenkar, O. (2004), 'Introduction', in B.J. Punnett and O. Shenkar (eds), *Handbook for International Management Research*, Ann Arbor, MI: Michigan University Press, pp. 3–13.

Punnett, B.J. and Withane, S. (1990), 'Hofstede's value survey model: to embrace or abandon, that is the question', *Advances in International Comparative Management*, **5**, 69–89.

Puppin, A.B. (1994), 'Mulheres em cargos de comando', in C. Bruschini, B. Sorj (orgs), *Novos olhares: mulheres e relações de gênero no Brasil*, São Paulo: Marco Zero: Fundação Carlos Chagas, pp. 13–36.

Ragins, B.R. (1989), 'Barriers to mentoring: the female manager's dilemma', *Human Relations*, **42**, 1–22.

Ragins, B.R. (1999), 'Gender and mentoring relationships: a review and research agenda', in G.N. Powell (ed.), *Handbook of Gender & Work*, Thousand Oaks, CA: Sage, pp. 347–70.

Ragins, B.R. and Cotton, J. (1991), 'Easier said than done: gender differences in perceived barriers to gaining a mentor', *Academy of Management Journal*, **34**, 939–51.

Ragins, B.R. and McFarlin, D.B. (1990), 'Perceptions of mentor roles in cross-gender mentoring relationships', *Journal of Vocational Behavior*, **37**, 3231–339.

Ragins, B.R. and Scandura, T. (1994), 'Gender differences in expected outcomes of mentoring relationships', *Academy of Management Journal*, **37**, 957–71.

Ragins, B.R., Townsend, B. and Mattis, M. (1998), 'Gender gap in the executive suite: CEOs and female executives report on breaking the glass ceiling', *Academy of Management Executive*, **12** (1), 28–36.

Ranson, G. (2000), 'The best of both worlds? Work, family life and the retention of women in engineering', presented at the National Conference for the Advancement of Women in Engineering, Science & Technology, St John's, Newfoundland.

Ray, E. (1988), 'The concrete ceiling', *Executive Female*, **11** (6), November/December, 34–8.

Reavley, M.A., Lituchy, T. and McClelland, E. (2005), 'Exporting success: a two country comparison of women entrepreneurs in international trade', *International Journal of Entrepreneurship and Small Business*, **2** (1), 57–8.

Rhode, D.L. (2001), 'Balanced lives: changing the culture of legal practice', American Bar Association, Commission on Women in the Profession.

Riger, S. and Galligan, P. (1980), 'Women in management: an exploration of competing paradigms', *American Psychologist*, **35**, 902–10.

Riska, E. (2001), *Medical Careers and Feminist Agendas: American, Scandinavian, and Russian Women Physicians*, New York: Aldine de Gruyter.

Rosa, P., Hamilton, S., Carter, S. and Burns, H. (1994), 'The impact of gender on small business management: preliminary findings of a British study', *International Small Business Journal*, **12** (3), 25–32.

Rosen, B. and Jerdee. T.H. (1974), 'Influence of sex-role stereotypes on personnel decisions', *Journal of Applied Psychology*, **59**, 9–14.

Rosener, J.B. (1990), 'Ways women lead', *Harvard Business Review*, **68**, 119–25.

Rosenthal, P. (1995), 'Gender differences in managers' attributions for successful work performance', *Women in Management Review*, **10** (6), 26–31.

Rowe, F.W. (1980), *A History of Newfoundland and Labrador*, Toronto: McGraw-Hill Ryerson.

Ryan, H.K. and Haslam, S.A. (2005), 'The glass cliff: evidence that women are over-represented in precarious leadership positions', *British Journal of Management*, **16** (2), 81–90.

Sánchez, R. (1989), 'Contaminación de la industria fronteriza: Riesgos para la salud y el medio ambiente', in B. González-Aréchiga and R. Barajas Escamilla (eds), *Las maquiladoras: Ajuste estructural y desarrollo regional*, Tijuana, BC: El Colegio de la Frontera Norte.

Santos, N.M.B.F. (1999), *Clima organizacional: pesquisa e diagnóstico*, São Paulo: Stiliano.

Santos, N.M.B.F. (2000), *Cultura organizacional e desempenho: pesquisa, teoria e aplicação*, São Paulo: Stiliano.

Sargent, J. and Matthews, L. (1999), 'Exploitation or choice? Exploring the relative attractiveness of employment in the maquiladoras', *Journal of Business Ethics*, **18**, 213–27.

Scandura, T.A. (1992), 'Mentorship and career mobility: an empirical investigation', *Journal of Organizational Behavior*, **13**, 169–74.

Scandura, T.A. and Viator. R.E. (1994), 'Mentoring in public accounting firms: an analysis of mentor protégé relationships, mentorship functions, and protégé turnover intentions', *Accounting, Organizations and Society*, **19**, 717–34.

Schein, V., Mueller, R., Lituchy, T. and Liu, J. (1996), 'Think manager think male: a global phenomenon?', *Journal of Organizational Behavior*, **17**, 33–41.

Schein, V.E. (1973), 'The relationship between sex role stereotypes and requisite management characteristics', *Journal of Applied Psychology*, **57**, 95–100.

Schein, V.E. (1975), 'Relationships between sex role stereotypes and requisite management characteristics among female managers', *Journal of Applied Psychology*, **60**, 340–44.

Schneer, J.A. (1985), 'Gender context: an alternative perspective on sex differences in organizations', paper presented at the Academy of Management, San Diego.

Schneier, C. and Bartol, K.M. (1980), 'Sex effects in emergent leadership', *Journal of Applied Psychology*, **65**, 341–5.

Schwartz, E.B. (1979), 'Entrepreneurship: a new female frontier', *Journal of Contemporary Business*, **8** (1), Winter, 47–76.

Schwartz, S.H. (1992), 'Universals in the content and structure of values: theoretical advances and empirical tests in 20 countries', in M.P. Zanna (ed.), *Advances in Experimental Social Psychology*, New York: Academic Press, pp. 1–65.

Schwartz, S.H. (1999), 'A theory of cultural values and some implications for work', *Applied Psychology: An International Review*, **48**, 23–47.

Schwartz, S.H. and Sagiv, L. (1995), 'Identifying culture-specifics in the content and structure of values', *Journal of Cross Cultural Psychology*, **26**, 92–116.

Sekaran, U. (1986), *Dual-Career Families: Contemporary Organizational and Counseling Issues*, San Francisco, CA: Jossey-Bass.

Selamé, T.M. (2004), *Brechas de Equidad y Mercado de Trabajo en Chile*, Santiago: OIT y PNUD.

Sellers, P. (2003), 'Power: do women really want it?', *Fortune*, European edition, **148** (8), October, 58–65.

Sennholz, H.F. (1982), 'Argentina on the brink', *The Freeman*, a publication of The Foundation for Economic Education, Inc., December, **32** (12), www.libertyhaven. com/countriesandregions/argentina/argen-brink.shtml, 12 July 2005.

Serdjenian, E. (1994), 'Women managers in France', in N.J. Adler and D.N. Izraeli (eds), *Competitive Frontiers: Women Managers in a Global Economy*, Cambridge, MA: Blackwell, pp. 190–205.

Servicio nacional de la Mujer (Sernam) (2006), http://www.sernam.cl/publico/seccion.php?sec=3, 10 January 2006

Shaw, L.B., Champli, D.P., Hartmann, H. and Spalter-Roth, R.M. (1994), 'The impact of the glass ceiling and structural change on minorities and women', US Government Reports, Glass Ceiling: Background Papers.

Shenkar, O. (2004), 'Cultural distance revisited', in B.J. Punnett and O. Shenkar (eds), *Handbook for International Management Research*, Ann Arbor, MI: Michigan University Press, pp. 168–88.

Sherer, M., Maddux, J.E., Mercandante, B., Prentice-Dunn, S., Jacobs, B. and Rogers, R.W. (1982), 'The self-efficacy scale: construction and validation', *Psychological Reports*, **51**, 663–71.

Sherk, S. (2000), 'Women in Canada's oil and gas sector', presented at the National Conference for the Advancement of Women in Engineering, Science & Technology, St John's, Newfoundland.

Simon, A.B. and Alonzo, A.A. (2004), 'The demography, career pattern, and motivation of locum tenens physicians in the United States', *Journal of Healthcare Management*, **49** (6), 363–75.

Simpson, J.M. (2000), *The Jamaican Woman: A Celebration*, New York: Atlas Books.

Sistema de información, monitoreo y evaluación de programas sociales (SIEMPRO) (1999), www.siempro.gov.ar/index.htm.

Snell, W., Hargrove, I. and Falbo, T. (1986), 'Birth order and achievement motivation configurations in women and men', *Individual Psychology*, **42** (3), 428–38.

Snyder, T., Pittaway, T., Forb, M. and Colapinto, R. (1999), '100 top women entrepreneurs', *Chatelaine*, **72** (11), 72–89.

Soares, T.A. (2001), 'Mulheres em ciência e tecnologia: ascensão limitada', *Química Nova*, **24** (2), 281–5.

Søndergaard, M. (1994), 'Hofstede's consequences: a study of reviews, citations and replications', *Organization Studies*, **15**, 447–56.

Spector, P.E. (1988), 'Development of the work locus of control scale', *Journal of Occupational Psychology*, **61**, 335–40.

Spector, P.E, Cooper, C.L., Sanchez, J.I., O'Driscoll, M., Sparks, K., Bernin, P., Bussing, A., Dewe, P., Hart, P., Lu, L., Miller, K., De Morales, L.R., Ostrognay, G.M., Pagon, M., Pitariu, H.D., Poelmans, S.A., Radhakrishnan, P., Russinova, V., Salamatov, V., Salgado, J.F., Shima, S., Siu, O., Stora, J.B., Teichmann, M., Theorell, T., Vlerick, P., Westman, M., Widerszal-Bazyl, M., Wong, P.T.P., Yu, S. (2002), 'Locus of control and well-being at work: how generalizable are Western findings?', *Academy of Management Journal*, **45**, 453–66.

Statistics Canada (2005), 'Proportion of foreign-born population, by provinces and territories (1991 to 2001 censuses)', www40.statcan.ca/l01/cst01/demo46a.htm, 30 June.

Still, L.V. (1997), 'Glass ceilings and sticky floors: barriers to the careers of women in the Australian finance industry', Commonwealth of Australia, Human Rights and Equal Opportunity Commission.

Stotland, E., Sherman, S.E. and Shaver, K.G. (1971), *Empathy and Birth Order: Some Experimental Explorations*, Lincoln, NA: University of Nebraska Press.

Stroh, L.K. and Reilly, A.H. (1997), 'Gender and careers: present experiences and emerging trends', in G.N. Powell (ed.), *Handbook of Gender and Work*, Thousand Oaks, CA: Sage, pp. 307–24.

Stroh, L.K, Varma, A. and Valy-Durbin, S. (2000), 'Why are women left at home: are they unwilling to go on international assignments?', *Journal of World Business*, **35** (3), 241–55.

Tepper, K., Shaffer, B.C. and Tepper, B.J. (1996), 'Latent structure of mentoring function scales', *Educational and Psychological Measurement*, **56** (5), 848–57.

Tesch, B.J., Wood, H.M., Helwig, A.L. and Nattinger, A.B. (1995), 'Promotion of women physicians in academic medicine: glass ceiling or sticky floor?', *Journal of American Medical Association*, **273**, 1022–5.

Tharenou, P., Latimer, S. and Conroy, D. (1994), 'How do you make it to the top? An examination of influences on women's and men's managerial advancement', *Academy of Management Journal*, **37** (4), 899–931.

Thomas, D.A. (1990), 'The impact of race on managers' experiences of developmental relationships (mentoring and sponsorship): an intra-organizational study', *Journal of Organizational Behavior*, **2**, 479–92.

Thomas, D.A. (1993), 'Racial dynamics in cross-race developmental relationships', *Administrative Science Quarterly*, **38**, 169–94.

Thomas, D.A. and Gabarro, J.J. (1999), *Breaking Through: The Making of Minority Executives in Corporate America*, Cambridge, MA: Harvard University Press.

Tidwell, C.H. Jr (1999), 'Geert Hofstede's cultural value dimensions', www2. andrews.edu/~tidwell/bsad560/Hofstede.html, 12 July 2005.

Toman, W. (1993), *Family Constellation: Its Effects on Personality and Social Behavior*, 4th edition, New York: Springer.

Trei, L. (2002), 'Women lawyers continue to battle gender bias, Rhode tells conference', Stanford Report, 13 March.

Triandis, H.C. (1995), *Individualism & collectivism*, Boulder, CO: Westview Press.

Trompenaars, F. and C. Hampden-Turner (1998), *Riding The Waves of Culture: Understanding Diversity in Global Business*, 2nd edition, New York: McGraw-Hill.

Tyler, K. (2001), 'Don't fence her in', *HR Magazine*, **46** (3), 69–77.

Ueltschy, L., Laroche, M., Tamilia, R. and Yannopoulos, P. (2004), 'Cross-cultural invariance of measures of satisfaction and service quality', *Journal of Business Research*, **57**, 901–12.

United Nations (UN) (2005), 'Women 2000 and beyond: implementation of the Beijing platform for action and compliance with international legal instruments on women, as of 8 March 2005', www.un.org/women-watch/daw/country/ compliance-table-3.2005.pdf, 18 June.

United States Trade Representative (USTR) (2004), www.ustr.gov/Trade_Agreements/Bilateral/DR-CAFTA/Section_Index.html, 12 July 2005.

US Census (2002), www.census.gov/econ/census 02/sbo/sboadvance.htm, 12 July 2005.

US Department of Labor, Bureau of Labor Statistics (2004), *Women in the Labor Force: A Databook*, Washington, DC: US Department of Labor, Report 973, February.

US Department of Labor, Women's Bureau (2005), *Statistics and Data*, 6 May, http://www.dol.gov/wb/stats/main.html, 8 May 2005.

US Gender and Trade Network (2005), 'Breaking boundaries: the Free Trade Area of the Americas and women: understanding the connections', www.wola.org/economic/econ_trade.htm#gender, 18 February.

Valian, V. (1998), *Why So Slow?*, Cambridge, MA: MIT Press.

Van der Velde, M.E.G., Bossink, C.J.H. and Jansen, P.G.W. (2003), 'Gender differences in the influence of professional tenure on work attitudes', *Sex Roles*, **49** (3 and 4), 153–62.

Van Velsor, E. and Hughes, M.W. (1990), 'Gender differences in the development of managers: how women managers learn from experience', Technical Report No. 145, Center for Creative Leadership, Greensboro, NC.

Vilkinas, T. (2000), 'The gender factor in management: how significant others perceive effectiveness', *Women in Management Review*, **15** (5/6), 261–71.

Wallace, J.E. (2001), 'The benefits of mentoring for female lawyers', *Journal of Vocational Behavior*, **58**, 366–91.

Wallace, P.A. (1982), 'Increased labor force participation of women and affirmative action', in P.A. Wallace (ed.), *Women in the Workplace*, Boston, MA: Auburn House, pp. 1–24.

Washington Office on Latin America (WOLA) (2005), www.wola.org/economic/ cafta.htm, 12 July 2005.

Weiner, B. (1992), *Human Motivation: Metaphors, Theories and Research*, Newbury Park, CA: Sage.

Weiner, B., Frieze, I., Kukla, A., Reed, I., Rest, S. and Rosenbaum, R.M. (1972), 'Perceiving the causes of success and failure', in E. Jones, D. Kanouse, H.H. Kelley, R. Nisgett, S. Valins and B. Weiner (eds), *Attribution: Perceiving the Causes of Behavior*, Morristown, NJ: General Learning Press.

Wernick, E. (1994), 'Preparedness, career advancement, and the glass ceiling', US Government Reports, Glass Ceiling: Background Papers.

White, B. (1995), 'The career development of successful women', *Women in Management Review*, **10**, 4–15.

White, B. (1997), 'A portrait of successful women', *Women in Management Review*, **12** (1), 27–34.

White, B., Cox, C. and Cooper, C.L. (1997), 'A portrait of successful women', *Women in Management Review*, **12** (1), 27–34.

White, M.C., Crino, M.D. and DeSanctis, G.L. (1981), 'Ratings of prestige and desirability: effects of additional women entering selected business occupations', *Personality and Social Psychology Bulletin*, **7**, 588–92.

Whitley, W., Dougherty, T.W. and Dreher, G.F. (1991), 'Relationship of career mentoring and socioeconomic origin to managers' and professionals' early career progress', *Academy of Management Journal*, **34** (2), 331–51.

Wilson, B. (1993), 'Touchstones for change: equality, diversity, and accountability', report of the Canadian Bar Association Task Force on

Gender Equality in the Legal Profession, Ottawa: Canadian Bar Association.

Winn, J. (2004), 'Entrepreneurship: not an easy path to top management for women', *Women in Management Review*, **19** (3), 143–53.

Wirth, L. (2001), *Breaking Through the Glass Ceiling: Women in Management*, Geneva: ILO.

Women World Leaders (2005), 'Women world leaders 1945–2005', www.terra.es/ personal2/monolith/00women.htm, 10 May.

Women's Executive Network (2002), 'Moving forward 2002: barriers and opportunities for executive women/Canada', report prepared by POLL-LARA Inc.

Woo, D. (1994), 'The glass ceiling and Asian Americans: a research monograph', US Government Reports, Glass Ceiling: Background Papers.

Wood, G.J. and Lindorff, M. (2001), 'Sex differences in explanations for career progress', *Women in Management Review*, **16** (4), 152–62.

Wood, R., Bandura, A. and Bailey, T. (1990), 'Mechanisms governing organizational performance in complex decision-making environments', *Organizational Behavior and Human Decision Processes*, **46** (2), 181–201.

Woody, B. and Weiss, C. (1994), 'Barriers to work place advancement: the experience of the white female work force', US Government Reports, Glass Ceiling: Background Papers.

World Bank (2004), 'GNI per capita 2003, Atlas method and PPP', http://www.worldbank.org/data/databytopic/GNIPC.pdf, 2 March 2005.

World Bank Policy Research Report (2001), 'Engendering development: through gender equality in rights, resources, and voice', 21776, New York: Oxford University Press, www.gobiernodechile.cl, 5 May 2005.

World Economic Forum (2005), *Women's Empowerment: Measuring the Global Gender Gap*, Geneva: World Economic Forum.

Xie, Y. and Shauman, K.A. (1998), 'Sex differences in research productivity: new evidence about an old puzzle', *American Sociological Review*, **63**, 847–70.

Zabludovsky, G. (2001), 'Women managers and diversity programs in Mexico', *Journal of Management Development*, **20** (4), 354–70.

Zedeck, S. (1992), 'Introduction: exploring the domain of work and family concerns', in S. Zedeck (ed.), *Work, Families and Organizations*, San Francisco, CA: Jossey-Bass, pp. 1–32.

Index

Titles of publications are in *italics*.

Abarca, N. 218
academic women 41–3
  Brazil 185–6
achievement/ascription dimension of
    culture 65
achievement orientation
  measurement 81
  as success factor 11, 68, 98, 100
  women, Mexico 173–4
  women, St Vincent 89
  women, USA 153–4
  see also motivation
Adler, N. 38
advertising and gender discrimination,
    Mexico 165
age, impact on success 127
  Canada 140–41
Alsop, Marin 220–21
Altus, W.D. 47
American nationality as success factor
    157
Argentina 15, 17, 195–8
  gender discrimination 203–5
  success factors 61, 205–9
  Successful Women study 200–209
  women 198–200, 202–3
attributional theory of achievement
    motivation 35–6
attributions for success, women 35–6
  Argentina 205–8
  Canada 141–5
  Mexico 176–80
  St Vincent 85–6
  USA 153–7
authoritarian leadership style 108

Babcock, B.A. 43
Bailyn, L. 42
Bandura, A. 10

Barbados 78–80
  Successful Women pilot project 84,
    87, 90–93
  women, motivations for success
    60–61
barriers, *see* gender barriers
Bass, B.M. 58
BBC interviews, successful women
    220–21
Bernard, J. 41
Bhagat, R.S. 62
birth order, influence on success 47,
    116
  Mexico 172, 175
  USA 152
Blair-Loy, M. 55–6
Bliese, P.D. 10
Bond, M. 63
Boyacigiller, N. 62
Brazil 17–18, 183–5
  success factors 191–3
  successful women 185–94
  women in management 34
Brenner, O.C. 36
Brown, S.M. 57
Bruschini, C, 186
Brush, C.G. 41
Burke, S. 123

Canada 20–21, 131–6
  gender impact on success 139–40
  Hofstede values 73, 135
  success factors 141–6
  successful women study 136–48
  women entrepreneurs 39–40
  women in legal profession 44
  workforce trends 30–31
career development 48–50
career ladders 51

career-oriented mentoring 12–13, 49
career paths, law, gender differences
    43–4
Caribbean countries 19–20, 78–80
    Successful Women pilot project
        80–95
    women, motivations for success
        60–61
    see also Barbados; Jamaica; St
        Vincent and the Grenadines
Catholic faith as success factor, Brazil
    189
CEDAW (Convention on Elimination
    of All Forms of Discrimination
    against Women) 164
childhood, impact on successful
    women 47; see also birth order,
    influence on success
children, professional women 55
    Mexico 171–2, 175
    see also family responsibilities
Chile 18–19, 210–12
    Hofstede cultural dimensions
        212–13
    success factors 215
    successful women study 214–19
    women's status 213–14, 216–17
Chiu, C. 43
civil status
    and female workforce, Mexico 168
    successful women, Mexico 171
Clark, R.D. 47
class status and success 116
colleagues, supportive 120–21
collectivism, see individualism/
    collectivism
concentric influences model 6–7
concrete ceiling 52
confidence as success factor 101
    USA 153
Confucian dynamism as cultural
    variable 63–4
conscientiousness as success factor
    101–2
contingency theory and leadership
    styles 56–7
corporate culture, impact on women's
    career development 48
Cotton, J. 50, 122
Cox, T.H. 50

Cuba, R. 41
cultural characteristics, see cultural
    variables
cultural influences on success, women,
    Mexico 178–9
cultural regions, Canada 20–21
cultural system of business, and
    women in management 39
cultural value models 63–6; see also
    Hofstede cultural values
cultural variables 11–12; see also
    Hofstede cultural values;
    individualism/collectivism; power
    distance; uncertainty avoidance
culture
    Argentina 15, 197–8
    Brazil 183, 185
    Canada 135
    Chile 18, 212–13
    definitions 61–2
*Culture's Consequences: Comparing
    Values, Behaviours, Institutions and
    Organizations across Nations* 72
*Culture's Consequences: International
    Differences in Work-Related
    Values* 63
*Cultures and Organizations: Software of
    the Mind* 63

demographic factors and success 9,
    114–15, 116–17
    Brazil 187, 188–9
    Canada 139–41
    Mexico 175
developed and developing countries,
    Hofstede variables 70–72
developmental job assignments 48–9
dimensions of culture 63–6
discipline as success factor 101
Dobbins, G.H. 57
domestic work, women, Argentina 203
Doña, K. 219
Dorfman, P.W. 68
Dreher, G.F. 50
Duffy, J.A. 224

Earley, P.C. 63
earnings
    Canada 132
    women

Canada 30
Latin America 32
Mexico 170
USA 24, 30
economic development and Hofstede
  variables 70–72
economic leadership, women, USA
  149–50
economy
  Argentina 197
  Caribbean countries 19–20
  Chile 211–12
education
  Brazil 17–18
  Chile 212
  as success factor 124–5
    Brazil 189–90
    Canada 144
    Chile 215
    USA 156
  women
    Argentina 198
    Chile 216
    Mexico 22–3, 168, 175
Elimination of All Forms of
  Discrimination against Women,
  Convention on (CEDAW) 164
emergent career patterns 35
empirical model of influences on
  women's careers 7–8
employment, *see* labour force
  participation
engineering academics, women 42
engineers, women 45–6
entrepreneurs, female 39–41
  Brazil 186
Epstein, C.F. 45
ethnicity
  Brazil 17, 183
  Canada 133
  Chile 210
  influences on success
    Canada 140–41
    Mexico 178–9
    St Vincent 86
executive women, *see* managers,
  women
external locus of control 10–11
external success factors, women 117–30
  Argentina 206–7

Brazil 191–2
Canada 143–5
Chile 215
Mexico 177–8
USA 156–7
see also education; gender barriers;
  mentoring; role models; support

faith, *see* religious faith
Falbo, T. 47
Falkenberg, L. 37
family responsibilities, women 54–5
  impact on career 44, 46
  see also work–family balance
family status, successful women
  Argentina 202–3
  Mexico 167–8, 171–2, 175
family support as success factor
  118–20
  Brazil 192–3
  Canada 143–4
  Chile 215
  Mexico 177–8
  St Vincent 85
  USA 156
father's education as success factor,
  Mexico 172
female labour, *see* labour force
  participation, women
female leadership style, Chile 218–19
feminine management approach,
  Mexico 58–9
firstborn children and achievement 47
Florentine, R. 36
Fox, R. 122
Fox, S. 224
free trade agreements (FTAs), impact
  on women 3
friends as support 120–21
'From polar winds to tropical breezes'
  workshop 24–5

Galinsky, E. 53
gender
  impact on success, women
    Argentina 203–5
    Brazil 190–91
    Canada 139–40
    Mexico 178
    positive effect 129–30

St Vincent 86
  USA 157–9
and leadership styles 56–9
and perception of success 35
gender barriers 3–4, 126–9
  Chile 216–17
  legal profession 43–4
  in management 33
  USA 158–9
gender context perspective, women in
    management 37
gender differences
  entrepreneurs 40
  leadership styles 56–9
  locus of control 11
  work–family roles 54–5
gender discrimination
  Argentina 204
  legislation, Mexico 165
gender equity, Mexico 162, 164–7
gender socialization and career choices,
    Mexico 169
Giscombe, K. 48
glass barriers 51–3
glass ceiling 38, 51–2
  legal profession 43, 44
glass cliff 53, 221–2
glass walls 52
Godinho, T. 185
Goffee, R. 40
Gordon, J.R. 56
government policies on gender equity,
    Mexico 164
great leaders, *see* leaders admired by
    women
Greer, C.R. 58–9
Gregory, A. 37, 225–6

Hall, E.T. 66
Hampden-Turner, C. 64–6
happiness as success factor 102
hard work as success factor 98, 100
  Canada 142
Haslam, S.A. 53, 221
high-context cultures 66
Hofstede, G. 62, 63–4, 135, 183
Hofstede cultural values 63–4, 81–2
  Argentina 197–8
  Brazil 183, 185
  Canada 135

Caribbean countries 91, 92
Chile 212–13
and personal characteristics 68–75
women 74–5
  Brazil 187–8
  Mexico 173
homophily bias 39
homosocial reproduction 39
household management, *see*
    work–family balance
Howell, J.P. 68
Hughes, M.W. 48
husband as support 119–20
  Mexico 177–8

Ibarra, H. 50
Inderlied, S.D. 57
individualism and developing countries
    70
individualism/collectivism 12, 63, 82
  Argentina 198
  Chile 213
  and developing countries 70
  and personal characteristics 69
  women, St Vincent 88–9
inflexibility as barrier, women
    engineers 46
internal locus of control 10
internal success factors, women
  Argentina 205–6
  Brazil 191
  Canada 142
  Chile 215
  Mexico 176–7
  St Vincent 85
  USA 153–4
Izraeli, D.N. 38

Jago, A.G. 57
Jamaica 78–80
  Successful Women pilot project 84,
    87, 90–93
  women, motivations for success 60
Jex, S.M. 10
job advertisements, gender
    discrimination, Mexico 165
job satisfaction
  measurement 13
  as success factor 102
Judge, E. 221

Kanter, R.M. 37
Kelly, M.R. 51
Kirchmeyer, C. 35
Kirchner, Cristina Fernandez de 200
Kluckhohn, C. 62
Kluckhohn, F. 62, 64
Kram, K.E. 50
Krefting, L.A. 43
Kroeber, A.L. 62

labour force participation, women
    28–32, 248–50
  Argentina 199
  Brazil 185–6
  Canada 30–31, 136
  Chile 19, 212, 214
  Latin America 31–2
  Mexico 21–2, 165–9
  USA 23–4, 30
Latin America
  wage rates, women 32
  women managers 33–4
  work–family balance 55
  workforce trends 31–2
law, gender barriers 43–4
  academics 42
  Canada 140, 146–7
leaders admired by women 108–13
  Mexico 181–2
  St Vincent 86–7
  USA 61
leadership positions, women, Chile
    217–19
leadership roles, women, St Vincent 85
leadership styles
  and gender 56–9
  women 104–8
    Argentina 207–8
    Brazil 192
    Canada 142–3
    Mexico 179–80
    St Vincent 86
    USA 154–5
Leavitt, N. 42
legal profession, *see* law, gender
    barriers
legislation on gender discrimination,
    Mexico 165
Lituchy, T.R. 223
locus of control 10–11, 67–8, 81

women
  Mexico 173
  St Vincent 88
  USA 155–6
Loden, M. 57
long-term/short-term orientation
    63–4
low-context cultures 66
luck as success factor 125–6
  Canada 144–5
  USA 155

machismo, Brazil, impact on women's
    careers 190–91
Maier, M. 48
management style, *see* leadership
    styles
managers, women 32–4, 38–9
  Canada 21
  Latin America 33–4
  and social support 54–6
  theoretical perspectives 36–8
  USA 33
maquiladora industry, Mexico 165–7
Marin, D.A.J. 51
Marshall, J. 37
masculinity as cultural variable 63
Massachusetts Institute of Technology
    (MIT) and women 42
Mattis, M.C. 41, 48
Mavin, S. 51
McBrier, D.B. 42
McFarlin, D.B. 50
McQuarrie, F.A.E. 48
medical careers, gender differences
    44–5
mentoring 12–13, 49–50, 121–4
  Argentina 206–7
  Brazil 187
  Canada 138, 145
  Caribbean countries 91, 92
  female lawyers 44
  Mexico 174
  St Vincent 85, 88
  USA 156–7
Mexico 21–3, 161–82
  famous women 163
  female workforce 165–9
  Successful Women Worldwide study
    169–82

women managers 34
women's management style 58–9,
    179–80
Mistral, Gabriela 18, 210
MIT (Massachusetts Institute of
    Technology) and women 42
Monserrat, S.I. 223–4
Moore, D.P. 40–41
Morris, D. 4
mother's education as success factor,
    women, Mexico 172
motherhood
    and female workforce, Mexico
        167–8
    see also work–family balance
motivation as success factor
    Brazil 191
    Canada 142
    see also internal success factors
Muller, H.J. 54, 58–9

Naked Woman, The 4
National Service for Women
    (SERNAM) 214
nationality as success factor, women,
    USA 157
need for achievement, *see* achievement
    orientation
network exclusion as barrier, women
    engineers 46
neutral/emotion dimension of culture
    65
Newfoundland 134–5
    culture, impact on women's success
        141, 148

O'Neil, A. 35
occupational segregation
    Canada 30–31
    see also gender socialization and
        career choices
Ohlott, P.J. 48
only children and achievement 47
opportunity as success factor 126
    Brazil 191–2
ordered career patterns 35
organization-centred perspective,
    women in management 37
organizational culture as barrier,
    women engineers 46

parental education as success factor,
    women, Mexico 172
parental relationships, impact on
    success 47
parental support as success factor
    Brazil 192–3
    Mexico 177
Parsons, T. 64
passion as success factor 102
people skills as success factor 102
perceptions of success
    Argentina 201–2
    Brazil 193–4
    Canada 145–6
    Mexico 175, 180–81
Perón, Eva 199, 204, 209
persistence as success factor 98, 100
person-centred view, women in
    management 36–7
personal satisfaction, successful
    women, Brazil 193–4
personality characteristics and success
    9–11, 66–8, 98–103
    Argentina 205–6
    Brazil 187, 19
    Canada 141–2
    Caribbean countries 90–91, 92
    Chile 215
    Mexico 173–4, 176–7
    St Vincent 85
    USA 153–4
physicians, women 44–5
politics and women
    Argentina 199–200
    Chile 213, 214
    USA 149
polychronic cultures 66
Porter, J. 133
Powell, G. 39, 57
power distance 12, 63, 82
    Argentina 197–8
    Chile 212
    and developing countries 70, 72
    and personal characteristics 69–70
    women, St Vincent 88–9
Preston, A.E. 42
private sector and gender equity,
    Mexico 164
professional satisfaction, successful
    women, Brazil 193–4

professional women, research on
38–59
psychosocial mentoring 12, 49
Punnett, B.J. 24, 60, 68, 76, 222–3
Puppin, A.B. 186

Quebec 21, 134

Ragins, B.R 50, 52, 122
recruitment and gender discrimination,
Mexico 165
regionalism, Canada 133–5
relational orientations 64
religious faith as success factor 102–3,
117
Brazil 117, 189
Mexico 180
St Vincent 85
Rice, G.A. 47
Rincon, P. 221
risk taking as success factor 142
role models
Canadian women 145
Mexican women 181–2
see also leaders admired by women
role-modelling 49
Rosa, P. 41
Rosener, J.B. 58
Rowell, M. 54, 58–9
Ryan, H.K. 53, 221
Rychel, C.J. 37

satisfaction with life
Brazil 188, 193–4
St Vincent 86
Scase, R. 40
Schein, V.E. 36
Schuhmann, R. 122
Schwarz values model 66
science academics, women 42
Segal, A.T. 38
Selamé, T.M. 212
self-confidence as success factor 101
self-efficacy 10, 67, 81
women, St Vincent 87–8
women, USA 153
sense of purpose as success factor
102–3
SERNAM (National Service for
Women) 214

Shenkar, O. 60, 62
Singh, H. 63
Snell, W. 47
social networks 50
social role theory 57–8
social support
as success factor, Canadian women
143–4
women managers 54–6
see also family support
social system of business, effect on
women in management 39
specific/diffuse dimension of culture
65
Spector, P.E. 11
St Vincent and the Grenadines 78–80
motivations for success 60
Successful Women pilot project
84–95
status characteristics theory 57–8
Stephens, G.K. 58–9
Strodtbeck, F. 64
structural barriers
women entrepreneurs 40
women managers 51–3
structural characteristics and success
51–3
struggle as success factor, Argentina
208–9
students, Successful Women pilot
project 91, 92
success and gender 35
success factors, *see* attributions for
success
success measurement 13, 35
Mexico 170
success perceptions, *see* perceptions of
success
Successful Women Worldwide (SWW)
project 76–7
interview questions 242–3
pilot project 77–8, 80–95
presentations 244–5
statistical results 246–7
survey questions 228–41
see also individual countries
support as success factor 12–13, 114,
115, 118–24
Brazil 192–3
Canada 143–4

Tesch, B.J. 45
Trahan, W. 57
training 48–9
trait perspectives theory, leadership
    styles 56
transactional leadership 58
transformational leadership 58
Triandis, H.C. 66
Trompenaars, F. 64–6

uncertainty avoidance 12, 63, 72, 82
    Argentina 198
    Chile 212–13
    and personal characteristics 69
    women, St Vincent 88–9
unemployment rates, Canada 133
universalism/particularism 64–5
USA 23–4
    identification of great leaders 61
    successful women study 151–60
    women entrepreneurs 39
    women in leadership 149–50
    women in legal profession 43
    women managers 33
    workforce trends 30

Van Velsor, E. 48
Vertical Mosaic, The 133
vocational choices, gender differences,
    Mexico 169

Vroom, V.H. 57

wage rates, *see* earnings
Wernick, E. 51
West Indies, *see* Caribbean countries
Wharton, A.S. 55–6
Whelan-Berry, K.S. 56
White, B. 35, 47–8, 51
women
    attributions for success, *see*
        attributions for success
    impact of FTAs 3
    managers, *see* managers, women
    wage rates, *see* earnings
    in the workforce, *see* labour force
        participation
work–family balance 54–6
    Argentina 203
    Canada 144, 147
    women engineers 46
workforce trends 28–32
    Canada 30–31
    Latin America 31–2
    USA 30
    worldwide 248–50
    see also labour force
        participation

Zabludovsky, G. 164
Zellner, W. 38